Building the Infrastructure for Cloud Security

A Solutions view

Raghu Yeluri

Enrique Castro-Leon

Apress
open

Building the Infrastructure for Cloud Security

Raghu Yeluri and Enrique Castro-Leon

Copyright © 2014 by Apress Media, LLC, all rights reserved

ISBN-13 (pbk): 978-1-4302-6145-2

ISBN-13 (electronic): 978-1-4302-6146-9

President and Publisher: Paul Manning
Lead Editors: Steve Weiss (Apress); Patrick Hauke (Intel)
Coordinating Editor: Melissa Maldonado
Cover Designer: Anna Ishchenko

Distributed to the book trade worldwide by Springer Science+Business Media New York, 233 Spring Street, 6th Floor, New York, NY 10013. Phone 1-800-SPRINGER, fax (201) 348-4505, e-mail orders-ny@springer-sbm.com, or visit www.springeronline.com.

For information on translations, please e-mail rights@apress.com, or visit www.apress.com.

About ApressOpen

What Is ApressOpen?

- ApressOpen is an open access book program that publishes high-quality technical and business information.

- ApressOpen eBooks are available for global, free, noncommercial use.

- ApressOpen eBooks are available in PDF, ePub, and Mobi formats.

- The user friendly ApressOpen free eBook license is presented on the copyright page of this book.

To Sunita, Sonia, and Rajeev. Without your motivation, patience, and sacrifice, I couldn't have succeeded. Many thanks for maintaining and managing normalcy while I spent hours writing this book.

—Raghu Yeluri

To Kitty, for her infinite patience and both explicit and tacit support during the long hours it took to put together this book project.

—Enrique Castro-Leon

Contents at a Glance

Contents

About the Authors

Raghu Yeluri is a Principal Engineer and lead Security Solutions Architect in the Data Center & Cloud Products Group at Intel Corporation, with focus on virtualization and cloud security usages, solution architectures, and technology initiatives. In this role, he drives security solution pathfinding and development to deliver hardware-assisted security solutions that enable deep visibility, orchestration, and control in multi-tenant clouds. Prior to this role, he has worked in various engineering and architecture positions in systems development and deployment, focusing on service-oriented architectures and large data analytics, in information technology and manufacturing technology groups during the last 15+ years at Intel. Raghu has multiple patents filed in security, attestation, and control in virtualization and cloud computing, and he is a co-author of a book, *Creating the Infrastructure for Cloud Computing: An Essential Handbook for IT Professionals*. He holds an MS degree in Computer Science, and a B.S in Electrical Engineering, and was involved in multiple artificial intelligence/knowledge-engineering startup ventures prior to joining Intel.

Enrique Castro-Leon is an Enterprise Architect and Technology Strategist with the Intel Architecture Group at Intel Corporation, working in enterprise IT solution integration, cloud computing, and service engineering. As a technology strategist, Enrique has been investigating the disruptive effects of emerging technologies in the marketplace. He is the lead author of a book on the convergence of virtualization, service-oriented methodologies, and distributed computing, titled *The Business Value of Virtual Service Grids: Strategic Insights for Enterprise Decision Makers*. He is also the lead author of a second book, *Creating the Infrastructure for Cloud Computing: An Essential Handbook for IT Professionals*. Enrique holds a Ph.D. in Electrical Engineering and M.S. degrees in Electrical Engineering and Computer Science from Purdue University, and a BSEE degree from the University of Costa Rica. Enrique is also a co-founder and President of Neighborhood Learning Center (NLC), a tax-exempt organization providing computer education and tutoring services to K-12 in Oregon. Since its inception in 2000, the NLC has served over 300 children at risk of falling behind in the school system, and currently serves over 60 families. It has received recent grant awards from the Meyer Memorial Trust, the Templeton Foundation, and the Rose E. Tucker Charitable Trust.

About the Technical Reviewers

Martin Guttmann is a Principal Engineer at Intel Corporation. He has 30+ years of extensive experience ranging from computer systems and software to operating systems, including the data center operation, security solutions, and enterprise architecture. As member of the office of the CTO at Intel, he was responsible for defining end-to-end manageability and security architecture for enterprise IT and data center infrastructure, systems, products, and solutions.

Uttam Shetty is Director of Cloud Security Solutions at Intel Corporation, leading the engineering groups delivering security solutions that provide platform-derived trust assurance of the cloud Infrastructure. He has extensive experience (25+ years) in leading global development centers in delivering technologies and solutions that enable key transformation with Intel for e-business, manufacturing systems, and infrastructure technology.

Mitch Koyama is a subject-matter expert on Intel's enterprise products, solutions, and technologies. Emergence of cloud computing keeps Mitch busy with Intel's security technologies, where he has been working with various technology suppliers and vendors to provide solutions addressing the barriers for cloud adoption. Mitch has been in this field for more than 10 years, working in multiple locations.

Ren Wu is a technology-integration engineer for security technologies in Intel Corporation's data center group. Ren has rich and varied experience both at Intel and at AT&T Bell Labs and Lucent Technologies as a systems and solution architect and has contributed to their optical network architectures, standards, and the long-haul DWDM systems.

Acknowledgments

This book is an embodiment of work by many different Intel Corporation communities of engineers, architects, technical and product marketing engineers, software architects, and researchers at Intel labs, as well as many external software and solution partners. The work could not have been created without the multi-year effort and development of Security Technologies by Intel's Data Center Group and Software and Services Group. Their technical whitepapers, industry engagements, and eco-system development work provided the impetus for the development of the solution architectures, solution components, and reference implementations discussed in this book. It is not feasible to name all the people involved, but here is a very likely nonexhaustive list of folks we would like to acknowledge: Monty Wiseman, Joe Cihula, Steve Orrin, James Blakley, James Greene, Iddo Kadim, Lynn Comp, Tracie Zenti, Hemma Prafullchandra, Vince Lubsey, Murugiah Souppaya, Michael Bartock and Nikhil Sharma. Special acknowledgement to the Intel Cloud Security team, including Ravi Varanasi, Uttam Shetty, Sudhir S. Bangalore, Jonathan Buhacoff, Kamal Natesan and Jerry Wheeler. This team has been at the forefront of the solution definition and development that are covered in this book.

The authors gratefully acknowledge the time, guidance, and expertise of the technical reviewers, Martin Guttmann, Uttam Shetty, Ren Wu, and Mitch Koyama.

Authors would like to offer special thanks to acknowledge a small set of contributors who provided particular content to these chapters:

- Chapter 1 – *Blake Dournaee*.

- Chapter 4, 5 - *Jonathan Buhacoff and Sudhir Bangalore*.

- Chapter 6 – *William Bathurst, M2Mi, Inc.*

- Chapter 7 – *Abhilasha Bhargav and Ned Smith*.

- Chapter 9 – *Gregsie Leighton and Pete Nicoletti, VirtuStream, Inc.*

Foreword

I've worn a lot of hats in my career, from investment banker to venture capitalist to business entrepreneur. And I've been fortunate to have been at the forefront of a number of technology waves, from mainframe to client/server computing, the Internet boom, and now the continuing rise of mobile and cloud computing. Each new wave brings technology disruption driven by an industry in transformation, and each enables new levels of efficiency and operational productivity. However, in line with that, each new wave also brings new security risks and operational concerns.

Virtualization and cloud technologies are no different. They're bringing about the most significant data center transformation in the last 20 years, and are enabling enormous benefits in terms of cost savings, flexibility, and business agility. But at the same time, there's been a correspondingly significant shift in the security risk posture. The new platform that cloud environments create brings together all an organization's critical systems, applications, and data, which, in essence, leads to a concentration of risk. That on its own should get executives to stop, sit up, and take notice. Without the proper controls in place (as you can very well imagine) a data center–and thus business–disaster can ensue. Critical systems and data might be accessed, copied, and deleted in one fell swoop or at touch of a button. Servers that IT used to think of as physical boxes that can be racked and stacked are now simply sets of files. The data center is becoming a software abstraction that can entirely be managed remotely.

Further, in this new environment, godlike privileges are enabled over the entire set of virtualized resources. A single systems administrator—or someone hijacking someone's privileges to escalate an attack—can copy a virtual machine or delete an entire virtual data center in a matter of minutes. Misconfigurations can now cause serious downtime owing to the greater number of systems. And, audit failures are more likely to happen given that now the new platform is subject to audit.

And we aren't done yet. Technology is moving toward software-defined networks and storage to enable the "software-defined data center." This concentrates risk further and creates additional security and compliance challenges.

Such radical changes demand a new approach to security and chain of trust—one that addresses these risks *specifically*. It's more critical than ever, given these factors: (1) concentration of risk, as noted; (2) attackers becoming much more sophisticated; and (3) higher stakes, such as insider risk and data leaks, and advanced external threats and privilege hijacking and to escalate attacks. A few good examples include Edward Snowden's leak of classified NSA documents; the theft of hundreds of millions of Target customers' personal information; and the Adobe breach that compromised tens of millions of user accounts and payments information, not to mention top-secret source code.

The new chain of trust must start from the hardware as well as the virtual infrastructure, to ensure you can trust the operating systems and applications that are running on virtual machines. It needs to work across private, hybrid, and public clouds so that the policies required for workloads can be dictated and enforced automatically. And it must be tied to data security to ensure VMs are encrypted unless they're running in authorized environments.

Looking ahead, cloud security from hardware-to-data will be critical to enabling faster adoption of cloud services.

This book is a great read for those looking to build secure foundations for cloud environments. As seasoned experts in virtualization, enterprise architectures, and security technologies, Raghu and Enrique provide a pivotal discussion of cloud security issues, the challenges companies face as they move into the cloud, and the infrastructure solution components required to address the new security requirements and controls.

—Eric Chiu, President & Co-Founder, Hytrust, Inc.

Introduction

Security is an ever-present consideration for applications and data in the cloud. It is a concern for executives trying to come up with criteria for migrating an application, for marketing organizations in trying to position the company in a good light as enlightened technology adopters, for application architects attempting to build a safe foundation and operations staff making sure bad guys don't have a field day. It does not matter whether an application is a candidate for migration to the cloud or it already runs using cloud-based components. It does not even matter that an application has managed to run for years in the cloud without a major breach: an unblemished record does not entitle an organization to claim to be home free in matters of security; its executives are acutely aware that resting on their laurels regardless of an unblemished record is an invitation to disaster; and certainly past performance is no predictor for future gains.

Irrespective of whom you ask, security is arguably the biggest inhibitor for the broader adoption of cloud computing. Many organizations will need to apply best practices security standards that set a much higher bar than that for on-premise systems, in order to dislodge that incumbent on-premise alternative. The migration or adoption of cloud services then can provide an advantage, in that firms can design, from the ground up, their new cloud-based infrastructures with security "baked-in;" this is in contrast to the piecemeal and "after the fact" or "bolted-on" nature of security seen in most data centers today. But even a baked-in approach has its nuances, as we shall see in Chapter 1. Cloud service providers are hard at work building a secure infrastructure as the foundation for enabling multi-tenancy and providing the instrumentation, visibility, and control that organizations demand. They are beginning to treat security as an integration concern to be addressed as a service like performance, power consumption, and uptime. This provides a flexibility and granularity wherein solution architects design in as much security as their particular situation demands: security for a financial services industry (FSI) or an enterprise resource planning (ERP) application will be different from security for a bunch of product brochures, yet they both may use storage services from the same provider, which demands a high level of integrity, confidentiality, and protection.

Some practices—for instance, using resources in internal private clouds as opposed to public, third-party hosted clouds—while conferring some tactical advantages do not address fundamental security issues, such as perimeter walls made of virtual Swiss cheese where data can pass through anytime. We would like to propose a different approach: to anchor a security infrastructure in the silicon that runs the volume servers in almost every data center. However, end users running mobile applications don't see the servers. What we'll do is define a logical chain of trust rooted in hardware, in a manner not unlike a geometry system built out of a small set of axioms. We use the hardware to ensure the integrity of the firmware: BIOS code running in the chipset and firmware taking care of the server's housekeeping functions. This provides a solid platform on which to run software: the hypervisor environment and operating systems. Each software component is "measured" initially and verified against a "known good" with the root of trust anchored in the hardware trust chain, thereby providing a trusted platform to launch applications.

We assume that readers are already familiar with cloud technology and are interested in a deeper exploration of security aspects. We'll cover some cloud technology principles, primarily with the purpose of establishing a vocabulary from which to build a discussion of security topics (offered here with no tutorial intent). Our goal is to discuss the principles of cloud security, the challenges companies face as they move into the cloud, and the infrastructure requirements to address security requirements. The content is intended for a technical audience and provides architectural, design, and code samples as needed to show how to provision and deploy trusted clouds. While documentation for low-level technology components such as trusted platform modules and the basics of secure boot is not difficult to find from vendor specifications, the contextual perspective—a usage-centric approach describing how the different components are integrated into trusted virtualized platforms—has been missing from the literature. This book is a first attempt at filling this gap through actual proof of concept implementations and a few initial commercial implementations. The implementation of secure platforms is an emerging and fast evolving issue. This is not a definitive treatment by a long measure, and trying to compile one at this early juncture would be unrealistic. Timeliness is a more pressing consideration, and the authors hope that this material will stimulate the curiosity of the reader and encourage the community to replicate the results, leading to new deployments and, in the process, advancing the state of the art.

There are three key trends impacting security in the enterprise and cloud data centers:

- *The evolution of IT architectures.* This is pertinent especially with the adoption of virtualization and now cloud computing. Multi-tenancy and consolidation are driving significant operational efficiencies, enabling multiple lines of business and tenants to share the infrastructure. This consolidation and co-tenancy provide a new dimension and attack vector. How do you ensure the same level of security and control in an infrastructure that is not owned and operated by you? Outsourcing, cross-business, and cross-supply chain collaboration are breaking through the perimeter of traditional security models. These new models are blurring the distinction between data "inside" an organization and that which exists "outside" of those boundaries. The data itself is the new perimeter.

- *The sophistication of attacks.* No longer are attacks targeted at software and no longer are the hackers intent on gaining bragging rights. Attacks are sophisticated and targeted toward gaining control of assets, and with staying hidden. These attacks have progressively moved closer to the lower layers of the platform: firmware, BIOS, and the hypervisor hosting the virtual machine operating environment. Traditionally, controls in these lower layers are few, allowing malware to hide. With multi-tenancy and consolidation through virtualization, taking control of a platform could provide significant leverage and a large attack surface. How does an organization get out of this quandary and institute controls to verify the integrity of the infrastructure on which their mission-critical applications can run? How do they prove to their auditors that the security controls and procedures in effect are still enforced even when their information systems are hosted at a cloud provider?

- *The growing legal and regulatory burden.* Compliance requirements have increased significally for IT practitioners and line-of-business owners. The cost of securing data and the risks of unsecured personally identifiable data, intellectual property, or financial data, as well as the implications of noncompliance to regulations, are very high. Additionally, the number of regulations and mandates involved are putting additional burdens on IT organizations.

Clearly, cloud security is a broad area with cross-cutting concerns that involve technology, products, and solutions that span mobility, networks security, web security, messaging security, protection of data or content and storage, identity management, hypervisor and platform security, firewalls, and audit and compliance, among other concerns. Looking at security from a tools and products perspective is an interesting approach. However, an IT practitioner in an enterprise or a cloud service provider iscompelled to look at usages and needs at the infrastructure level, and to provide a set of cohesive solutions that address business security concerns and requirements. Equally intriguing is to look at the usages that a private cloud or a public cloud have so as to address the following needs:

- For service providers to deliver enterprise-grade solutions. What does this compliant cloud look like? What are its attributes and behaviors?

- For developers, service integrators, and operators to deliver protected applications and workloads from and in the cloud. Irrespective of the type of cloud service, how does a service developer protect the static and the dynamic workload contents and data?

- For service components and users alike to granularly manage, authenticate, and assign trust for both devices and users.

Intel has been hard at work with its partners and as fellow travelers in providing comprehensive solution architectures and a cohesive set of products to not only address these questions but also deploy e solutions in private clouds, public clouds at scale. This book brings together the contributions of various Intel technologists, architects, engineers, and marketing and solution development managers, as well as a few key architects from our partners.

The book has roughly four parts:

- Chapters 1 and 2 cover the context of cloud computing and the idea of security, introducing the concept of trusted clouds. They discuss the key usage models to enable and instantiate the trusted infrastructure, which is a foundational for those trusted clouds. Additionally, these chapters cover the use-models with solution architectures and component exposition.

- Chapters 3, 4, and 5 cover use-cases, solution architectures, and technology components for enabling the trusted infrastructure, with emphasis on trusted compute, the role of attestation, and attestation solutions, as well as geo-fencing and boundary control in the cloud.

- Chapters 6 and 7 provide an interesting view of identity management and control in the cloud, as well as network security in the cloud.

- Chapter 8 extends the notion of trust to the virtual machines and workloads, with reference architecture and components built on top of the trusted compute pools discussed in earlier chapters. Then, Chapter 9 provides a comprehensive exposition of secure cloud bursting reference architecture and a real-world implementation that brings together all the concepts and usages discussed in the preceeding chapters.

These chapters take us on a rewarding journey. Starting with a set of basic technology ingredients rooted in hardware, namely the ability to carry out the secure launch of programs; not just software programs, but also implemented in firmware in server platforms: the BIOS and the system firmware. We have also added other platform sensors and devices to the mix, such as TPMs, location sensors. Eventually it will be possible integrate information from other security related telemetry in the platform: encryption accelerators, secure random generators for keys, secure containers, compression accelerators, and other related entities.

With a hardened platform defined it now becomes possible to extend the scope of the initial set of security features to cloud environments. We extend the initial capability for boot integrity and protection to the next goal of data protection during its complete life cycle: data at rest, in motion and during execution. Our initial focus is on the server platform side. In practical terms we use an approach similar to building a mathematical system, starting with a small set of assertions or axioms and slowly extending the scope of the assertions until the scope becomes useful for cloud deployments. On the compute side we extend the notion of protected boot to hypervisors and operating systems running on bare metal followed by the virtual machines running on top of the hypervisors. Given the intense need in the industry secure platforms, we hope this need will motivate application vendors and system integrators to extend this chain of trust all the way to application points of consumption.

The next abstraction beyond trust established by secure boot is to measure the level of trust for applications running in the platform. This leads to a discussion on attestation and frameworks and processes to accomplish attestation. Beyond that there are a number of practical functions needed in working deployments, including geo-location monitoring and control (geo-fencing), extending trust to workloads, the protected launch of workloads and ensuring run time integrity of workloads and data.

The cloud presents a much more dynamic environment than previous operating environments, including consolidated virtualized environments. For instance, virtual machines may get migrated for performance or business reasons, and within the framework of secure launch, it is imperative to provide security for these virtual machines and their data while they move and where they land. This leads to the notion of trusted compute pools.

Security aspects for networks comes next. One aspect left to be developed is the role of hardened network appliances taking advantage of secure launch to complement present safe practices. Identity management is an ever present challenge due to the distributed nature of the cloud, more so than its prior incarnation in grid computing because distribution, multi-tenancy and dynamic behaviors are carried out well beyond the practices of grid computing.

Along with the conceptual discussions we sprinkle in a number of case studies in the form of proofs of concept and even a few deployments by forward thinking service providers. For the architects integrating a broad range of technology components beyond those associated with the secure launch foundation these projects provides invaluable proofs of existence, an opportunity to identify technology and interface gaps and to provide very precise feedback to standards organizations. This will help accelerate the technology learning curve for the industry as a whole, enabling a rapid reduction in the cost and time to deploy specific implementations.

The compute side is only one aspect of cloud. We'll need to figure out how to extend this protection to the network and storage capabilities in the cloud. The experience of building a trust chain starting from a secure boot foundation helps: network and storage appliances also run on the same components used to build servers. We believe that if we follow the same rigorous approach used to build a compute trust chain, it should be possible to harden network and storage devices to the same degree we attained with the compute subsystem. From this perspective the long journey is beginning to look more than like a trailblazing path.

Some readers will shrewdly note that the IT infrastructure in data centers encompasses more than servers; it also includes networks and storage equipment. The security constructs discussed in this book relate mostly to application stacks running on server equipment, and they are still evolving. It must be noted that network and storage equipment also runs on computing equipment, and therefore one strategy for securing network and storage equipment will be precisely to build analogous trust chains applicable to the equipment. These topics are beyond the scope of this book but are certainly relevant to industry practitioners and therefore are excellent subjects for subject-matter experts to document in future papers and books.

The authors acknowledge the enormous amount of work still to be done, but by the same token, these are enormously exciting areas to explore, with the potential of delivering equally enormous value to a beleaguered security industry—an industry that has been rocked by a seemingly endless stream of ever-more sophisticated and brazen exploits. We invite industry participants in any role, whether executive, architecture, engineering, system integration, or development, to join us in broadening this path. Actually, the path to innovation will never end—this is the essence of security. However, along the way, industry participants will build a much more robust foundation to the cloud, bringing some well-deserved assurances to customers.

CHAPTER 1

■ ■ ■

Cloud Computing Basics

In this chapter we go through some basic concepts with the purpose of providing context for the discussions in the chapters that follow. Here, we review briefly the concept of the cloud as defined by the U.S. National Institute of Standards and Technology, and the familiar terms of IaaS, PaaS, and SaaS under the SPI model. What is not often discussed is that the rise of cloud computing comes from strong historical motivations and addresses shortcomings of predecessor technologies such as grid computing, the standard enterprise three-tier architecture, or even the mainframe architecture of many decades ago.

From a security perspective, the main subjects for this book—perimeter and endpoint protection—were pivotal concepts in security strategies prior to the rise of cloud technology. Unfortunately these abstractions were inadequate to prevent recurrent exploits, such as leaks of customer credit card data, even before cloud technology became widespread in the industry. We'll see in the next few pages that, unfortunately for this approach, along with the agility, scalability, and cost advantages of the cloud, the distributed nature of these third-party-provided services also introduced new risk factors. Within this scenario we would like to propose a more integrated approach to enterprise security, one that starts with server platforms in the data center and builds to the hypervisor operating system and applications that fall under the notion of *trusted compute pools,* covered in the chapters that follow.

Defining the Cloud

We will use the U.S. government's National Institute of Standards and Technology (NIST) cloud framework for purposes of our discussions in the following chapters. This provides a convenient, broadly understood frame of reference, without our attempts to treat it as a definitive definition or to exclude other perspectives. These definitions are stated somewhat tersely in *The NIST Definition of Cloud Computing*[1] and have been elaborated by the Cloud Security Alliance.[2]

---

[1]Peter Mell and Timothy Grance, *The NIST Definition of Cloud Computing*. NIST Special Publication 800-145, September 2011.
[2]*Security Guidance for Critical Areas of Focus in Cloud Computing*, Cloud Security Alliance, rev. 2.1 (2009).

The model consists of three main layers (see Figure 1-1), laid out in a top-down fashion: global essential characteristics that apply to all clouds, the service models by which cloud services are delivered, and how the services are instantiated in the form of deployment models. There is a reason for this structure that's rooted in the historical evolution of computer and network architecture and in the application development and deployment models. Unfortunately most discussions of the cloud gloss over this aspect. We assume readers of this book are in a technology leadership role in their respective fields, and very likely are influential in the future direction of cloud security. Therefore, an understanding of the dynamics of technology evolution will be helpful for the readers in these strategic roles. For this purpose, the section that follows covers the historical context that led to the creation of the cloud.

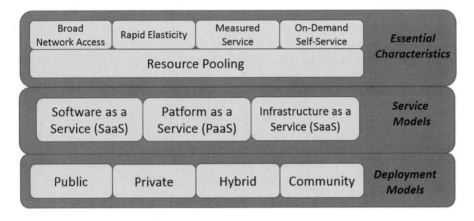

Figure 1-1. *NIST cloud computing definition*

The Cloud's Essential Characteristics

The main motivation behind the pervasive adoption of cloud use today is economic. Cloud technology allows taking a very expensive asset, such as a $200 million data center, and delivering its capabilities to individual users for a few dollars per month, or even for free, in some business models. This feat is achieved through *resource pooling*, which is essentially treating an asset like a server as a fungible resource; a resource-intensive application might take a whole server, or even a cluster of servers, whereas the needs of users with lighter demands can be packed as hundreds or even thousands to a server.

This dynamic range in the mapping of applications to servers has been achieved through virtualization technology. Every intervening technology and the organizations needed to run them represent overhead. However, the gains in efficiency are so large that this inherent overhead is rarely in question. With applications running on bare-metal operating systems, it is not unusual to see load factors in the single digits. Cloud applications running on virtualized environments, however, typically run utilizations up to 60 to 80 percent, increasing the application yield of a server by several-fold.

Cloud applications are inherently distributed, and hence they are necessarily *delivered over a network*. The largest applications may involve millions of users, and the conveyance method is usually the Internet. An example is media delivery through Netflix, using infrastructure from Amazon Web Services. Similarly, cloud applications are expected to have automated interfaces for setup and administration. This usually means they are accessible *on demand* through a *self-service* interface. This is usually the case, for instance, with email accounts through Google Gmail or Microsoft `Outlook.com`.

With the self-service model, it is imperative to establish methods for *measuring service*. This measuring includes guarantees of service provider performance, measurement of services delivered for billing purposes, and very important from the perspective of our discussion, measurement of security along multiple vectors. The management information exchanged between a service provider and consumers is defined as *service metadata*. This information may be facilitated by auxiliary services or *metaservices*.

The service provider needs to maintain a service pool large enough to address the needs of the largest customer during peak demand. The expectation is that, with a large customer base, most local peaks and valleys will cancel out. In order to get the same quality of service (QoS), an IT organization would need to size the equipment for expected peak demand, leading to inefficient use of capital. Under some circumstances, large providers can smooth out even regional peaks and valleys by coordinating their geographically disperse data centers, a luxury that mid-size businesses might not be able to afford.

The expectation for cloud users, then, is that compute, network, and data resources in the cloud should be provided on short order. This property is known as *elasticity*. For instance, virtual machines should be available on demand in seconds, or no more than minutes, compared to the normal physical server procurement process that could take anywhere from weeks to years.

At this point, we have covered the *what* question—namely, the essential characteristics of the cloud. The next section covers service models, which is essentially the *how* question.

The Cloud Service Models

The unit of delivery for cloud technology is a *service*. NIST defines three service models, affectionately known as the SPI model, for SaaS, PaaS, and IaaS, or, respectively, software, platform, and infrastructure services.

Under the *SaaS* service model, applications run at the service provider or delegate services under the service network paradigm described below. Users access their applications through a browser, thin client, or mobile device. Examples are Google Docs, Gmail, and MySAP.

PaaS refers to cloud-based application development environments, compilers, and tools. The cloud consumer does not see the hardware or network directly, but is able to determine the application configuration and the hosting environment configuration.

IaaS usually refers to cloud-based compute, network, and storage resources. These resources are generally understood to be virtualized. For simplicity, some providers may require running pre-configured or highly paravirtualized operating system images. This is how a pool of physical hosts is able to support 500 or more virtual machines each. Some providers may provide additional guarantees—for instance, physical hosts shared with no one else or direct access to a physical host from a pool of hosts.

The bottom layer of the NIST framework addresses *where* cloud resources are deployed, which is covered in the next section.

The Cloud Deployment Models

The phrase *cloud deployment models* refers to the environment or placement of cloud services as deployed. The quintessential cloud is the multi-tenant *public cloud,* where the infrastructure is pooled and made available to all customers. Cloud customers don't have a say in the selection of the physical host where their virtual machines land. This environment is prone to the well-known noisy and nosy neighbor problems, with multiple customers sharing a physical host.

The *noisy neighbor* problem might manifest when a customer's demand on host resources impacts the performance experienced by another customer running on the same host; an application with a large memory footprint may cause the application from another customer to start paging and to run slowly. An application generating intense I/O traffic may starve another customer trying to use the same resource.

As for the *nosy neighbor* problem, the hypervisor enforces a high level of isolation between tenants through the virtual machine abstraction—much higher, for instance, than inter-process isolation within an operating system. However, there is no absolute proof that the walls between virtual machines belonging to unrelated customers are completely airtight. Service-level agreements for public clouds usually do not provide assurances against tenants sharing a physical host. Without a process to qualify tenants, a virtual machine running a sensitive financial application could end up sharing the host with an application that has malicious intent. To minimize the possibility of such breaches, customers with sensitive workloads will, as a matter of practice, decline to run them in public cloud environments, choosing instead to run them in corporate-owned infrastructure. These customers need to forfeit the benefits of the cloud, no matter how attractive they may seem.

As a partial remedy for the nosy neighbor problem, an entity may operate a cloud for exclusive use, whether deployed on premises or operated by a third party. These clouds are said to be *private clouds*. A variant is a *community cloud,* operated not by one entity but by more than one with shared affinities, whether corporate mission, security, policy, or compliance considerations, or a mix thereof.

The community cloud is the closest to the model under which a predecessor technology, *grid computing,* operated. A computing grid was operated by an affinity group. This environment was geared toward high-performance computing usages, emphasizing the allocation of multiple nodes—namely, computers or servers to run a job of limited duration—rather than an application running for indefinite time that might use a fractional server.

The broad adoption of the NIST definition for cloud computing allows cloud service providers and consumers alike to establish an initial set of expectations about management, security, and interoperability, as well as determine the value derived from use of cloud technology. The next section covers these aspects in more detail.

The Cloud Value Proposition

The NIST service and deployment models—namely public, private, and hybrid—get realized through published APIs, whether open or proprietary. It is through these APIs that customers can elicit capabilities related to management, security, and interoperability for cloud computing. The APIs get developed through diverse industry efforts, including the Open Cloud Computing Interface Working Group, Amazon EC2 API, VMware's DMTF-submitted vCloud API, Rackspace API, and GoGrid's API, to name just a few. In particular, open, standard APIs will play a key role in cloud portability, federation, and interoperability, as will common container formats such as the DMTF's Open Virtualization Format or OVF, as specified by the Cloud Security Alliance in the citation above.

Future flexibility, security, and mobility of the resultant solution, as well as its collaborative capabilities, are first-order considerations in the design of cloud-based solutions. As a rule of thumb, de-perimeterized solutions have the potential to be more effective than perimeterized solutions relying on the notion of an enterprise perimeter to be protected, especially in cloud-based environments that have no clear notion of inside or outside. The reasons are complex. Some are discussed in the section "New Enterprise Security Boundaries," later in this chapter. Careful consideration should also be given to the choice between proprietary and open solutions, for similar reasons.

The NIST definition emphasizes the flexibility and convenience of the cloud, enabling customers to take advantage of computing resources and applications that they do not own for advancing their strategic objectives. It also emphasizes the supporting technological infrastructure, considered an element of the IT supply chain managed to respond to new capacity and technological service demands without the need to acquire or expand in-house complex infrastructures.

Understanding the dependencies and relationships between the cloud computing deployment and the service models is critical for assessing cloud security risks and controls. With PaaS and SaaS built on top of IaaS, as described in the NIST model above, inherited or imported capabilities introduce security issues and risks. In all cloud models, the risk profile for data and security changes is an essential factor in deciding which models are appropriate for an organization. The speed of adoption depends on how fast security and trust in the new cloud models can be established.

Cloud resources can be created, moved, migrated, and multiplied in real time to meet enterprise computing needs. A trusted cloud can be an application accessible through the Web or a server provisioned as available when needed. It can involve a specific set of users accessing it from a specific device on the Internet. The cloud model delivers convenient, on-demand access to shared pools of hardware and infrastructure, made possible by sophisticated automation, provisioning, and virtualization technologies. This model decouples data and software from the servers, networks, and storage systems. It makes for flexible, convenient, and cost-effective alternatives to owning and operating an organization's own servers, storage, networks, and software.

However, it also blurs many of the traditional, physical boundaries that help define and protect an organization's data assets. As cloud- and software-defined infrastructure becomes the new standard, the security that depends on static elements like hardware, fixed network perimeters, and physical location won't be guaranteed. Enterprises seeking the benefits of cloud-based infrastructure delivery need commensurate security and compliance. Covering this topic is the objective for this book. The new perimeter is defined in terms of data, its location, and the cloud resources processing it, given that the old definition of on-premise assets no longer applies.

Let's now explore some of the historical drivers of the adoption of cloud technology.

Historical Context

Is it possible to attain levels of service in terms of security, reliability, and performance for cloud-based applications that rival implementations using corporate-owned infrastructure? Today it is challenging not only to achieve this goal but also to measure that success except in a very general sense. For example, consider doing a cost rollup at the end of a fiscal year. There's no capability today to establish operational metrics and service introspection. A goal for security in the cloud, therefore, is not to just match this baseline but to surpass it. In this book, we'd like to claim that is possible.

Cloud technology enables the disaggregation of compute, network, and storage resources in a data center into pools of resources, as well as the partitioning and re-aggregation of these resources according to the needs of consumers down the supply chain. These capabilities are delivered through a network, as explained earlier in the chapter. A virtualization layer may be used to smooth out the hardware heterogeneity and enable configurable software-defined data centers that can deliver a service at a quality level that is consistent with a pre-agreed SLA.

The vision for enterprise IT is to be able to run varied workloads on a software-defined data center, with ability for developers, operators, or in fact, any responsible entity to use self-service unified management tools and automation software. The software-defined data center must be abstracted from, but still make best use of, physical infrastructure capability, capacity, and level of resource consumption across multiple data centers and geographies. For this vision to be realized, it is necessary that enterprise IT have products, tools, and technologies to provision, monitor, remediate, and report on the service level of the software-defined data center and the underlying physical infrastructure.

Traditional Three-Tier Architecture

The three-tier architecture shown in Figure 1-2 is well established in data centers today for application deployment. It is highly scalable, whereby each of the tiers can be expanded independently by adding more servers to remove choke points as needed, and without resorting to a forklift upgrade.

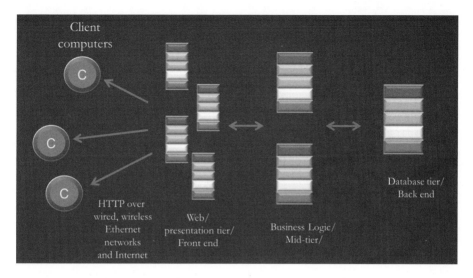

Figure 1-2. *Three-tier application architecture*

While the traditional three-tier architecture did fine in the scalability department, it was not efficient in terms of cost and asset utilization, however. This was because of the reality of procuring a physical asset. If new procurement needs to go through a budgetary cycle, the planning horizon can be anywhere from six months to two years. Meanwhile, capacity needs to be sized for the expected peak demand, plus a generous allowance for demand growth over the system's planning and lifecycle, which may or may not be realized. This defensive practice leads to chronically low utilization rates, typically in the 5 to 15 percent range. Managing infrastructure in this overprovisioned manner represents a sunk investment, with a large portion of the capacity not used during most of the infrastructure's planned lifetime. The need for overprovisioning would be greatly alleviated if supply could somehow be matched with demand in terms of near-real time—perhaps on a daily or even an hourly basis.

Server consolidation was a technique adopted in data centers starting in the early 2000s, which addressed the low-utilization problem using virtualization technology to pack applications into fewer physical hosts. While server consolidation was successful at increasing utilization, it brought significant technical complexity and was a static scheme, as resource allocation was done only at planning or deployment time. That is, server consolidation technology offered limited flexibility in changing the machine allocations during operations, after an application was launched. Altering the resource mix required significant retooling and application downtime.

Software Evolution: From Stovepipes to Service Networks

The low cost of commodity servers made it easy to launch application instances. However, little thought was given to how the different applications would interact with one another. For instance, the information about the employee roster in an organization is needed for applications as diverse as human resources, internal phone directory, expense reporting, and so on. Having separate copies of these resources meant allocating infrastructure to run these copies, and running an infrastructure was costly in terms of extra software licensing fees. Having several copies of the same data also introduced the problem of keeping data synchronized across the different copies.

■ **Note**   Cloud computing has multiplied the initial gains in efficiency delivered by server consolidation by allowing dynamic rebalancing of workloads at run time, not just at planning or deployment time.

The initial state of IT applications circa 2000 ran in stovepipes, shown in Figure 1-3 on the left, with each application running on assigned hardware. Under cloud computing, capabilities common across multiple stacks, such as the company's employee database, are abstracted out in the form of a service or of a limited number of service instances that would certainly be smaller than the number of application instances. All applications needing access to the employee database, for instance, get connected to the employee database service.

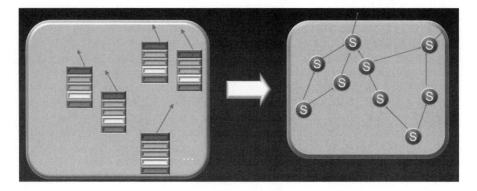

Figure 1-3. *Transition from stovepipes to a service network ecosystem*

Under these circumstances, duplicated stacks characterizing stovepiped applications now morph into a graph, with each node representing a coalesced capability. The capability is implemented as a reusable service. The abstract connectivity of the service components making up an application can be represented as a network—a *service network*. The stovepipes, thus, have morphed into service networks, as depicted on the right side of Figure 1-3. We call these nodes *servicelets*; they are service components designed primarily to be building blocks for cloud-based applications, but they are not necessarily self-contained applications.

With that said, we have an emerging service ecosystem with composite applications that are freely using both internally and third-party servicelets. A strong driver for this application architecture has been the consumerization of IT and the need to make existing corporate applications available through mobile devices.

For instance, front-end services have gone through a notable evolution, whereby the traditional PC web access has been augmented to enable application access through mobile devices. A number of enterprises have opened applications for public access, including travel reservation systems, supply chain, and shopping networks. The capabilities are accessible to third-party developers through API managers that make it relatively easy to build mobile front ends to cloud capabilities; this is shown in Figure 1-4. A less elegant version of this scheme is the "lipstick on a pig" approach of retooling a traditional three-tier application and slapping a REST API on top, to "servitize" the application and make it accessible as a component for integration into other third-party applications. As technology evolves, we can expect more elegantly architected servicelets built from the ground up to function as such.

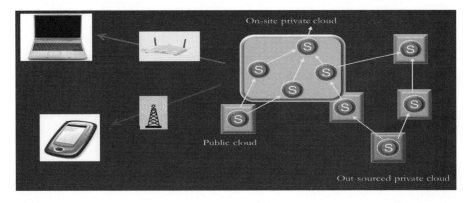

Figure 1-4. *Application service networks*

So, in Figure 1-4 we see a composite application with an internal API built out of four on-premise services hosted in an on-premise private cloud, the boundary marked by the large, rounded rectangle. The application uses four additional services offered by third-party providers and possibly hosted in a public cloud. A fifth service, shown in the lower right corner, uses a third-party private cloud, possibly shared with other corporate applications from the same company.

Continuing on the upper left corner of Figure 1-4, note the laptop representing a client front end for access by nomadic employees. The mobile device on the lower left represents a mobile app developed by a third-party ISV accessing another application API posted through an API manager. An example of such an application could be a company's e-commerce application. The mobile app users are the company's customers, able to check stock and place purchase orders. However, API calls for inventory restocking and visibility into the supply chain are available only through the internal API. Quietly, behind the scenes, the security mechanisms to be discussed in the following chapters are acting to ensure the integrity of the transactions throughout.

In this section we have covered the evolution of application architecture from application stovepipes to the current service paradigm. IT processes have been evolving along with the architecture. Process evolution is the subject of the next section.

The Cloud as the New Way of Doing IT

The cloud represents a milestone in technology maturity for the way IT services are delivered. This has been a common pattern, with more sophisticated technologies taking the place of earlier ones. The automobile industry is a fitting example. At the dawn of the industry, the thinking was to replace horses with the internal combustion engine. There was little realization then of the real changes to come, including a remaking the energy supply chain based on petroleum and the profound ripple effects on our transportation systems. Likewise, servicelets will become more than server replacements; they will be key components for building new IT capabilities unlimited by underlying physical resources.

▓ **Note**   An important consideration is that the cloud needs to be seen beyond just a drop-in replacement for the old stovepipes. This strategy of using new technology to re-implement existing processes would probably work, but can deliver only incremental benefits, if any at all. The cloud represents a fundamental change in how IT gets done and delivered. Therefore, it also presents an opportunity for making a clean break with the past, bringing with it the potential for a quantum jump in asset utilization and, as we hope to show in this book, in greater security.

Here are some considerations:

- *Application development time scales are compressing,* yet the scope of these applications keeps expanding, with new user communities being brought in. IT organizations need to be ready to use applications and servicelets from which to easily build customized applications in a fraction of the time it takes today. Unfortunately, the assets constituting these applications will be owned by a slew of third parties: the provider may be a SaaS provider using a deployment assembled by a systems integrator; the systems integrator will use offerings from different software vendors; IaaS providers will include network, computing, and storage resources.

- *A high degree of operational transparency is required to* build a composite application out of servicelets—that is, in terms of application quantitative monitoring and control capability. A composite application built from servicelets must offer end-to-end service assurance better than the same application built from traditional, corporate-owned assets. The composite application needs to be more reliable and secure than incumbent alternatives if it's to be accepted. Specific to security, operational transparency means it can be used as a building block for auditable IT processes, an essential security requirement.

- *QoS constitutes an ever-present concern and a barrier;* today's service offerings do not come even close to reaching this goal, and that limits the migration of a sizable portion of corporate applications to cloud. We can look at security as one of the most important QoS issues for applications, on a par with performance.

On the last point, virtually all service offerings available today are not only opaque when it comes to providing quantifiable QoS but, when it comes to QoS providers, they also seem to run in the opposite direction of customer desires and interests. Typical messsages, including those from large, well-known service providers, have such unabashed clauses as the following:

> "Your access to and use of the services may be suspended . . . for any reason . . ."

> "We will not be liable for direct, indirect or consequential damages . . ."

> "The service offerings are provided 'as is' . . . "

> "We shall not be responsible for any service interruptions . . . "

These customer agreements are written from the perspective of the service provider. The implicit message is that the customer comes as second priority, and the goal of the disclaimers is to protect the provider from liability. Clearly, there are supply gaps in capabilities and unmet customer needs with the current service offerings. Providers addressing the issue head on, with an improved ability to quantify their security risks and the capability of providing risk metrics for their service products, will have an advantage over their competition, even if their products are no more reliable than comparable offerings. We hope the trusted cloud methods discussed in the following chapters will help providers deliver a higher level of assurance in differentiated service offerings. We'd like to think that these disclaimers reflect service providers' *inability,* considering the current state of the art, to deliver the level of security and performance needed, rather than any attempts to dodge the issue.

Given that most enterprise applications run on servers installed in data centers, the first step is to take advantage of the sensors and features already available in the server platforms. The next chapters will show how, through the use of Intel Trusted Execution Technology (TXT) and geolocation sensors, it is possible to build more secure platforms.

We believe that the adoption, deployment, and application of the emerging technologies covered in this book will help the industry address current quandaries with service-level agreements (SLAs) and enable new market entrants. Addressing security represents a baby step toward cloud service assurance. There is significant work taking place in other areas, including application performance and power management, which will provide a trove of material for future books.

Security as a Service

What would be a practical approach to handling security in a composite application environment? Should it be baked-in—namely, every service component handling its own security—or should it be bolted on after integration? As explained above, we call these service components *servicelets,* designed primarily to function as application building blocks rather than as full-fledged, self-contained applications.

Unfortunately, neither approach constitutes a workable solution. A baked-in approach requires the servicelet to anticipate every possible circumstance for every customer during the product's lifetime. This comprehensive approach may be overkill for most applications. It certainly burdens with overwrought security features the service developer trying to quickly bring a lightweight product to market. The developer may see this effort as a distraction from the main business. Likewise, a bolted-on approach makes it difficult both to retrofit security on the servicelet and to implement consistent security policies across the enterprise.

One possible approach out of this maze is to look at security as a horizontal capability, to be handled as another service. This approach assumes the notion of a virtual enterprise service boundary.

New Enterprise Security Boundaries

The notion of a security perimeter for the enterprise is essential for setting up a first line of defense. The perimeter defines the notion of what is inside and what is outside the enterprise. Although insider attacks can't be ruled out, let's assume for the moment that we're dealing with a first line of defense to protect the "inside" from outsider attacks. In the halcyon days, the inside coincided with a company's physical assets. A common approach was to lay out a firewall to protect unauthorized access between the trusted inside and untrusted outside networks.

Ideally, a firewall can provide centralized control across distributed assets with uniform and consistent policies. Unfortunately, these halcyon days actually never existed. Here's why:

- A firewall only stands a chance of stopping threats that attempt to cross the boundary.

- Large companies, and even smaller companies after a merger and acquisition, have or end up having a geographically disperse IT infrastructure. This makes it difficult to set up single-network entry points and it stretches the notion of what "inside" means.

- The possibility of composite application with externalized solution components literally turns the concept of "inside" inside out. In an increasingly cloud-oriented world, composite applications are becoming the rule more than the exception.

- Mobile applications have become an integral part of corporate IT. In the mobile world, certain corporate applications get exposed to third-party consumers, so it's not just matter of considering what to do with external components supporting internal applications; also, internal applications become external from the application-consumer perspective.

The new enterprise security perimeter has different manifestations depending on the type of cloud architecture in use—namely, whether private, hybrid, or public under the NIST classification.

The *private cloud* model is generally the starting point for many enterprises, as they try to reduce data center costs by using a virtualized pooled infrastructure. The physical infrastructure is entirely on the company's premises; the enterprise security perimeter is the same as for the traditional, vertically owned infrastructure, as shown in Figure 1-5.

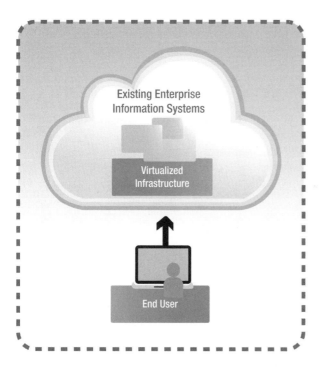

Figure 1-5. *Traditional security perimeter*

The next step in sophistication is the *hybrid cloud*, shown in Figure 1-6. A hybrid cloud constitutes the more common example of an enterprise using an external cloud service in a targeted manner for a specific business need. This model is hybrid because the core business services are left in the enterprise perimeter, and some set of cloud services are selectively used for achieving specific business goals. There is additional complexity, in that we have third-party servicelets physically outside the traditional enterprise perimeter.

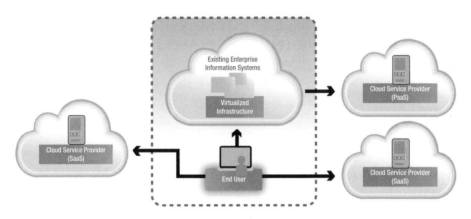

Figure 1-6. *Security perimeter in the hybrid cloud*

The last stage of sophistication comes with the use of *public clouds*, shown in Figure 1-7. Using public clouds brings greater rewards for the adoption of cloud technology, but also greater risks. In its pure form, unlike the hybrid cloud scenario, the initial on-premise business core may become vanishingly small. Only end users remain in the original perimeter. All enterprise services may get offloaded to external cloud providers on a strategic and permanent basis. Application components become externalized, physically and logically.

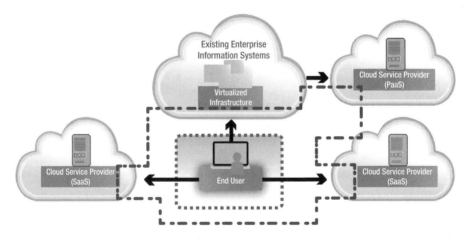

Figure 1-7. *Generalized cloud security perimeter*

Yet another layer of complexity is the realization that the enterprise security perimeter as demarcation for an IT fortress was never a realistic concept. For instance, allowing employee access to the corporate network through VPN is tantamount to extending a bubble of the internal network to the worker in the field. However, in practical situations, that perimeter must be semipermeable, allowing a bidirectional flow of information.

A case in point is a company's website. An initial goal may have been to provide customers with product support information. Beyond that, a CIO might be asked to integrate the website into the company's revenue model. Examples might include supply-chain integration: airlines making their scheduling and reservation systems, or hotel chains publishing available rooms, not only for direct consumption through browsers but also as APIs for integration with other applications. Any of these extended capabilities will have the effect of blurring the security boundaries by bringing in external players and entities.

■ **Note** An IT organization developing an application is not exclusively a servicelet consumer but also is making the company become a servicelet provider in the pursuit of incremental revenue. The enterprise security boundary becomes an entity enforcing the rules for information flow in order to prevent a free-for-all, including corporate secrets flying out the window.

If anything, the fundamental security concerns that existed with IT delivered out of corporate-owned assets also apply when IT functions, processes, and capabilities migrate to the cloud. The biggest challenge is to define, devise, and carry out these concepts into the new cloud-federated environment in a way that is more or less transparent to the community of users. An added challenge is that, because of the broader reach of the cloud, the community of users expands by several orders of magnitude. A classic example is the airline reservation system, such as the AMR Sabre passenger reservation system, later spun out as an independent company. Initially it was the purview of corporate staff. Travel agents in need of information or making reservations phoned to access the airline information indirectly. Eventually travel agents were able to query and make reservations directly. Under the self-service model of the cloud today, it is customary for consumers to make reservations themselves through dozens of cloud-based composite applications using web-enabled interfaces from personal computers and mobile devices.

Indeed, security imperatives have not changed in the brave new world of cloud computing. Perimeter management was an early attempt at security management, and it is still in use today. The cloud brings new challenges, though, such as the nosy neighbor problem mentioned earlier. To get started in the cloud environments, the concept of trust in a federated environment needs to be generalized. The old concept of inside vs. outside the firewall has long been obsolete and provides little comfort. On the one hand, the federated nature of the cloud brings the challenge of ensuring trust across logically and geographically distributed components. On the other hand, we believe that the goal for security in the cloud is to match current levels of security in the enterprise, preferably by removing some of the outstanding challenges. For instance, the service abstraction used internally provides additional opportunities for checks and balances in terms of governance, risk management, and compliance (GRC) not possible in earlier monolithic environments.

We see this transition as an opportunity to raise the bar, as is expected when any new technology displaces the incumbent. Two internal solution components may trust each other, and therefore their security relationships are said to be implicit. If these components become servicelets, the implicit relationship becomes explicit: authentication needs to happen and trust needs to be measured. If these actions can't be formalized, though, the provider does not deliver what the customer wants. The natural response from the provider is to put liability-limiting clauses in place of an SLA. Yet there is trouble when the state-of-the-art can't provide what the customer wants. This inability by service providers to deliver security assurances leads to the brazen disclaimers mentioned above.

Significant progress has been achieved in service performance management. Making these contractual relationships explicit in turn makes it possible to deliver predictable cost and performance in ways that were not possible before. This dynamic introduces the notion of service metadata, described in Chapter 10. We believe security is about to cross the same threshold. As we've mentioned, this is the journey we are about to embark on during the next few chapters.

The transition from a corporate-owned infrastructure to a cloud technology poses a many-layered challenge: every new layer addressed then brings a fresh one to the fore. Today we are well past the initial technology viability objections, and hence the challenge *du jour* is security, with security cited as a main roadblock on the way to cloud adoption.

A Roadmap for Security in the Cloud

Now that we have covered the fundamentals of cloud technology and expressed some lingering security issues, as well as the dynamics that led to the creation of the cloud, we can start charting the emerging technology elements and see how they can be integrated in a way that can enhance security outcomes. From a security perspective, there are two necessary conditions for the cloud to be accepted as a mainstream medium for application deployment. We covered the first: essentially embracing its federated nature and using it to advantage. The second is having an infrastructure that directly supports the security concerns inherent in the cloud, offering an infrastructure that can be trusted. In Chapter 2, we go one level deeper, exploring the notion of "trusted cloud." The trusted cloud infrastructure is not just about specific features. It also encompasses processes such as governance, assurance, compliance, and audits.

In Chapter 3, we introduce the notions of *trusted infrastructure* and *trusted distributed resources* under the umbrella of *trusted compute pools* and enforcement of security policies steming from a hardware-based root of trust. Chapter 4 deals with the idea of *attestation*, an essential operational capability allowing the authentication of computational resources.

In a federated environment, location may be transparent. In other cases, because of the distributed nature of the infrastructure, location needs to be explicit: policies prescribing where data sets and virtual machine can travel, as well as useful *ex post facto* audit trails. The topic of geolocation and geotagging is covered in Chapter 5. Chapter 6 surveys security considerations for the network infrastructure that links cloud resources.

Chapter 7 considers issues of identity management in the cloud. And Chapter 8 discusses the idea of identity in a federated environment. The latter is not a new problem; federated identity management was an important feature of the cloud's predecessor technology, grid computing. However, as we'll show, considerations of federation for the cloud are much different.

Summary

We started this chapter with a set of commonly understood concepts. We also observed the evolution of security as IT made of corporate-owned assets to that of augmented with externalized resources. The security model also evolved from an implicit, essentially "security by obscurity" approach involving internal assets to one that is explicit across assets crossing corporate boundaries. This federation brings new challenges, but it also has the possibility of raising the bar in terms of security for corporate applications. This new beginning can be built upon a foundation of trusted cloud infrastructure, which is discussed in the rest of this book.

CHAPTER 2

The Trusted Cloud: Addressing Security and Compliance

In Chapter 1 we reviewed the essential cloud concepts and took a first look at cloud security. We noted that the traditional notion of perimeter or endpoint protection left much to be desired in the traditional architecture with enterprise-owned assets. Such a notion is even less adequate today when we add the challenges that application developers, service providers, application architects, data center operators, and users face in the emerging cloud environment.

In this chapter we'll bring the level of discourse one notch tighter and focus on defining the issues that drive cloud security. We'll go through a set of initial considerations and common definitions as prescribed by industry standards. We'll also look at current pain points in the industry regarding security and the challenges involved in addressing those pains.

Beyond these considerations, we first take a look at the solution space: the concept of a trusted infrastructure and usages to be implemented in a trusted cloud, starting with a trust chain that consists of hardware that supports boot integrity. Then, we take advantage of that trust chain to implement data protection, equally at rest and in motion and during application execution, to support application run-time integrity and offer protection in the top layer.

Finally, we look briefly at some of the "to be" scenarios for users who are able to put these recommendations into practice.

Security Considerations for the Cloud

One of the biggest barriers to broader adoption of cloud computing is security—the real and perceived risks of providing, accessing, and controlling services in a multi-tenant cloud environment. IT managers would like to see higher levels of assurance before they can declare their cloud-based services and data ready for prime time, similar to the level of trust they have in corporate-owned infrastructure. Organizations require their compute platforms to be secure and compliant with relevant rules, regulations, and laws. These requirements must be met, whether deployment uses a dedicated service available via a private cloud or is a service shared with other subscribers via a public cloud. There's no margin for error when it comes to security. According to a research study conducted by the Ponemon Institute and Symantec, the average cost to an organization of a data breach in 2013 was $5.4 million, and the corresponding cost of lost business came to about $3 million.[1] It is the high cost of such data breaches and the inadequate security monitoring capabilities offered as part of the cloud services that pose the greatest threats to wider adoption of cloud computing and that create resistance within organizations to public cloud services.

From an IT manager's perspective, cloud computing architectures bypass or work against traditional security tools and frameworks. The ease with which services are migrated and deployed in a cloud environment brings significant benefits, but they are a bane from a compliance and security perspective. Therefore, this chapter focuses on the security challenges involved in deploying and managing services in a cloud infrastructure. To serve as an example, we describe work that Intel is doing with partners and the software vendor ecosystem to enable a security-enhanced platform and solutions with security anchored and rooted in hardware and firmware. The goal of this effort is to increase security visibility and control in the cloud.

Cloud computing describes the pooling of an on-demand, self-managed virtual infrastructure, consumed as a service. This approach abstracts applications from the complexity of the underlying infrastructure, allowing IT to focus on enabling greater business value and innovation instead of getting bogged down by technology deployment details. Organizations welcome the presumed cost savings and business flexibility associated with cloud deployments. However, IT practitioners unanimously cite security, control, and IT compliance as primary issues that slow the adoption of cloud computing. These considerations often denote general concerns about privacy, trust, change management, configuration management, access controls, auditing, and logging. Many customers also have specific security requirements that mandate control over data location, isolation, and integrity. These requirements have traditionally been met through a fixed hardware infrastructure.

At the current state of cloud computing, the means to verify a service's compliance are labor-intensive, inconsistent, non-scalable, or just plain impractical to implement. The necessary data, APIs, and tools are not available from the provider. Process mismatches occur when service providers and consumers work under different operating models. For these reasons, many corporations deploy less critical applications in the public cloud and restrict their sensitive applications to dedicated hardware and traditional IT architecture running in a corporate-owned vertical infrastructure. For business-critical applications and processes, and for sensitive data, third-party attestations of security controls usually aren't enough. In such cases, it is absolutely critical for organizations to be able to ascertain that the underlying cloud infrastructure is secure enough for the intended use.

---

[1] https://www4.symantec.com/mktginfo/whitepaper/053013_GL_NA_WP_Ponemon-2013-Cost-of-a-Data-Breach-Report_daiNA_cta72382.pdf

This requirement thus drives the next frontier of cloud security and compliance: implementing a level of transparency at the lowest layers of the cloud, through the development of standards, instrumentation, tools, and linkages to monitor and prove that the IaaS cloud's physical and virtual servers are actually performing as they should be and that they meet defined security criteria. The expectation is that the security of a cloud service should match or exceed the equivalent in house capabilities before it can be considered an appropriate replacement.

Today, security mechanisms in the lower stack layers (for example, hardware, firmware, and hypervisors) are almost absent. The demand for security is higher for externally sourced services. In particular, the requirements for transparency are higher: while certain monitoring and logging capabilities might not have been deemed necessary for an in-house component, they become absolute necessities when sourced from third parties to support operations, meet SLA compliance, and have audit trails should litigation and forensics become necessary. On the positive side, the use of cloud services will likely drive the re-architecturing of crusty applications with much higher levels of transparency and scalability with, we hope, moderate cost impact due to the greater efficiency the cloud brings.

Cloud providers and the IT community are working earnestly to address these requirements, allowing cloud services to be deployed and managed with predictable outcomes, with controls and policies in place to monitor trust and compliance of these services in cloud infrastructures. Specifically, Intel Corporation and other technology companies have come together to enable a highly secure cloud infrastructure based on a hardware root of trust, providing tamper-proof measurements of physical and virtual components in the computing stack, including hypervisors. These collaborations are working to develop a framework that integrates the secure hardware measurements provided by the hardware root of trust with adjoining virtualization and cloud management software. The intent is to improve visibility, control, and compliance for cloud services. For example, making the trust and integrity of the cloud servers visible will allow cloud orchestrators to provide improved controls of on boarding services for their more sensitive workloads, offering more secure hardware and subsequently better control over the migration of workloads and greater ability to deliver on security policies.

Security requirements for cloud use are still works in progress, let alone firming up the security aspects proper. Let's look at some of the security issues being captured, defined, and specified by the government and standards organizations.

Cloud Security, Trust, and Assurance

There is significant focus on and activity across various standards organizations and forums to define the challenges facing cloud security, as well as solutions to those challenges. The Cloud Security Alliance (CSA), NIST, and the Open Cloud Computing Interface (OCCI) are examples of organizations promoting cloud security standards. The Open Data Center Alliance (ODCA), an alliance of customers, recognizes that security is the biggest challenge organizations face as they plan for migration to cloud services. The ODCA is developing usage models that provide standardized definitions for security in the cloud services and detailed procedures for service providers to demonstrate compliance with those standards. These attempts seek to give organizations an ability to validate adherence to security standards within the cloud services.

Here are some important considerations dominating the current work on cloud security:

- **Visibility, compliance, and monitoring**. Ways are needed to provide seamless access to security controls, conditions, and operating states within a cloud's virtualization and hardware layers for auditability and at the bottom-most infrastructure layers of the cloud security providers. The measured evidence enables organizations to comply with security policies and with regulated data standards and controls such as FISMA and DPA (NIST 2005).

- **Data discovery and protection**. Cloud computing places data in new and different places—not just user data but also application and VM data (source). Key issues include data location and segregation, data footprints, backup, and recovery.

- **Architecture**. Standardized infrastructure and applications provide opportunities to exploit a single vulnerability many times over. This is the BORE (Break Once, Run Everywhere) principle at work. Considerations for the architecture include:

  - *Protection*. Protecting against attacks with standardized infrastructure when the same vulnerability can exist at many places, owing to the standardization.

  - *Support for multi-tenant environments*. Ensuring that systems and applications from different tenants are isolated from one another appropriately.

  - *Security policies*. Making sure that security policies are accurately and fully implemented across cloud architectures.

- **Identity management**. Identity management (IdM) is described as "the management of individual identities, their authentication, authorization, roles, and privileges/permissions within or across system and enterprise boundaries, with the goal of increasing security and productivity while decreasing cost, downtime, and repetitive tasks." From a cloud security perspective, questions like, "How do you control passwords and access tokens in the cloud?" and "How do you federate identity in the cloud?" are very real, thorny questions for cloud providers and subscribers.

- **Automation and policy orchestration**. The efficiency, scale, flexibility, and cost-effectiveness that cloud computing brings are because of the automation—the ability to rapidly deploy resources, and to scale up and scale down with processes, applications, and services provisioned securely "on demand." A high degree of automation and policy evaluation and orchestration are required so that security controls and protections are handled correctly, with minimal errors and minimal intervention needed.

Trends Affecting Data Center Security

The industry working groups that are addressing the issues identified above are carrying on their activities with some degree of urgency, driven as they are by a number of circumstances and events. There are three overriding security considerations applicable to data centers, namely:

- New types of attacks

- Changes in IT systems architecture as a transformation to the cloud environment takes place

- Increased governmental and international compliance requirements because of the exploits

The nature and types of attacks on information systems are changing dramatically. That is, the threat landscape is changing. Attackers are evolving from being hackers working on their own and looking for personal fame into organized, sophisticated attackers targeting specific types of data and seeking to gain and retain control of assets. These attacks are concerted, stealthy, and organized. The attacks have predominantly targeted operating systems and application environments, but new attacks are no longer confined to software and operating systems. Increasingly, they are moving lower down in the solution stacks to the platform, and they are affecting entities such as the BIOS, various firmware sites in the platform, and the hypervisor running on the bare-metal system. The attackers find it is easy to hide there, and the number of controls at that level is still minimal, so leverage is significant. Imagine, in a multi-tenant cloud environment, what impact malware can have if it gets control of a hypervisor.

Similarly, the evolving IT architecture is creating new security challenges. Risks exist anywhere there are connected systems. It does not help that servers, whether in a traditional data center or in a cloud implementation, were designed to be connected systems. Today, there is an undeniable trend toward virtualization, outsourcing, and cross-business and cross-supply chain collaboration, which blurs the boundaries between data "inside" an organization and data "outside" that organization. Drawing perimeters around these abstract and dynamic models is quite a challenge, and that may not even be practical anymore. The traditional perimeter-defined models aren't as effective as they once were. Perhaps they never were, but the cloud brings these issues to the point they can't be ignored anymore. The power of that cloud computing and virtualization lies in the abstraction, whereby workloads can migrate for efficiency, reliability, and optimization.

This fungibility of infrastructure, therefore, compounds the security and compliance problems. A vertically owned infrastructure at least provided the possibility of running critical applications with high security and with successfully meeting compliance requirements. But this view becomes unfeasible in a multi-tenant environment. With the loss of visibility comes the question of how to verify the integrity of the infrastructure on which an organization's workloads are instantiated and run.

Adding to the burden of securing more data in these abstract models is a growing legal or regulatory compliance demand to secure personally identifiable data, intellectual property, or financial data. The risks (and costs) of non-compliance continue to grow. The Federal Information Security Management Act (FISMA) and the Federal Risk and Authorization Management Program (FedRAMP) are two examples of how non-compliance prevents the cloud service providers from competing in the public sector. But even if cloud providers aren't planning to compete in the public sector by offering government agencies their cloud services, it's still important that they have at least a basic understanding of both programs. That's because the federal government is the largest single producer, collector, consumer, and disseminator of information in the United States. Any changes in regulatory requirements that affect government agencies will also have the potential of significantly affecting the commercial sector. These trends have major bearing on the security and compliance challenges that organizations face as they consider migrating their workloads to the cloud.

As mentioned, corporate-owned infrastructure can presumably provide a security advantage by virtue of its being inside the enterprise perimeter. The first defense is security by obscurity. Resources inside the enterprise, especially inside a physical perimeter, are difficult for intruders to reach. The second defense is genetic diversity. Given that IT processes vary from company to company, an action that breaches one company's security may not work for another company's. However, these presumed advantages are unintended, and therefore difficult to quantify; in practice, they offer little comfort or utility.

Security and Compliance Challenges

The four basic security and compliance challenges that organizations face are as follows:

- **Governance**. Cloud computing abstracts the infrastructure, and in order to prove compliance and satisfy audit requirements, organizations rely on the cloud providers to supply logs, reports, and attestation. When companies outsource parts of their IT infrastructure to cloud providers, they effectively give up some control of their information infrastructure and processes, even as they are required to bear greater responsibility for data confidentiality and compliance. While enterprises still get to define how their information is handled, who gets access to that information, and under what conditions in their private or hybrid clouds, they must largely take cloud providers at their word that their SLA trusting security policies and conditions are being met. Even then, service customers may have to compromise to have the capabilities that cloud providers can deliver. The organization's ability to monitor actual activities and verify security conditions within the cloud is usually very limited, and there are no standards or commercial tools to validate conformance to policies and SLAs.

- **Co-Tenancy and Noisy or Adversarial Neighbors.** Cloud computing introduces new risks resulting from multi-tenancy, an environment in which different users within a cloud share physical resources to run their virtual machines. Creating secure partitions between co-residental virtual machines has proved challenging for many cloud providers. Results range from the unintentional, noisy-neighbor syndrome whereby workloads that consume more than their fair share of compute, storage, or I/O resources starve the other virtual tenants on that host; to the deliberately malicious efforts, such as when malware is injected into the virtualization layer, enabling hostile parties to monitor and control any of the virtual machines residing on the system. To test this idea, researchers at UCSD and MIT were able to pinpoint the physical server used by programs running on the EC2 cloud, and then extract small amounts of data from these programs by inserting their own software and launching a side-channel attack.[2]

- **Architecture and Applications.** Cloud services are typically virtualized, which adds a hypervisor layer to a traditional IT application stack. This new layer introduces opportunities for improvements in security and compliance, but it also creates new attack surfaces and different risk exposure. Organizations must evaluate the new monitoring opportunities and the risks presented by the hypervisor layer, and account for them in their policy definition and compliance reporting.

- **Data.** Cloud services raise access and protection issues for user data and applications, including source code. Who has access, and what is left behind when an organization scales down a service? How is corporate confidential data protected from the virtual infrastructure administrators and cloud co-tenants? Encryption of data, at rest, in transit, and eventually in use, becomes a basic requirement, yet it comes with a performance cost (penalty). If we truly want to encrypt everywhere, how is it done in a cost-effective and efficient manner? Finally, data destruction at end of life is a subject not often discussed. There are clear regulations on how long data has to be retained. The assumption is that data gets destroyed or disposed of once the retention period expires. Examples of these regulations include Sarbanes-Oxley Act (SOX), Section 802: seven years (U.S. Security and Exchange Commission 2003); HIPAA, 45 C.F.R. §164.530(j): six years; and FACTA Disposal Rule (Federal Trade Commission 2005).

---

[2]S. Curry, J. Darbyshire, Douglas Fisher, et al., *RSA Security Brief*, March 2010. Also, T. Ristenpart, E. Tromer, et al., *Hey, You, Get Off of My Cloud: Exploring Information Leakage in Third-Party Compute Clouds*, CCS'09, Chicago.

With many organizations using cloud services today for non-mission-critical operations or for low-confidentiality applications, security and compliance challenges seem manageable, but this is a policy of avoidance. These services don't deal with data and applications governed by strict information security policies such as health regulations, FISMA regulations, and the Data Protection Act in Europe. But the security and compliance challenges mentioned above would become central to cloud providers and subscribers once these higher-value business functions and data begin migrating to private cloud and hybrid clouds. Industry pundits believe that the cloud value proposition will increasingly drive the migration of these higher value applications, as well as information and business processes, to cloud infrastructures. As more and more sensitive data and business-critical processes move to these cloud environments, the implications for security officers in these organizations will be to provide a transparent and compliant framework for information security, with monitoring.

So how do IT people address these challenges and requirements? With the concept of *trusted clouds*. This answer addresses many of these challenges and provides the ability for organizations to migrate both regular and mission-critical applications so as to leverage the benefits of cloud computing.

Trusted Clouds

There are many definitions and industry descriptions for the term *trusted cloud*, but at the core these definitions all have four foundational pillars:

- A trusted computing infrastructure

- A trusted cloud identity and access management

- Trusted software and applications

- Operations and risk management

Each of these pillars is broad and goes deep, with a rich cohort of technologies, patterns of development, and of course security considerations. It is not possible to cover all of them in one book. Since this book deals with the infrastructure for cloud security, we focus on the first pillar, the trusted infrastructure, and leave the others for future work. (Identity and access management are covered very briefly within the context of the trusted infrastructure.) But before we delve into this subject, let's review some key security concepts to ensure clarity in the discussion. These terms lay the foundation for what visibility, compliance, and monitoring entail, and we start with baseline definitions for *trust* and *assurance*.

- **Trust**. The assurance and confidence that people, data, entities, information, and processes will function or behave in expected ways. Trust may be human-to-human, machine-to-machine (e.g., handshake protocols negotiated within certain protocols), human-to-machine (e.g., when a consumer reviews a digital signature advisory notice on a website), or machine-to-human. At a deeper level, trust might be regarded as a consequence of progress toward achieving security or privacy objectives.

- **Assurance**. Evidence or grounds for confidence that the security controls implemented within an information system are effective in their application. Assurance can be shown in:

  - Actions taken by developers, implementers, and operators in the specification, design, development, implementation, operation, and maintenance of security controls.

  - Actions taken by security control assessors to determine the extent to which those controls are implemented correctly, operating as intended, and producing the desired outcomes with respect to meeting the security requirements for the system.

With these definitions established, let's now take a look at the *trusted computing infrastructure,* where computing infrastructure embraces three domains: compute, storage, and network.

Trusted Computing Infrastructure

Trusted computing infrastructure systems consistently behave in expected ways, with hardware and software working together to enforce these behaviors. The behaviors are consistent across compute on servers, storage, and network elements in the data center.

In the traditional infrastructure, hardware is a bystander to security measures, as most of the malware prevention, detection, and remediation is handled by software in the operating system, applications, or services layers. This approach is no longer adequate, however, as software layers have become more easily circumvented or corrupted. To deliver on the promise of trusted clouds, a better approach is the creation of a *root of trust* at the most foundational layer of a system—that is, in the hardware. Then, that root of trust grows upward, into and through the operating system, applications, and services layers. This new security approach is known as *hardware-based* or *hardware-assisted* security, and it becomes the basis for enabling the trusted clouds.

Trusted computing relies on cryptographic and measurement techniques to enforce a selected behavior by authenticating the launch and authorizing processes. This authentication allows an entity to verify that only authorized code runs on a system. Though this typically covers initial booting, it may also include applications and scripts. Establishing trust for a particular component implies also an ability to establish trust for that component relative to other trusted components. This transitive trust path is known as the *chain of trust*, with the initial component being the root of trust.

A system of geometry is built on a set of postulates assumed to be true. Likewise, a trusted computing infrastructure starts with a root of trust that contains a set of trusted elemental functions assumed to be immune from physical and other attacks. Since an important requirement for trust is that conditions be tamper-proof, cryptography or some immutable unique signature is used to identify a component. The hardware platform is usually a good proxy for the root of trust; for most attackers, the risk, cost, and difficulty of tampering with hardware exceeds the potential benefits of attempting to do so.

With the use of hardware as the initial root of trust, you can then measure (which means taking a hash, like an MD5 or SHA1, of the image of component or components) the software, such as the hypervisor or operating system, to determine whether unauthorized modifications have been made to it. In this way, a chain of trust relative to the hardware can be established. Trust techniques include hardware encryption, signing, machine authentication, secure key storage, and attestation. Encryption and signing are well-known techniques, but these are hardened by the placement of keys in protected hardware storage. Machine authentication provides a user with a higher level of assurance, as the machine is indicated as known and authenticated. Attestation, which is covered in Chapter 4, provides the means for a third party (also called a trusted third party) to affirm that loaded firmware and software are correct, true, or genuine. This is particularly important for cloud architectures based on virtualization.

Trusted Cloud Usage Models

In this abstracted and fungible cloud environment, the focus needs to be on enabling security across the three infrastructure domains. Only then can an enterprise have an infrastructure that is trusted to enable the broad migration of critical applications. Mitigating risk becomes more complex, as cloud use introduces an ever-expanding, transient chain of custody for sensitive data and applications. Only when security is addressed in a transparent and auditable way can enterprises and developers have:

- Confidence that their applications and workloads are equally safe in multi-tenant clouds

- Greater visibility and control of the operational state of the infrastructure, to balance the loss of physical control that comes with this abstracted environment

- Capability to continuously monitor for compliance

Cloud consumers may not articulate the needs in this fashion. From their perspective, there are key mega-needs, such as:

- How can I trust the cloud enough to use it?

- How can I protect my application and workloads in the cloud—and from the cloud?

- How can I broker between device and cloud services to ensure trust and security?

A cloud provider has to address these questions in a meaningful way for its tenants. These needs translate into a set of *foundational usage models for trusted clouds* that apply across the three infrastructure domains, as shown in Figure 2-1.

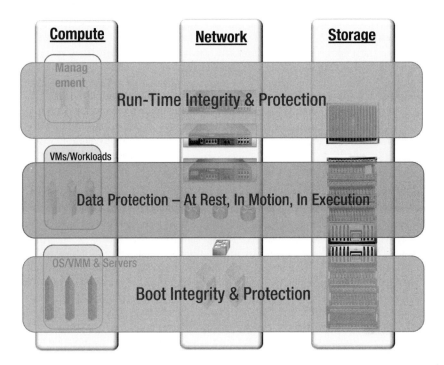

Figure 2-1. *A framework for the trusted cloud*

1. Boot integrity and protection

2. Data governance and protection, at rest, in motion, and during execution

3. Run-time integrity and protection

The scope and semantics of these usage models changes across the three infrastructure domains, but the purpose and intent are the same. How they manifest and are implemented in each of the domains could differ. For example, data protection in the context of the compute domain entails protection (both confidentiality and integrity) of the virtual machines at rest, in motion, and during execution; this applies to their configuration, state, secrets, keys, certificates, and other entities stored within. The same data-protection usage for the network domain has a different focus; it is on protection of the network flows, network isolation, confidentiality on the pipe, tenant-specific IPS, IDS, firewalls, deep packet inspection, and so on. In the storage domain, data protection pinpoints strong isolation/segregation, confidentiality, sovereignty, and integrity. Data confidentiality, which is a key part of data protection across the three domains, uses the same technological components and solutions—that is, encryption.

As a solution provider, methodical development and instantiation of these usage models across all the domains will provide the necessary assurance for organizations migrating their critical applications to a cloud infrastructure, and will enable establishment of the foundational pillar for trusted clouds.

In the rest of this chapter, we provide an exposition of the usage models listed above. We include enough definition of these four usage models for them to provide a broad overview. Subsequent chapters go into greater detail on each of these models and offer solutions, including the solution architecture and a reference implementation using commercial software and management components.

The Boot Integrity Usage Model

Boot integrity represents the first step toward achieving a trusted infrastructure. This model applies equally well to the compute, network, and storage domains. As illustrated in Figure 2-1, every network switch, router, or storage controller (in a SAN or NAS) runs a compute layer operating specialized OS to provide networking and storage functions, so this model enables a service provider to make claims about the boot integrity of the network, storage, and compute platforms, as well as the operating system and hypervisor instances running in them. As discussed earlier, boot integrity supported in the hardware makes the system robust and less vulnerable to tampering and targeted attacks. It enables an infrastructure service provider to make quantifiable claims about the boot-time integrity of the pre-launch and the launch components. This provides a means, therefore, to observe and measure the integrity of the infrastructure. In a cloud infrastructure, these security features refer to the virtualization technology in use, which comprises two layers:

- The boot integrity of the BIOS, firmware, and hypervisor. We identify this capability as *trusted platform boot.*

- The boot integrity of the virtual machines that host the workloads and applications. We want these applications to run on *trusted virtual machines.*

Understanding the Value of Platform Boot Integrity

To attain trusted computing, cloud users need systems hardened against emerging threats such as rootkits. Historically, many have viewed these threats as someone else's problem or as a purely hypothetical issue. This position is untenable in view of today's threats.

The stealthy, low-level threats are real and they occur in actual operating environments. The recent Mebromi BIOS rootkit low-level attack on a shipping platform was an eye-opener, as it took the industry by surprise. Unfortunately, as is often the case, it takes an actual exploit to change the mindset and drive change. And indeed, there are many more IT managers and security professionals taking action to improve the situation. As of 2012, a growing number of entities, including the U.S. National Institute of Standards and Technologies (NIST), are developing recommendations for protecting a system's boot integrity. These recommendations contain measures for securing very basic, but highly privileged platform components.

Given the crucial role played by the hypervisor as essential software responsible for managing the underlying hardware and allocating resources such as processor, disk, memory, and I/O to the guest virtual machines and arbitrating the accesses and privileges among guests, it is imperative to have the highest levels of assurance so that it is uncompromised. This was the rationale for conducting the survey shown in Figure 2-2. With this growing awareness and concern has come a corresponding growth in vendors looking to define the solutions.

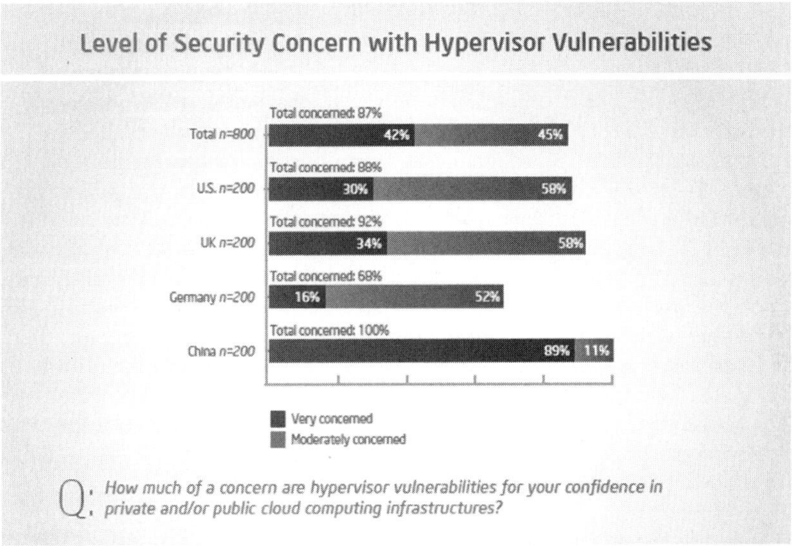

Level of Security Concern with Hypervisor Vulnerabilities

	Very concerned	Moderately concerned	Total concerned
Total n=800	42%	45%	87%
U.S. n=200	30%	58%	88%
UK n=200	34%	58%	92%
Germany n=200	16%	52%	68%
China n=200	89%	11%	100%

Q: How much of a concern are hypervisor vulnerabilities for your confidence in private and/or public cloud computing infrastructures?

Figure 2-2. Survey results showing concerns over hypervisor integrity across regions

For the various devices/nodes across the infrastructure domains (compute, storage, and network), the integrity of the pre-launch and launch environment can be asserted anytime during the execution's lifecycle. This is done by verifying that the identity and values of the components have not changed unless there has been a reset or a reboot of the platform by the controlling software. This assertion of integrity is deferred to a trusted third party that fulfills the role of a trust authority, and the verification process is known as *trust attestation*. The trust authority service is an essential component of a trusted cloud solution architecture.

The Trusted Virtual Machine Launch Usage Model

A trusted platform boot capability provides a safe launch environment for provisioning virtual machines running workloads. This environment has the mechanisms to evaluate the integrity of pre-launch and launch components on a platform, from the BIOS to the operating system and hypervisor. The service provider thus attests to the trust-ability

31

of the launch environment. However, no specific claims can be made about the virtual machines being launched, other than indicating that they are being launched on a measured and attested hypervisor platform. Although virtual machine monitors (VMM) or hypervisors are naturally good at isolating workloads from each other because they mediate all access to physical resources by virtual machines, they cannot by themselves attest and assert the state of the virtual machine that is launched.

The trusted virtual machine launch usage model applies the same level of trustability to the pre-launch and launch environment of the virtual machines and workloads. Each virtual machine launched on a virtual machine manager and hypervisor platform benefits from a hardware root of trust by storing the launch measurements of the virtual machines' sealing and remote attestation capabilities. However, this requires virtualizing the TPM, with a virtual TPM (vTPM) for each of the virtual machines. Each of these virtual TPM vTPM instances then emulates the functions of a hardware TPM. Currently, there are no real virtualized TPM implementations available, owing to the challenges related to virtualizing the TPM. The difficulty lies not in providing the low-level TPM instructions but in ensuring that the security properties are supported and established with an appropriate level of trust. Specifically, we have to extend the chain of trust from the physical TPM to each virtual TPM by carefully managing the signing keys, certificates, and lifecycle of all necessary elements. An added dimension is the mobility of the virtual machines and how these virtual TPMs would migrate with the virtual machines.

There are other ways of enabling a measured launch of virtual machines, such as storing the measurements in memory as part of a trusted hypervisor platform without the use of virtual TPMs but still ensuring that the chain of trust is extended from the physical TPM. Irrespective of the design approach, day-to-day operations on virtual machines—such as suspend and resume, creating snapshots of running virtual machines, and playing them back on other platforms or live migration of virtual machines—become challenging to implement.

There are no real production-quality implementations of these architectures. There are few academic and research implementations of vTPMs and other memory structure–based approaches, each with its own pros and cons. Trusted virtual machine usages are still evolving at the time of this writing; hence it's not possible to be definitive. Chapter 8 covers aspects of the measured VM launch and some architectural elements. Chapter 3 covers in depth the matter of boot integrity and trusted boot of platforms and the hypervisors, as well as the associated trusted compute pools concept that aggregates systems so specific policies can be applied to those pools. The discussion also includes the solution architecture, and a snapshot of industry efforts to support the enabling of trusted compute pools. Chapter 4 covers the trust attestation or remote attestation architecture, including a reference implementation.

The Data Protection Usage Model

This usage model is about protecting data in the cloud that is at rest, in motion, and undergoing execution. It applies uniformly across infrastructure domains (compute, storage, and network). On the compute domain, the protection is for the virtual machines and workloads that have the applications, configurations, state, keys, secrets, and needed mechanisms to ensure confidentiality and integrity.

For virtual machine and workload data protection, cloud user organizations need a method to securely place workloads into the cloud, as well as store and use data there. Current provisioning and bursting models include either storing the virtual machine and application images and data in the clear (unencrypted), or having these images and data encrypted by the keys controlled by the service provider—keys which are likely applied uniformly to all the tenants. But increasingly, virtual machine images—effectively, containers for operating system and application images, configuration files, data, and other entities—need confidentiality protection in a multi-tenant cloud environment. That is, images need to be encrypted by keys under tenant control, and also decrypted for provisioning by the keys under tenant control in a manner that is transparent to the cloud service provider. The usage model also calls for not only leveraging hardware for encryption and decryption but also ensuring that the service or entity acquiring the decryption keys does it on a need-to-know basis, is trusted and attested, and is running on a platform whose boot integrity has been attested. This provides a more effective last line of defense to protect from misuse or abuse by other tenants or cloud administrators. Chapter 8 covers this usage model for virtual machine protection, including a reference architecture and implementation.

The Run-time Integrity and Attestation Usage Model

Having a trusted foundation for the platform is extremely important. Roots of trust in hardware, and with a credible static and binary remote attestation process, ensure that a service provider can make assertions about the boot integrity of the platforms on which the tenant workloads execute. But that is only half the answer. The integrity of the platform could be assured at boot time, and remote attestation can measure and attest the state of healthiness at that point—only for integrity to be degraded and compromised at run time for a variety of reasons, such as configuration errors or, worse, the presence of run-time rootkits. These mechanisms compromise the integrity of the platforms and yet static binary remote attestation doesn't catch them; instead, this situation calls for remote run-time attestation. However, for this solution to be viable, there needs to be a way of representing and approximating the run-time integrity of the system via a set of policies or properties. A system or platform stays healthy only to the extent that these properties stay healthy.

Determining what constitutes the minimum and sufficient set of properties that indicate the run-time health of a hypervisor or virtual machine monitor is a tough computer science problem that has long track record of research in software integrity. For example, if the integrity properties cover the system call table—the call table being the basis for measurement, monitoring, and attestation—a new rootkit can be deployed that manipulates other function pointers, such as device driver jump tables, and it will stay undetected. Clearly, there are no commercial implementations, since the threat vectors are too many to consider and modeling the threats, as well as mitigation, is still an active research area.

One promising research effort has been to define what are called "scoped invariants" as an important class of integrity properties. According to the authors of this research, scoped invariants are code or data with a constant value in some context (*scope*). For example, one scoped invariant is the Interrupt Descriptor Table (IDT) entry for page fault, containing a constant function pointer once the virtual machine monitor or operating system finishes initialization. Scoped invariants are building blocks for more general integrity properties, and they are amenable to integrity checking. A case study was done to identify a core set of scoped invariants of the open-source Xen virtual machine monitor. In addition to the IDT, another core invariant property was demonstrated in this research; the addressable memory limit of a guest OS must not include Xen's code and data, and this proved indispensable for Xen's guest isolation mechanism. Violation of this property can let an attacker modify a single byte in the Global Descriptor Table (GDT) to achieve a virtual machine escape goal.

At the current state of the art, run-time integrity monitoring and attestation is a broad and complex topic, and commercial implementations are still works in progress at many system and security organizations.

Trusted Cloud Value Proposition for Cloud Tenants

While a tenant organization's compliance and security policies won't change when IT processes migrate to the cloud, the way that organization enforces those policies and proves compliance will change significantly. For most compliance officers and infosec (information security) professionals, the cloud becomes, for practical purposes, a black box. In contrast, a cloud tenant that is landing a workload in a trusted pool can expect the following:

- The assurance that the compute, network, and storage elements in that segment of the cloud or the virtualized data center are trusted. The service provider or the management infrastructure asserts the integrity of the security and trust of these elements.

- The assurance that the information (data and content) s stored, processed, and migrated is always protected for confidentiality, integrity, and privacy.

- The assurance that workloads and applications are not tampered with, and that the infrastructure will launch and execute what is expected, and can provide a chain of trust that is rooted in hardware.

- The assurance that the devices and users accessing the workloads and services in these trusted clouds are authenticated, and that the workloads run on hardware with demonstrated integrity; likewise, for the controlling software. This ensures that services are being accessed over a reliable and secure network and location.

The Advantages of Cloud Services on a Trusted Computing Chain

The advantages to delivering cloud services on computing resources that have a demonstrated chain of trust rooted in hardware include:

- *Reducing the risks for co-residency.* It ensures that the infrastructure is trusted and has demonstrated integrity. This prevents the launch and execution of untrusted components. It protects not only against malware but also from benign conditions, such as the improper migration or deployment of virtual machines. To illustrate, if a cloud orchestrator (like OpenStack) attempts to move virtual machines from an unsecured computing platform to a trusted one, the policy management software will prevent the incoming virtual machines from landing, since the action originated from an unsecured platform.

- *Preventing the unsafe transit of secure virtual machines.* In the same way that virtual machines arriving from an unsecured platform are not allowed to move to secured platforms, virtual machines originating on secured platforms are not allowed to move to unsecured ones. For instance, if an administrator attempted to transfer a secured virtual machine to a new server, the virtualization management console would first perform a policy check on the outgoing virtual machine and then measure the security configurations of the new server against accepted standards. If the new server does not meet the secure standards required to host the virtual machine, the virtualization management console or security policy engine prevents the virtual machine from migrating and logs the attempt.

- *Maximizing and scaling operational efficiency by creating trusted pools of systems.* Once platform trustworthiness can be measured, cloud providers can put such measurements to use by building trusted pools of systems, all with identical security profiles. Hypervisors can then make more efficient use of secure clouds, moving virtual machines with similar security profiles within zones of identically secured systems for load balancing and other administrative purposes—all the while protecting data in conformance with regulated standards and policies.

The authors believe that ubiquitous adoption of trusted computing chains will address a number of fundamental user concerns about cloud security that currently prevent many applications from being deployed in a cloud setting, thereby barring them from realizing the potential cost reductions that could stem from using cloud technology and limiting the greater business impact that would come from broader deployment.

Summary

We covered the challenges of cloud security and compliance, as well as introduced the concept of trusted clouds. We discussed the needs for trusted clouds and introduced four usage models to enable a trusted computing infrastructure, the foundation for trusted clouds. These models provide a foundation for enhanced security that can evolve with new technologies from Intel and others in the hardware and software ecosystem.

There are no silver bullets for security, such as a single technology solving all problems, because the matter of security is a multifaceted one. But it is clear that a new set of security capabilities is needed, and that starts at the most foundational elements. Trusted platforms provide such a foundation. These platforms can provide:

- Increased visibility of critical controlling software in the cloud environment through attestation capabilities.

- A new control point capable of identifying and enforcing local known good configurations of the host operating environment, and able to report the resultant launch trust status to cloud and security management software for subsequent use.

In the next few chapters we will discuss each of the usage models in detail, including some solution architectures and technologies to bring them to reality.

■ ■ ■

CHAPTER 3

Platform Boot Integrity: Foundation for Trusted Compute Pools

In Chapter 2, we introduced the concept of trusted clouds and the key usage models to enable a trusted infrastructure. We provided a brief exposition of the boot integrity usage model, and its applicability across the three infrastructure domains—compute, storage, and network. In this chapter we will take a deeper look into ensuring the boot integrity of a compute platform, which boils down to ensuring the integrity of a number of platform components: the pre-launch and launch components covering firmware, BIOS, and hypervisor. Boot integrity is foundational in embodying the concept of a trusted infrastructure.

This chapter provides an introduction to the concept of roots of trust in a trusted computing platform, the measured boot process, and the attestation that are critical steps for ensuring boot integrity. It also provides an overview of Intel's Trusted Executed Technology (TXT), an example of root of trust technology for asserting platform boot integrity. Complementary to this is the concept of *trusted compute pools*, which is a logical or physical grouping of computing platforms with demonstrated platform boot integrity. Trusted compute pools embody the integrity of the virtual infrastructure, which can then enable granular controls, an essential requirement for virtualized data centers. Here, also, we present a solution reference architecture for building a trusted compute pool in a virtualized data center, and provide a case study of its implementation at the Taiwan Stock Exchange, with a number of typical use cases and the solution components of a successful implementation of trusted compute pools.

The Building blocks for Trusted Clouds

Organizations using or planning to use cloud services are starting to require that cloud service providers offer improved security at the hardware layer and greater transparency of system activities within and below the hypervisor. This means that cloud providers should be able to:

- Give organizations greater visibility into the security states of the hardware platforms running the IaaS for their private clouds.

- Produce automated and standardized reports on the configuration of the physical and virtual infrastructure hosting the customers' virtual machines and data.

- Set policy concerning the physical location of the servers on which the virtual machines are running, and control of the placement and migration of these virtual machines to acceptable locations based on such policy specifications (as some FISMA and DPA requirements dictate).

- Provide measured evidence that their services infrastructure complies with security policies and meets regulated data standards.

What is needed is a set of building blocks for the development of "trustworthy clouds." These building blocks consist of:

- A chain of trust rooted in hardware that extends to the hypervisor.

- A hardening of the virtualization environment using known best methods.

- Provision of visibility for compliance and audit purposes.

- Trust as an integral part of policy management for cloud activity.

- A leveraging of infrastructure and services to address data protection requirements.

- Automation to bring it all together and achieve economies of scale and management efficiency.

Cloud providers and other members of the IT community are carrying out research and development to address this need. A growing ecosystem of technology companies is collaborating to develop a new, interoperable trusted computing infrastructure. The goal is to reduce the risk of attack, such as come from virtual rootkits, by building a hardware-based root of trust founded on the assumption that a hardware-based, bottom-up approach can make this infrastructure more impervious to exploits than does today's mostly software-based approach.

Platform Boot Integrity

As described in the previous chapter, a trusted computing platform is said to have platform boot integrity—or boot integrity, for short—if the key controlling components (namely firmware, BIOS, and hypervisors) have demonstrated integrity. Two steps are needed to assert the integrity of the pre-launch and launch components:

1. A measured boot process.

2. Assurance and enforcement of the executed components as trusted components. This process is called attestation; without this, there is no assurance that the platform is in a trusted state.

Before we describe these two steps, we have to look at roots of trust on a platform, as this is fundamental to a trusted computing platform.

Roots of Trust–RTM, RTR, and RTS in the Intel TXT Platform

Hardware-based roots of trust, when coupled with an enabled operating system, hypervisor, and solutions, lay the foundation for a more secure computing platform. This secure platform ensures hypervisor and VMM integrity at boot from rootkits and other low-level attacks. It establishes the trustworthiness of the server and the host platforms.

There are three roots of trust in a trusted platform:

- Root of trust for measurement (RTM)

- Root of trust for reporting (RTR)

- Root of trust for storage (RTS)

RTM, RTR, and RTS are the system elements that must be trusted, because misbehavior in these normally would not be detectable in the higher layers. In an Intel TXT-enabled platform, the RTM is the Intel microcode, the Core-RTM (CRTM). An RTM is the first component to send integrity-relevant information (measurements) to the RTS. Trust in this component, thus, is the basis for trust in all the other measurements. The RTS contains the component identities (measurements) and other sensitive information. A trusted platform module (TPM) provides the RTS and RTR capabilities in a trusted computing platform.

A trustworthy CRTM reliably measures the integrity of the next piece of code following in the boot sequence. The result of this measurement is extended into the platform configuration register (PCR) in the TPM before the control is transferred to the next program in the sequence. If each component in the sequence in turn measures the next before handing off control, there's a chain of trust established. If this measurement chain continues throughout the entire boot sequence, the resulting PCR values transitively reflect the measurement of all files used.

In the unlikely event that one of the components in the chain gets compromised, it is re-measured before its execution during the next reboot. Even if the control is transferred to the malicious software, and the malicious software attempts to fake the measurements, it will have to run a cryptographic gauntlet, where the fake measurements extended to PCR would equal the value it would have had after an uncompromised boot. Thus, the cryptographic strength of the SHA-1 hashing algorithm makes it computationally unlikely for the tampered code to calculate an extension value that would "adjust" the PCR values.

Now that we have exppplained what RTM and RTS are, let's look at the measured boot process, which is one of the two steps listed above that are used to assert the integrity of the pre-launch and launch components of a platform.

Measured Boot Process

A *measured boot process*, as shown in the Figure 3-1, is a boot sequence starting at a root of trust for measurement (RTM) initiating a series of measurements consisting of all the relevant trusted compute base (TCB) components into the root of trust for storage (RTS). The measured boot performs no evaluation or verification of any of the component's identities.

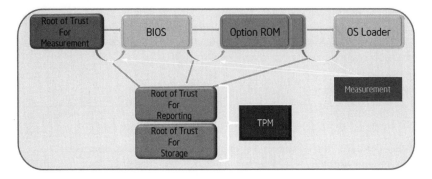

Figure 3-1. *Measured boot process*

There are two ways defined by the trusted compute group (TCG) to establish this trust during boot:

- Static root of trust (S-RTM)

- Dynamic root of trust (D-RTM)

Figure 3-2 depicts these two boot models and the associated trust chains. As the name *Static Root of Trust for Measurement* (S-RTM) suggests, the entire trust begins with the static, immutable piece of code, which is called the *core root of trust for measurement* (CRTM). On ordinary computing platforms, BIOS is the first component to be executed. Therefore, the trusted platform needs an additional entity to measure the BIOS and act as a CRTM. This entity is a fundamental trusted building block (TBB) that remains unchanged during the lifetime of the platform. The CRTM can be an integrated part of the BIOS itself (e.g., Microsoft Windows 8), like a BIOS boot block. The CRTM can also be a set of CPU instructions that are normally stored within a chip on the motherboard. This latter method can be more resistant to tampering, as exemplified by the Intel TXT.

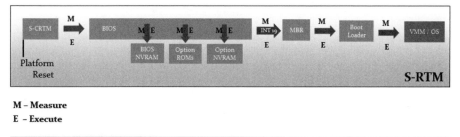

M – Measure

E – Execute

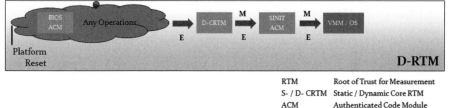

RTM	Root of Trust for Measurement
S- / D- CRTM	Static / Dynamic Core RTM
ACM	Authenticated Code Module

Figure 3-2. *S-RTM and D-RTM trusted chains*

In the static root of trust method, all trust starts with a fixed or immutable piece of trusted code in the BIOS. This trusted piece of code measures the next piece of code to be executed and extends a platform configuration register (PCR) in the TPM based on the measurement before that control is transferred to the next program. If each new program in turn measures the next one before transferring control, there's a chain of trust established. If this measurement chain continues through the entire boot sequence, the resultant PCR values will reflect the measurement of all files used. This "measurement before execution" model therefore leads to a chain of trust that's observable by a remote party wanting to assess the trustworthiness of a system. Hence, S-RTM enables trust on the entire boot chain, including the master boot record, boot loader, kernel, drivers, and all files referenced or executed during boot. These are all parts of a trusted computing base (TCB). In other words, a TCB encompasses the sum of all the components that affect a system's assurance.

However, S-RTM has two shortcomings:

- **Scalability and Inclusivity.** The number of components in a boot chain is large. Each component's trusted computing base (TCB), and hence security, depends on the many layers of code that have been executed earlier in the chain. Windows and Linux have an ill-defined TCB and therefore they require all executable content to be measured, including executables, libraries, and shell scripts. Components determining the chain of trust (including TCB) are subject to frequent patching and updating with their myriad configuration variations. Also, the launch order of elements in the chain may vary, leading to different measurement values in PCRs. Keeping track of the expected values for integrity measurements becomes a nettlesome task.

- **Uncontrolled Scope.** The execution of an S-RTM sequence pulls in code for the evaluation of an OS TCB that's unrelated to the operation of the platform. This forces mostly unnecesary evaluations of software and firmware, including BIOS components loaded and run during the boot process, only to be discarded just to verify the integrity of the TCB.

These shortcomings were identified by the TCG. The newer TCG 1.2 specifications define a new mechanism for an authenticated boot: dynamic root of trust for measurement, or D-RTM.

Dynamic root of trust for measurement (D-RTM) reduces the complexity of the TCB, making the evaluation of the platform state more tractable. With D-RTM, the trust properties of the components are ignored until a secure event, such as an enabled hypervisor launch, triggers and initializes the system, starting the initial root of trust measurement. Components that were staged before the D-RTM secure event are excluded from the TCB and not allowed to execute after the trust properties of the system are established. D-RTM is much more streamlined compared to S-RTM.

The server platforms used in virtualization and cloud data centers present challenging boot scenarios where D-RTM alone won't suffice. The TCB in a true D-RTM implementation will not include the system management modules (SMM), which are needed to support server RAS (reliability, availability, scalability) features. SMM is part of the pre-boot BIOS, and a pure D-RTM implementation excludes these items. Intel TXT provides a hybrid implementation of S-RTM and D-RTM, as described above, to establish trust during the boot process. The book *Intel Trusted Execution Technology for Server Platforms* from Apress has exhaustive coverage of S-RTM and D-RTM.

Attestation

The second step in ensuring boot integrity of a platform is to guarantee that the executed and launched components are trusted components. This process is called *attestation*, and without this step there is no assurance that the platform is in a trusted state. Why is attestation important from a cloud perspective? There are two main considerations for use cases to be instantiated and delivered in a cloud:

- How would the entity needing this information know if a specific platform is Intel TXT enabled, or if a specific server has a defined or compliant BIOS or VMM running on it (i.e., can it be trusted)?

- Why should the entity requesting this information (which, in a cloud environment, could be a resource scheduler or orchestrator trying to schedule a service on a set of available nodes or servers) trust the response from the platform?

An attestation service provides definitive answers to these questions. Chapter 4 covers attestation in detail, including description of a reference attestation platform for Intel-based platforms, code-named Mt. Wilson. But here is a quick summary of the capability.

Attestation ratchets up the notion of roots of trust by making the information from various roots of trust visible and usable by other entities. In a TPM-based implementation of RTS and RTR, it provides a digital signature of platform configuration registers (PCR), with a set of registers in a TPM extended with specific measurements for various launch modules of the software and the requestor validating the signature and the PCR contents. To validate, first the requestor invokes, via an agent on the host or device, the TPM_Quote command, specifying an attestation identity key to perform the digital signature on the set of PCRs to quote, and a cryptographic nonce to ensure freshness of the digital signature. Next, the attestation service validates the signature and determines the trust of the launched server by comparing the measurements from the TPM quote with known-good measurements. It is a critical IT operations challenge to manage the known-good measurement for hypervisors, operating systems, and BIOS software to ensure they are all protected from tampering and spoofing. This capability can be internal to a company, offered by a service provider, or delivered remotely as a service by a trusted third party (TTP). The process is described in detail in Chapter 4.

The measured boot and the attestation thus enable a server/host to demonstrate its boot integrity. Failure of a measured boot process or attestation can initiate a series of remediation steps that are managed and controlled by the policies in the data center. Barring any hardware or configuration issues, then, a failed attestation would mean one of following two conditions:

- Someone or something has tampered with one or more launch components.

- A wrong version (compared to the known-good or whitelist) of BIOS, OS, drivers, and so on has been installed and attempted to launch at the server/host.

Security tools like security information and event management (SIEMs), compliance tools, and configuration checkers would flag these alerts to drive the appropriate remediation actions. In short, having the ability to assert the integrity of a platform is both valuable and necessary. With a set of platforms that have demonstrated integrity, they can be aggregated to do interesting things. This aggregation of platforms is what we refer to as a *trusted compute pool* (TCP).

Trusted Compute Pools

The notion of a trusted compute pool (TCP) relies on the establishment and propagation of a new data center management attribute: *platform trust*. Platform trust derives directly from the boot integrity demonstrated by the server. TCP is a leading approach to aggregate trusted systems and to segregate them from untrusted resources, which results in a split between higher value, more sensitive workloads and commodity application workloads. The principles of TCP operation (see Figure 3-3) are to:

- Create a cloud subsystem that meets the specific and varying security requirements of users.

- Control administrative access to subsystems so that the right workloads get deployed and maintained there.

- Secure, federated, and multi-factored authentication of users and devices accessing the services.

- Continuous monitoring and, on detection of a change in host trust or geolocation, generation of alerts and implementation of configured remediation measures.

- Audits of that segment of the cloud that enables users to verify compliance.

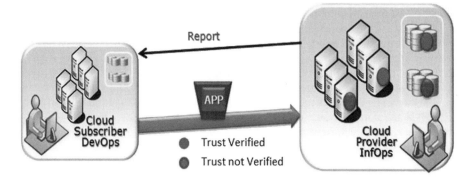

Figure 3-3. *Trusted compute pools*

These trusted pools allow IT to gain the benefits of the dynamic cloud environment while enforcing higher levels of protection for their more critical and security-sensitive workloads. The resources tagged green in Figure 3-3 are trusted, and the resources tagged red are untrusted, as they have not asserted their boot integrity. Critical policies can be defined such that security-sensitive cloud services can be launched only on these resources or migrated only to other trusted platforms within these pools. Also, use of TCPs eliminates the need for air-gapped (i.e., isolated from the rest of the data center) clusters of servers.

TCP Principles of Operation

How is a trusted compute pool created? Platform trust is the primary attribute used by management orchestration and operational software to create a trusted pool. Initially, platform trust is achieved through the use of a trusted platform launch (which, for server platforms, is based on TXT). Once this initial platform trust is established, TCP incorporates additional protections, including visibility of the integrity of the infrastructure and control of the placement and migration of workloads. Figure 3-4 shows a progression of TCP functionality with increasing levels of trust and compliance.

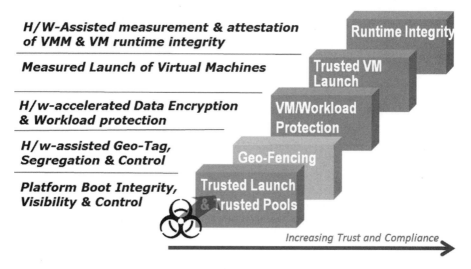

Figure 3-4. *Progression of trusted compute pool usage*

When a trusted pool is created, systems and workloads can be tagged with specific security policies, enabling the monitoring, control, and audits for the placement and migration of workloads into, across, and outside the pool. The most obvious premise behind this is that highly confidential and sensitive applications and workloads must be constrained by policy to run only on systems that have proved to be trusted.

The rest of this section of the chapter describes the flows involved in supporting each of the use cases represented in Figure 3-5.

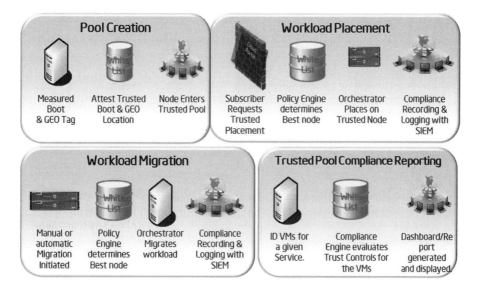

Figure 3-5. *Core use cases for trusted compute pools*

Pool Creation

This is the first step in TCP, involving the creation of a group of platforms with a common level of trust. Pool creation involves the following steps:

1. Virtualization management and orchestration software identifies and enumerates the platforms with demonstrated and attested platform boot integrity.

2. Virtualization management software incorporates the platforms into a trusted pool.

Workload Placement

Once a trusted pool of platforms has been created, workloads can be selected to be placed on that pool based on their security requirements. A typical flow for workload placement would involve the following:

1. A cloud subscriber requests the workload be placed in a trusted pool.

2. Security management tools identify and tag workloads for classification according to certain security properties.

3. Security management tools match platform trust to workload classification according to existing policies.

4. Orchestrator and scheduler software determines the best server to place the workload within the trusted pool, pursuant to existing server selection and security policies. The scheduler requests an attestation of the integrity of the server before the workload is placed on the server, to reaffirm its boot integrity.

5. A compliance record is created to register the launch of the workload in the trusted pool. This record is tied to the hardware root of trust of the server, and can be associated with a set of security controls to meet compliance requirements.

Workload Migration

Infrastructure as a service (IaaS) cloud multi-tenant environments typically use virtualization capability to migrate virtual machines across physical hosts. When it comes to security-sensitive workloads, it is desirable, or perhaps even essential, to meet customer requirements that these migrations occur only between prequalified trusted platforms. A flow representing how to achieve this goal in a TCP environment might occur as follows:

1. A migration of workload is triggered either manually or based on resource orchestrator/scheduler policies.

2. The resource scheduler determines the set of servers that best meets the policy, based on the security standards associated with the workload. (The scheduler requests an attestation of the integrity of the target host.) The first server in the set that meets the integrity requirements is picked.

3. The orchestration software migrates the workload to the new server.

4. A compliance record is created to register the migration of the workload to this new location, including the attestation of integrity at the time of selection.

Compliance Reporting for a Workload/Cloud Service

Being able to prove to an auditing entity that the security requirements of a given workload have been fulfilled is just as important as actually fulfilling those requirements. A flow for compliance reporting might be as follows:

1. The compliance tool enumerates all the virtual machines in the service or workload.

2. The compliance tool evaluates the security controls for each virtual machine; these controls include determining the trail of hosts and the migration of records throughout the virtual machine lifecycle.

3. A report is generated to provide proof that security properties associated with the workload running on TCP have been met. This verifiable proof is linked to the hardware root of trust (provided by TXT) in the participating hosts.

Solution Reference Architecture for the TCP

The Intel TXT-enabled launch is not sufficient to support the TCP uses mentioned in the previous section. Measurement and attestation tell the data center and security management software whether a given host can be trusted, but there is more to it than that. Exposing, transporting, storing, and ultimately consuming platform trust measurements in support of the use cases is an integration challenge across different software and management elements. Successfully doing this requires a well-defined and seamless integration model of multiple security management and data center/cloud management software components; in other words, there needs to be an underlying solution architecture.

Figure 3-6 depicts a reference architecture for these trusted compute pool usages. It prescribes four distinct layers, with each layer serving one of the four functions:

1. Reporting of the source of the platform trust/boot integrity measurements

2. Interface with the boot integrity information via secure protocols

3. Verifification/appraisal of the boot integrity measurements

4. Consumer of the boot integrity verification for policy enforcement, compliance reporting, and remediation

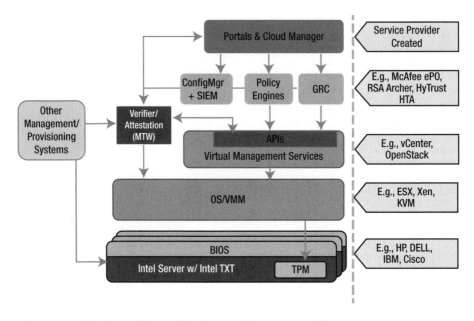

Figure 3-6. *Solution architecture for the trusted compute pools*

Here's a brief overview of the four layers of this software architecture, starting from the base and moving upward.

Hardware Layer

At the base of the architecture we have the physical server hardware. For virtualization and the cloud computing environment, the hardware typically consists of x86 architecture-based servers. These are servers hosting the virtualization and cloud workloads. Intel TXT enables trusted compute pool usages. (See sidebar for a brief introduction to the technology.) In addition to having TXT-enabled CPUs and chipsets, there needs to be Intel Virtualization Technology (VT) and a trusted platform module, or TPM. TXT needs support in the BIOS, as well. By default, TXT and TPM are not enabled in the BIOS in the current generation of servers. Unfortunately, the method for turning on TXT and TPM support varies by vendor; there is no standard for carrying out this operation. There are, however, well-published documents on how to enable TXT and TPM for various OEM vendors, available from Intel and few security management companies supporting Intel TXT.

One of the challenges in scale deployments and enablement of TXT is meeting the need for physical access and the assertion of presence to enable the TPM and TXT on a server platform via the BIOS interface. This limits automation and large-scale enablement. Though each of the OEM provides custom implementation and interfaces for doing this, unless there are architectural solutions such as a physical presence interface (PPI), the provisioning and configuration task won't become any simpler.

Operating System / Hypervisor Layer

Moving up the stack, the second layer is the OS/hypervisor. To participate in a measured launch, an OS or hypervisor has to be enabled for TXT. The changes related to TXT are in the initialization code, and also during termination and shutdown. Additionally, basic enablement means that the operating system or hypervisor can invoke the secure launch process. This entails including a pre-kernel module that can ensure the right SINIT (authenticated code modules from Intel) module is selected and assure the orderly evaluation of the launch components of the software. Intel provides a reference implementation called Trusted Boot (tboot) for the pre-kernel module that can be integrated into OS/hypervisors toward enabling for Intel TXT, and it is the maintainer of this open-source "tboot" project.

Tboot is by far the most widely used mechanism offered by software vendors to enable their OS or hypervisor. SINIT modules on server platforms are generally embedded in the platform BIOS, and are processor- and chipset generation-specific. The tboot components provided by Intel are integrated into the operating systems or hypervisors (by the respective ISVs) and work across multiple generations of platforms. This makes sense, as it allows the most qualified party (in this case, the ISV) to determine which modules are essential for the trusted compute base (TCB) of their software, and therefore which modules to include in the measured launch and in which order.

Tboot technology is included in multiple open-source operating system/hypervisor environments from Linux, to Xen/KVM, to a number of commercial products, such as Red Hat and Citrix XenServer. Other vendors, like VMware, have implemented their own tboot-like functions. It is interesting to note that the percentage of TCB measured by vendors as part of the launch process varies significantly. As of this writing, VMware by far has the most coverage of the TCB. Other OS/VMM vendors have the core kernel and few modules measured. All of these vendors have been actively working toward increasing the amount of TCB that they measure. For detailed coverage of the measured launch environments (MLE) developer guidance, check out the book *Intel Trusted Execution Technology for Server Platforms* from Apress.

With TXT and TPM correctly configured and enabled in hardware, when a TXT-enabled OS/hypervisor is launched, the platform goes through a measured D-RTM launch. Just to refresh your understanding of the TXT launch process, when a TXT launch happens, what you have is a measured launch of the firmware, BIOS, and controlling software like an OS or VMM. These measurements (which are the identities of the various components), as part of the launch process are stored in the various registers in the TPM (RTS and RTR) called PCRs (platform configuration registers) and are verified with an attestation system. TCG PC Spec provides the semantics for where the various measurements are stored in the TPM.

Virtualization/Cloud Management and Verification/Attestation Layer

This is the critical management and orchestration layer in a data center that controls the provisioning, deployment, and lifecycle management of the workloads and virtual machines. This layer serves one of four functions for the trusted compute pool use cases:

1. Provides a secure interface to the measured launch measurements on each of the servers

2. Provides an attestation mechanism to evaluate platform trust and assert its integrity

3. Consumes the trust information, essentially helping to identify which platforms are trusted and which ones are not

4. Makes use of this information to establish an enhanced security capability through policy definition and enforcement linked to platform trust

There are significant differences in terms of interfaces provided to support platform trust. Some, such as Citrix, have developed explicit APIs natively to their hypervisor software (Xen APIs) to provide TCG-compliant access to the launch measurements in the TPM. These APIs are available for any management software to use—for evaluation, attestation, reporting, alerting, and so on—and they maintain the integrity of the measurements. Others, such as VMWare, have tied access to these measurements to their primary virtualization resource management software—vCenter, in this case. VMware provides access to the measurements via run-time vCenter APIs, which when invoked instantiate a TCG-compliant remote attestation protocol to request the measurements for the attesting server/device. None of the virtualization and cloud management software vendors provides verification/attestation software for verification of the measurements. Since attestation is a relatively new concept, it is not yet integral to most of the virtualization and cloud management software. Having attestation services provided through the operating system or hypervisor would establish the function across many enterprise and cloud customers—thereby unlocking the most valuable use models.

Intel in collaboration with security ISVs have developed attestation software for attestation verification. This attestation software is a multi-hypervisor, multi-OS verification/attestation program providing a secure assertion of the hypervisor and platform integrity that is verified against a set of known-good, golden measurements, or whitelist values. Following the key tenet of cloud technology with regard to programmability and automation, the attestation platform exposes all its functionality via well-defined REST & SOAP APIs for querying trust assertions, as well as for provisioning, management, and whitelisting. The attestation process and the Intel attestation platform are covered in detail in Chapter 4. The trust assertion from the attestation/verification software is used by the cloud management software and the security management tools that are in the next layer of the architecture.

Security Management Layer

The security management layer is the top layer, where the platform trust assertion from the previous layer is requested and consumed. This security applications layer includes some classes of traditional security applications focused on event reporting and managing compliance and risk. Because the technologies and trusted compute pools involve platform integrity and trust, workload control, and policy enforcement, it makes perfect sense to have such applications aware of and enabled to detect, report, and act on the trust information available from the Intel TXT–enabled platforms.

In the context of the TCP use model, the security management tools of interest are:

- Workload/VM policy management

- SIEM/configuration management/monitoring

- GRC/compliance

These tools are critical for mainstreaming trust and elements of cloud security into any overall corporate security management systems. This is a crucial requirement, as IT managers do not want a new suite of tools for managing cloud security; they would very much rather see existing tools extended to include the new cloud and virtualized architectures as they adopt them. The primary motivation for these security management tools is to ensure that they have the visibility to platform trust and a set of control functions to management the lifecycle of the VMs/workloads. Though initially the monitoring and enforcement of trust might be periodic, over time we envision that these tools will provide continuous monitoring and enforcement of policies based on trust.

VM/Workload Policy Management

These tools provide the mechanism to specify and define the granular security requirements for the virtual machines and workloads, and to enforce these requirements during the lifetime of those virtual machines. Defining a security policy for a workload runs the gamut from the trivial, such as asserting "I want to run on trusted servers," to the sophisticated. For an example of the latter, a policy definition could include "Run on servers with trust level X and only on servers that are in geolocation Y, and don't co-exist with Z type of workloads." Today, there is no canon for policy definition, nor standards for tagging the workloads. Each of the policy management ISVs carries a particular language of definition and execution environments, with these definitions likely not to be portable or interoperable with other vendor offerings. As these capabilities mature, it is imperative that policy definitions and other matters of semantics become standardized and interoperable across vendors.

Policy tools also provide an interface to feed the following information to other security management tools in this layer of the stack, like the security event management and GRC tools. They provide:

- Auditable information about the policies that have been evaluated

- Evidence considered during policy evaluation

- Whitelists/manifests/known-good measurements considered for decision making

- Reports of decisions made, such as launch or deny workload creation or migration in a certain pool of compute servers

This information is provided in different formats while preserving integrity and maintaining the chain of trust. Hytrust VPA and McAfee ePO are examples of policy management tools for trusted compute pools.

GRC Tools—Compliance in the Cloud

GRC tools set requirements for platform trust and integrity based on workload requirements and security standards, followed by an assessment of the environment to determine security controls in place and to dashboard actual conditions against policy to determine compliance. SIEM tools allow trust events to be captured, reported, logged, and processed for correlation to determined responses or heuristics to indicate whether a larger attack is occurring. Although not every organization will need the high level of security afforded by a trusted computing environment, every organization using cloud services will benefit from the vastly improved control and transparency that a measured chain of trust enables.

Simply being able to verify conditions in the cloud services, down the stack through the hypervisor, brings significant value to users with its visibility into actual states and activities within the cloud and in its improved governance for cloud resources. Internal and private clouds built on a measured chain of trust will:

- Strengthen an organization's ability to enforce differentiated policies in private clouds

- Enhance monitoring for compliance at all layers within the cloud

- Streamline the auditing process

- Allow for more flexible usage and billing for secure computing resources

Organizations often see the completion of a regulatory audit as the end goal of their compliance efforts. The reality is that compliance is a continuous cycle that starts with technical and operational decisions on how to address control requirements. It's an accomplishment to have auditors give a thumbs-up to your technical and administrative controls. That goal notwithstanding, passing subsequent audits requires continuous maintenance and reporting on those controls. Cloud teams hold the key to making that happen in a scalable, automated manner. The most effective approach to achieving continuous compliance is to define and implement policies, guidelines, standards, and tools that secure the organization's computing systems as a whole, with an eye toward regulatory guidance, standards, and mandates themselves. Ensuring that the corresponding security controls meet or exceed the standards prescribed by the governing body will help ensure a successful audit.

RSA was one of the first ecosystem participants to demonstrate the value of platform trust for GRC uses, with a joint Intel–VMware-RSA demonstration at the RSA Security Show in 2010. Figure 3-7 shows a dashboard view of the status of a security control tied to platform trust. Intel is working with a number of other providers in these market segments to provide customers with ample choice of solutions and capabilities.

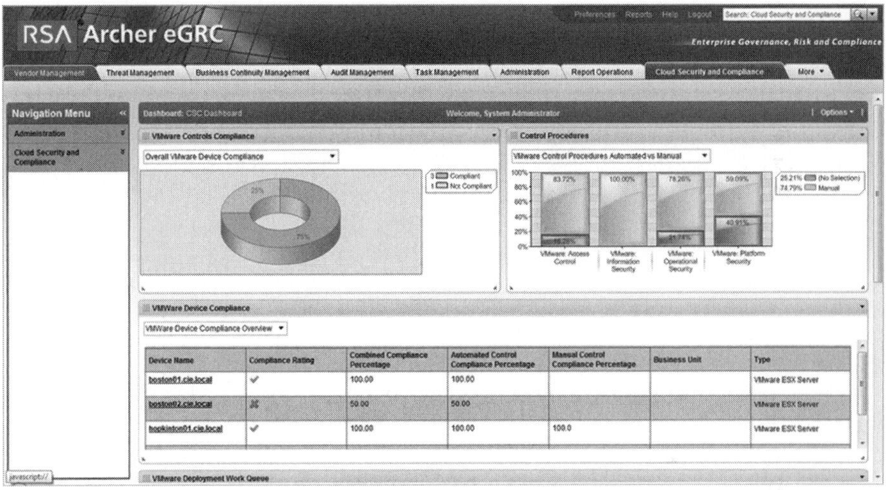

Figure 3-7. *GRC dashboard showing compliance to platform trust*

Now that we have laid out the details of the solution architecture for trusted compute pools, let's focus on a specific example and walk through one solution stack with a reference implementation of the use cases, so as to put these new concepts on a solid footing.

Reference Implementation: The Taiwan Stock Exchange Case Study

The Taiwan Exchange Stock Exchange Corporation (TWSE) is a stock exchange in Taiwan that supports the trading of 758 listed companies. Its primary business drivers are developing new financial products and boosting the number of services it offers. Cloud computing will be part of its ability to do so, but it realizes that strong security controls must first be part of the picture.

A fundamental business and technical requirement for the cloud infrastructure under construction at the TWSE infrastructure is to provide secure systems and trusted compute environments. It has established as crucial the ability to integrate software application solutions that provide TWSE with overall trust and security for its cloud infrastructure and that exploit hardware-based security and include roots of trust and platform attestation. The goals for the proof of concept built for this case study were to enable:

- Greater visibility into the security states of the hardware platforms running the infrastructure as a service (IaaS) for their private clouds.

- Production of automated, standardized reports on the configuration of the physical and virtual infrastructure hosting customer virtual machines and data.

- Controls based on the physical location of the server's virtual machines and control any migration of these virtual machines onto acceptable servers per policy specified.

- Generation of measured evidence that their services infrastructure complies with security policies and with regulated data standards.

To explore the capabilities and challenges of implementing such an infrastructure, TWSE engaged Intel and other key ecosystem partners to develop a multi-phased proof of concept (PoC) implementation of a more secure cloud based on familiar tools, platforms, and software. The basic capabilities under the proof of concept include:

- Measured boot for servers, with platform attestation

- Ability to create trusted compute pools

- Security-controlled workload placement in the trusted compute pools

- Security controlled workload migration into trusted compute pools

- Integration and extension of security and platform trust with McAfee ePolicy Orchestrator* (McAfee ePO)

Solution Architecture for TWSE

For the proof of concept, a number of systems and solutions were selected based on TWSE's current and future business directions and needs. They map directly onto the solution reference architecture layers discussed in the earlier section. As shown in Figure 3-8, these include:

- *Cloud system and infrastructure supported by Cisco.* This includes a Cisco UCS server with Intel Xeon processor E5 family and Intel TXT-enabled, equipped with the optional Cisco TPM part. Three blades were used to establish a mix of trusted and untrusted platforms in the PoC environment.

- *Virtualization solutions supported by VMware.* VMware ESXi 5.1 provides fullly integrated support for Intel TXT and enables remote platform attestation measurements to detect possible malicious changes to BIOS and other critical base-software components of the servers. VMware ESXi 5.1, in conjunction with TXT, measures the critical components of the hypervisor stack when the system boots and it stores these measurements in the platform configuration registers (PCR) of the TPM on the platform.

- *Trust and policy management supported by HyTrust and HyTrust Appliance.* HyTrust Appliance 3.5 provides extensive support for Intel TXT; the HyTrust Appliance verifies the integrity of the physical hardware of the host to ensure that the underlying platform is fully trusted and can implement policies based on this information. It can ensure that specified workloads are permitted to be instantiated only on specific hosts or clusters, the essence of TCP. It also intercepts all administrative access and change requests, determines whether a request is in accordance with the organization's defined policy, and permits or denies the request as appropriate. The HyTrust Appliance is not a physical piece of hardware; it is a VMware vSphere*compatible virtual appliance deployed alongside the rest of the virtual infrastructure. Finally, it provides direct sharing of trust and security information with McAfee ePolicy Orchestrator (McAfee ePO).

- *Security management solution supported by McAfee.* McAfee ePO unifies security management through an open platform, simplifies risk and compliance management, and provides security intelligence across endpoints, networks, data, and compliance solutions. It helps to manage security, streamline and automate compliance processes, and increase overall visibility across security management activities. McAfee with HyTrust ePO extensions enable communication with the HyTrust Appliance.

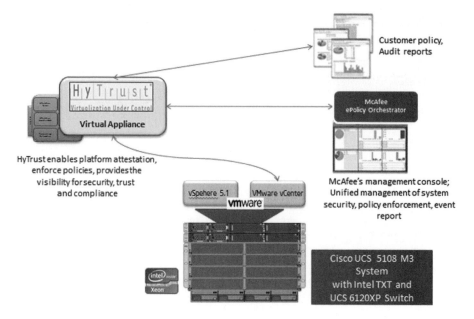

Figure 3-8. *TWSE proof of concept solution components*

Trusted Compute Pool Use Case Instantiation

Although all of the Cisco blades in this PoC were fully Intel TXT-capable, it was important to have a contrast between trusted and untrusted servers so as to differentiate trusted pools and prove the controls and status reporting mechanisms. For this reason, Intel TXT was disabled in the system BIOS configuration settings in one of the Cisco UCS blades to prohibit the system from executing a trusted launch. HyTrust Appliance had full integration of remote attestation capabilities. From VMWare ESXi side, the measured elements included the VMkernel, kernel modules, drivers, native management applications that run on ESXi, and any boot-time configuration options. As shown in Figure 3-9, the trust status dashboard of the HyTrust Appliance shows an unknown BIOS trust status, unknown VMM status, and overall unknown status for the second Cisco UCS blade as a consequence of disabling the Intel TXT support.

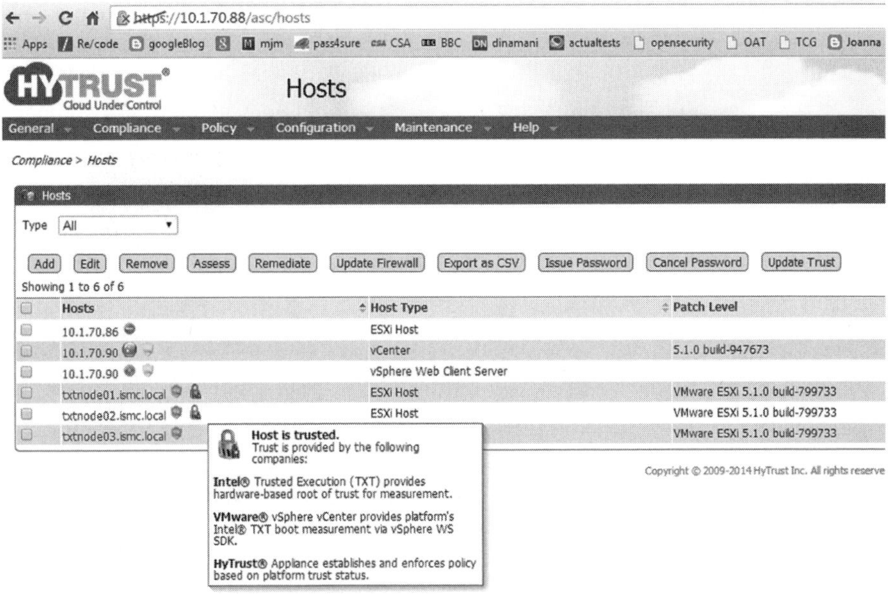

Figure 3-9. *HyTrust trust attestation service dashboard indicating two trusted hosts and one untrusted host*

Remote Attestation with HyTrust

The HyTrust Appliance provides extensive support for Intel TXT, plus policy control functionality for this use case—essentially establishing the parameters and policies for a trusted compute pool. As shown in Figure 3-10, the HyTrust Appliance provides management of critical platform attestation functionality, whitelisting of known-good measurements, and trust operation and report dashboards for trusted compute pools, as well as a broad set of other virtualization security controls for workloads, servers, and administrators. The HyTrust Appliance and these solutions were used to detect, measure, and report the trust of both the server platforms and the hypervisor, and to implement workload controls (VM migration, etc.) based on the required platform trust attributes.

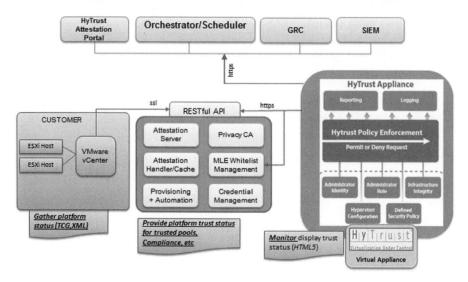

Figure 3-10. *HyTrust Appliance with remote trust attestation architecture*

To summarize, the remote attestation process provides an independent evaluation of the integrity measurements of the firmware, BIOS, and the VMM against known-good (whitelist) program components, and it securely makes that assertion available to the HyTrust Appliance policy enforcement and reporting components. The evaluation of the measurements is comprehensive and covers the core of the BIOS, the BIOS configurations, the VMM kernel, and various VMM modules loaded as part of the VMware ESXi launch. Figure 3-11 shows a snapshot of the actual measurements of an ESXi Server with the known-good or whitelist values.

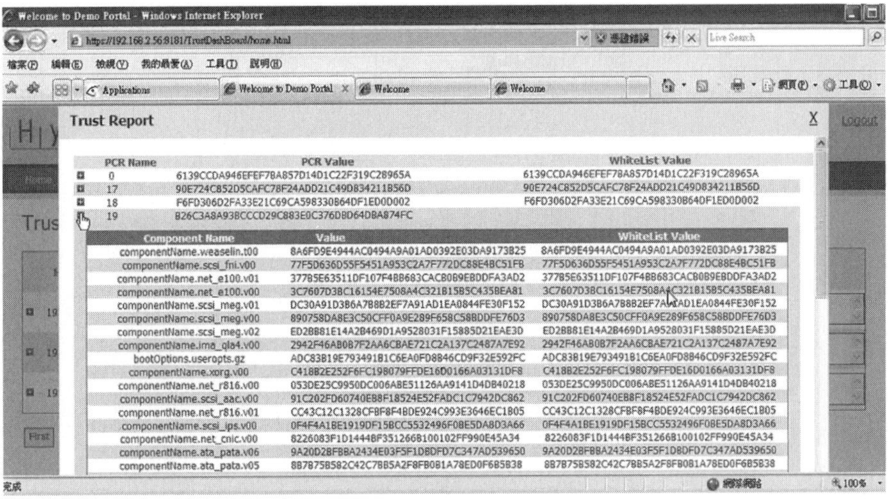

Figure 3-11. *Trust attestation service - trust report view*

Use Case Example: Creating Trusted Compute Pools and Workload Migration

Knowing the trust status of both the servers and the hypervisor highlighted the platform trust information to TWSE, as well as defined an appropriate set of operational policies and controls. The reference implementation demonstrated the operational details of the trusted compute pools use cases as follows:

- Creation of trusted compute pools

- Workload placement in the trusted compute pools

- Workload migration into the trusted compute pools

- Dashboard reporting with McAfee ePolicy Orchestrator* (McAfee ePO*)

The HyTrust Appliance enabled the team to intercept all administrative requests for the virtual infrastructure, determine whether the request was in accordance with defined policy, permit or deny that request, and record all administrative access and change requests.

To apply effective end-to-end trust policies for the cloud infrastructure, the team did the following:

- Created trusted compute pools with Intel TXT

- Identified and labeled the sensitive workloads that required protection

- Configured the trust policies to establish trust requirements

- Assigned and managed workload migration based on defined trust polices

- Enforced trust policies end-to-end

- Recorded all activities, including audit, and compliance; and provided reports

Integrated and Extended Security and Platform Trust with McAfee ePO

A TWSE requirement was the integration and reporting of all security events and enforcement decisions to a SIEM and GRC system. This gave TWSE another common and aggregated management view of its cloud infrastructure. The PoC used the HyTrust Appliance to extend and integrate the trust information for each hypervisor and the virtualized resource functionality to the McAfee ePO console.

The direct integration of the HyTrust Appliance dashboard showed users the Intel TXT trust status of the host on which each VM was running. HyTrust Appliance assessed compliance by comparing a host's current configuration with a hardening configuration template that was customized based on TWSE requirements. It then provided assessment data to the master ePO dashboard for reporting and analysis. HyTrust Appliance gave McAfee ePO a record of all administrative activities, including a unique user ID, and operations attempted by the privileged user, including denied or failed attempts. Figure 3-12 shows the aggregated view of trust within the McAfee ePO dashboard.

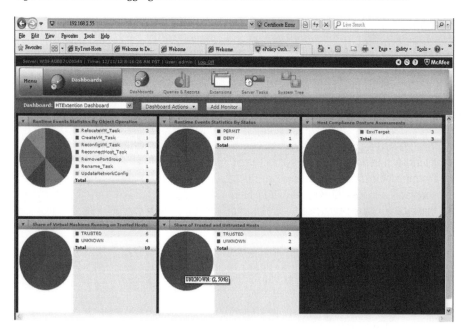

Figure 3-12. *McAfee ePO displaying administrator activity and trust status captured by HyTrust Appliance*

Figure 3-13 shows a drilldown view of the trust information in the McAfee ePO system as provided by the seamless integration between the HyTrust Appliance and the McAfee policy orchestrator.

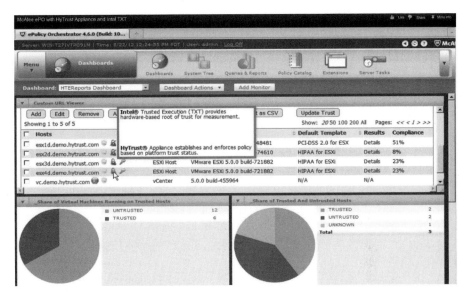

Figure 3-13. *McAfee ePO displaying a drilldown of the server trust status from the HyTrust Appliance*

McAfee ePO's flexible automation capability streamlined the workflows, dramatically reducing the cost and complexity of security and compliance administration.

INTEL TXT ARCHITECTURAL OVERVIEW

Intel TXT is a set of enhanced hardware components designed to protect sensitive information from software-based attacks. Intel TXT features include capabilities in the microprocessor, chipset, I/O subsystems, and other platform components. When coupled with an enabled operating system, hypervisor, and enabled applications, these capabilities provide confidentiality and integrity of data in a time of increasingly hostile environments.

Intel TXT incorporates a number of secure processing innovations (see Figure 3-14), including:

- *Protected execution.* Lets applications run in isolated environments so that no unauthorized software on the platform can observe or tamper with the operational information. Each of these isolated environments executes with the use of dedicated resources managed by the platform.

- *Sealed storage.* Provides the ability to encrypt and store keys, data, and other sensitive information within the hardware. This can be decrypted only by the same environment as encrypted it.

- *Attestation.* Enables a system to provide assurance that the protected environment has been correctly invoked and takes a measurement of the software running in the protected space. The information exchanged during this process is known as the attestation identity key credential, and is used to establish mutual trust between parties.

- *Protected launch.* Provides the controlled launch and registration of critical system software components in a protected execution environment.

- *Trusted extensions integrated into silicon* (processor and chipset). Allow for the orderly quiescence of all activities on the platform such that a tamper-resistant environment is enabled for the measurement and verification processes; and allows for protection of platform secrets in the case of "reset" and other disruptive attacks.

- *Authenticated code modules* (ACM). Authenticate platform-specific code to the chipset and execute in an isolated environment within the processor and the trusted environment (authenticated code mode) enabled by AC Modules to perform secure tasks.

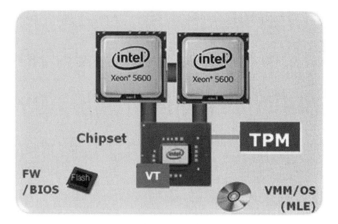

Figure 3-14. *Intel Trusted Execution Technology components*

Intel TXT Principles of Operation

Intel TXT works through the creation of a measured launch environment (MLE) enabling an accurate comparison of all the critical elements of the launch environment against a known-good source. Intel TXT creates a cryptographically unique identifier for each approved launch-enabled component and then provides a hardware-based enforcement mechanism to block the launch of the code that does not match that which is authenticated or, alternatively, indicates when an expected trusted launch has not happened. This hardware-based solution provides the foundation on which IT administrators can build trusted platform solutions to protect against aggressive software-based attacks and to better control their virtualized or cloud environments.

Figure 3-15 illustrates two different scenarios. In the first, the measurements match the expected values, so the launch of the BIOS, firmware, and VMM are allowed. In the second, the system has been compromised by a rootkit hypervisor, which has attempted to install itself below the hypervisor to gain access to the platform. In this case, the Intel TXT-enabled, MLE-calculated hash system measurements differ from the expected value, owing to the insertion of the rootkit. Therefore, the measured environment will not match the expected value and, based on the launch policy, Intel TXT could abort the launch of the hypervisor or report an untrusted launch into the virtualization or cloud management infrastructure for subsequent use.

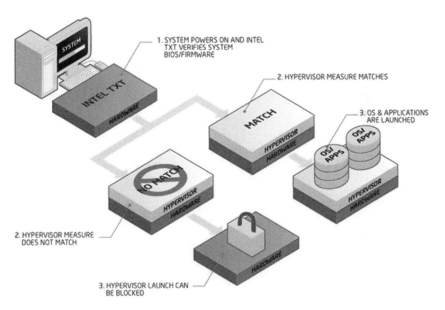

INTEL® TXT
INTEL TRUSTED EXECUTION TECHNOLOGY

Figure 3-15. How Intel Trusted Execution Technology protects the launch environment

Summary

In this chapter, we introduced the concept of platform boot integrity and trust. We covered the roots of trust in a trusted compute platform, and the two measured boot models, S-RTM and D-RTM. We introduced the concept of attestation as a critical requirement to assert the boot integrity, and presented the notion of trusted compute pools, including the use cases and the solution reference architecture for enabling trusted compute pools. By reviewing one solution stack and a reference implementation, we reinforced the concept and showed how to enable and use trusted compute pools. Platform trust is the new data center management attribute that can be used to orchestrate and manage the resources of virtualization and cloud data centers so as to meet the corresponding security challenges and requirements.

Looking ahead, Chapter 4 is a deep dive into attestation and view of a commercial implementation of a remote attestation software solution. In addition to platform trust and hardware roots of trust, more and more organizations and service providers are interested in providing visibility of and control to the physical location of the servers where the workloads and data are actually residing and executing. These controls are critical for federal agencies and regulated industries. Chapter 5 will introduce a new concept and control called hardware-assisted asset tag, which can be used to provide isolation, segregation, placement, and migration control of workload execution in multi-tenant cloud environments. Additionally, as a specialization of asset tags, geolocation/geotagging can be enabled to definitively provide visibility of the physical geolocation of the server, which can enable many controls that requirement hardware-based roots of trust to assert the location of the workloads and data. These attributes and the associated controls are dependent on the assertion of the boot integrity of the platform, and hence they become a great adjacency to trusted compute pools and boot integrity.

CHAPTER 4

■ ■ ■

Attestation: Proving Trustability

In the last few chapters we have looked at the first stages in a process toward establishing trust between systems. First, the establishment of roots of trust and the measured boot components; and second, the collection of evidence throughout the measurement process. We reviewed the different roots of trust in a compute platform—namely, the RTM, RTS, and RTR—and how the measured boot process (S-RTM and D-RTM) uses the RTM to measure and store the evidence in the RTS. The next stage in this process is the presentation of this evidence through attestation protocols and appraisal of the evidence that asserts the integrity of a platform. This stage is referred to as *attestation and verification* in this book, and it is our objective for this chapter.

We introduce the concept of attestation in this chapter, along with an attestation framework that defines a logical view of the assertion layers leading to attestation of specific target entities or components. The attestation provides evidence of trust and can include any device or target system participating in the trust chain. Additionally, the chapter covers one commercial implementation of the attestation solution authored by Intel and security management independent software vendors, code-named Mt. Wilson. We provide details about the solution architecture, attestation application programming interfaces (APIs), integration of these APIs into a security management function, and workload orchestration tools for decision making. We hope application developers and security specialists will gain a solid understanding of the inner workings of attestation solutions to the level of being able to carry out integration projects and even extend the paradigm.

Attestation

Attestation is a critical component for trusted computing environments, providing an essential proof of trustability and the means for conducting audits for target computing devices. That is, attestation allows a program or platform to authenticate itself. Remote attestation is a means for a system to make reliable statements about the pre-launch and launch components in a distributed system. A remote party can then make authorization decisions based on that information. The concept of attestation is still evolving, and hence the research community has not reached a common understanding of what it means. However, here is a practical definition for the purpose of working with trusted clouds. The Trusted Computing Group (TCG) defines attestation as:

> *The process of vouching for the accuracy of information. External entities can attest to shielded locations, protected capabilities, and Roots of Trust. A platform can attest to its description of platform characteristics that affect the integrity (trustworthiness) of a platform. Both forms of attestation require reliable evidence of the attesting entity.*

There are two properties that have to be addressed to assert this trust.

1. *Measurement properties.* Includes the degree of completeness for measuring the launch and running state of the targeted device or system, and the freshness of the measurements—that is, how recent the measurements are.

2. *Attestation properties.* Includes the authenticity of the evidence to the decision process, and a measure of semantic explicitness describing the appropriateness of the evidence to the decision-making process.

These two properties help us classify the remote attestation techniques. Most of the existing remote attestation techniques can be categorized into one of the two types.

- *Static remote attestation* techniques rely on the signatures or hashes of the firmware and binaries for determining the integrity of the platform state. Static remote attestation can't be extended to measure the behavior of a platform. Furthermore, even if the hash of the boot state (static state) does not reveal any tampering, it does not follow that the run-time behavior of the application will be trustworthy.

- *Dynamic remote attestation* techniques use monitoring instead of measuring the application binary. Dynamic remote attestation techniques are relatively difficult to integrate into existing operating systems and software applications, because there is no unequivocal reference point; that is, there is no commonly agreed upon definition of what constitutes trustworthy behavior in an operating system, virtual machine monitor, or application. Benchmarks for trustworthy behavior, defined in existing remote attestation techniques, are either vague or incomplete, with only a portion of the activities performed by an application during its execution monitored. The benchmarks don't apply to virtual machine monitors because the benchmark requirements are not yet well understood.

Both static and dynamic remote attestation are relevant to virtualization and cloud computing. As described in the previous chapters, the trusted compute pool uses models that begin with the boot integrity of the platform, asserted with the static attestation techniques. Meanwhile, asserting run-time integrity needs dynamic attestation techniques. Static attestation techniques are beginning to be adopted in practical cloud computing deployments. The static techniques provide a good foundation toward reaching a trusted infrastructure. Dynamic remote attestation is complementary and brings significant value by enforcing security; hence, we can expect a strong drive for adoption. However, in order to achieve the vision and goals of a trusted infrastructure, it is an imperative to have a dynamic remote attestation facility in working order.

For context, we provide a brief overview in this chapter of remote attestation techniques discussed in the research community, including reference implementations where available. Please note that, other than Integrity Measurement Architecture, none of the schemes has seen wide adoption, if any at all.

Integrity Measurement Architecture

Integrity Measurement Architecture (IMA) is a classic static remote attestation model developed by IBM[1] for measurement and reporting of the integrity of Linux-based systems. It takes a hash of the binaries of the software code that run on any system, and compares them against known-good hashes to assert that the system is high integrity. IMA extends the trusted boot process of the TCG beyond the bootstrapping of the Linux loader, to the chain of trust from the TPM, to applications running on the system. Through extensions to the kernel of the Linux system, IMA measures the code that's loaded into memory for execution by taking a SHA-1 hash of the code prior to that execution. A measurement archive is maintained for measurements previously taken.

Integrity Measurement Architecture was the first practical implementation of a TCG-based remote attestation technique. It allows a challenger to verify a platform status by measuring the executables running on that platform. IMA forms the basis for many remote attestation techniques that followed the original implementation. The requirement for using IMA is to download a kernel patch from IBM. The prototype of IMA was implemented as a Linux Security Module on RedHat 9.0 Linux distribution and kernel version 2.6.5.

Policy Reduced Integrity Measurement Architecture

Policy Reduced Integrity Measurement Architecture (PRIMA) is a variation of IMA. According to the authors of this architecture,[2] the static code and load-time measurement cannot be used to assess the run-time behavior. This architecture introduces the concept of measured security context or label of the subject, in addition to static code. The code/data digest also includes a role field so that additional identification of subjects and objects can be done. This approach allows remote attestation to be made on the basis of secure information-flow models. The approach is rather low level and cannot be used for distributed services in an organization or the information flows that occur within the organization and in outside world. There are no known implementations in a commonly available operating system environment.

---

[1]See http://researcher.watson.ibm.com/researcher/files/us-msteiner/ima.sailer_usenix_security_2004_slides.pdf

[2]Trent Jaeger et al., "PRIMA: PolicyReduced Integrity Measurement Architecture, SACMAT2006, June 7–9, 2006, Lake Tahoe, California. ACM 1595933549/06/0006.

Semantic Remote Attestation

Semantic Remote Attestation is an attempt at creating a platform-independent remote attestation technique.[3] The core idea is that of a trusted virtual machine (TVM) capable of enforcing the requirements for those applications running within this virtual machine. The model establishes trust on the TVM and uses this trust to enforce security requirements. It attempts to measure the behavior of the code running inside a trusted virtual machine. The architecture is an incremental improvement over the original remote attestation techniques and is more flexible compared with binary attestation techniques with regard to expressiveness. This model of attestation has not been implemented, or at least published, owing to the complexity of defining and analyzing the notion of trust.

The Attestation Process

Given the discussion in the above section about the state and maturity of attestation techniques, let's look at the details of the static attestation protocol and the overall integrity measurement flow.

The integrity measurement flow describes the steps required to measure the platform integrity measurements. It includes:

- A means of generating and collecting the measurements through an RTM.

- A means of storing the measurements that is either tamper resistant or tamper evident, with a TPM for RTS and RTR.

- A means of conveying the measurements to a challenger via the attestation agents, as described in the attestation protocol below.

- A means of analyzing the measured result, and a means of asserting the trustability of the machine based on the results of that determination through a trust assessment authority or trust attestation authority (TAA).

Remote Attestation Protocol

Figure 4-1 illustrates the attestation protocol providing the means for conveying measurements to the challenger. The endpoint attesting device must have a means of measuring the BIOS firmware, low-level device drivers, operating system, virtual machine monitor components, and be able to forward those measurements to the attestation authority. The attesting device must do this while protecting the integrity, authenticity, nonrepudiation, and some cases, the confidentiality of those measurements.

---

[3]Vivek Haldar et al., *Semantic Remote Attestation: a Virtual Machine Directed Approach to Trusted Computing*, VM2004 Proceedings of the 3rd conference on Virtual Machine Research and Technology Symposium, vol. 3 (Berkeley, CA: USENIX Association).

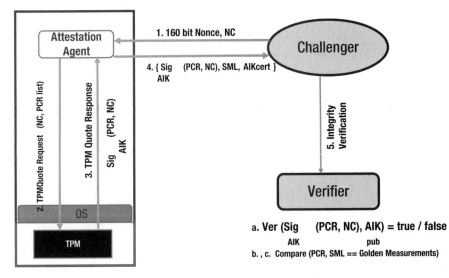

Figure 4-1. *Remote attestation protocol*

Let's walk through the steps of the remote attestation protocol:

1. The challenger, at the request of a requester, creates a nonpredictable nonce (NC) and sends it to the attestation agent on the attesting node, along with the selected list of platform configuration registers (PCRs).

2. The attestation agent sends that request to the TPM as a TPMQuote request with the nonce, and the PCR list.

3. In reponse to the TPMQuote request, the TPM loads the attestation identity key from protected storage in the TPM by using the storage root key (SRK), performs a TPM Quote command, which is used to sign the selected PCRs and the provided nonce (NC) with the private key, AIKpriv. Additionally, the attesting agent retrieves the stored measurement log (SML).

4. Called the integrity response, the attesting agent sends the response consisting of the signed quote, signed nonce (NC), and the SML to the challenger. The attesting agent also delivers the AIK credential, which consists of the AIKpub that was signed by a privacy CA.

5. The challenger validates if the AIK credential was signed by a trusted privacy CA thus belonging to a genuine TPM. The challenger also verifies whether AIKpub is still valid by checking the certificate revocation list of the trusted issuing party.

6. The challenger verifies the signature of the quote and checks the freshness of the quote.

7. Based on the received stored measurement log and the PCR values, the challenger processes the SML, compares the individual module hashes that are extended to the PCRs against the known-good or golden values, and recomputes the received PCR values. If the individual values match the golden values, and if the computed values match the signed aggregate, the remote node is asserted to be in a trusted state.

This protocol is highly resistant to replay attacks, tampering, and masquerading.

How does this remote attestation protocol get implemented and manifested in an IT environment? Figure 4-2 illustrates a sample IT architecture supporting the generation, forwarding, and analysis of platform boot integrity measurements, as well as assertion of the trustability of the attestation at each decision point via a trust assertion authority, or TAA. These solutions come from a set of compatible components available from a variety of suppliers.

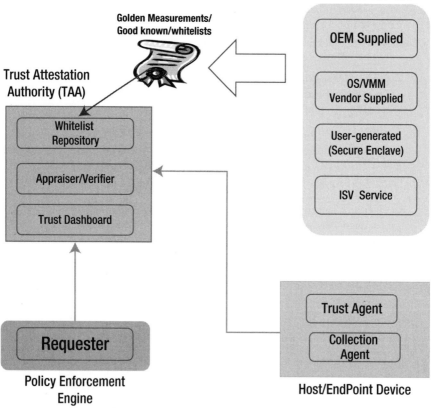

Figure 4-2. Trust attestation authority

Flow for Integrity Measurement

In assessing the measurements, the TAA references a set of properties. These properties represent attributes and measurements for the BIOS and the operating system and virtual machine monitors. These measurements are referred to as *golden measurements* or *whitelists*, and are:

- Provided and verified and validated through certificates by the original equipment manufacturer (OEM))

- Provided and vouched for by an ISV Service

- Collected by an authenticated administrator on first boot in an isolated or enclave type of environment

The process for carrying out the integrity measurement and verification is as follows:

1. When a new instance of a BIOS or an operating system or virtual machine monitor is made available, an initial set of trusted measurements (golden measurements) is taken on the image. These measurements are provided either through third parties such as an OEM, operating system, virtual machine monitor supplier, or through a trusted whitelist service provider to the trust authority, It may also be generated at initial provisioning by system administrators.

2. An RTM such as Intel TXT is used to take the measurement of the software components during server or device boot.

3. The measurements are stored in the TPM. A log from which the measurements can be reconstructed is stored in memory for transmission to the verifier to allow reconstruction of the measurements.

4. The TAA generates an authenticated request for measurements from the server/device, in response to an action by any requester, or the endpoint device requesting a service. This action follows the attestation protocol previously described. The trust agent receives this request and passes it to the TPM to obtain a TPMQuote for the requested PCR measurments. TPMQuote, along with the measurement log, are packaged as an integrity report, using the TCG Integrity Reporting Schema.

5. The trust agent transmits the data to the TAA's verifier. The TAA verifies the signature over the hashes by inspecting both the public key used to sign them and the signature itself, which will ensure that the nonce sent to the trust agent is the same one as the one used in the TPMQuote. It then compares those signed measurements with the golden measurements obtained earlier. There is more than a simple comparison. Depending upon the sophistication of the verifier, it can use the system measurement log (SML) to re-compute the aggregate measurements from the individual measurements, and then verify them against the golden measurements.

6. The results of the comparison, collated with other such comparisons from other machines and digitally signed, may be displayed via a user interface, such as a management console or dashboard, to the administrator or it can be provided through an API to an automated enforcement, policy engines, and orchestrators. Solutions use the results to apply, manage, enforce, and report on the trust level of the systems.

A First Commercial Attestation Implementation: The Intel Trust Attestation Platform

To provide a path toward broad use of trusted compute pools and to exemplify the vision of trusted infrastructure and cloud computing, Intel developed a remote attestation solution capable of working across a broad range of hardware and operating system and virtual machine monitor platforms: the Intel Trust Attestation Platform (TAP). The goals of the Intel Trust Attestation Platform are threefold:

- Provide a production-quality implementation of remote attestation and a trust assessment authority capable of providing verification and assessment across a broad range of devices. The Intel Trust Attestation Platform features high availability and security of the attestation platform and its interfaces.

- Provide stable and simplistic northbound and southbound application programming interfaces (APIs) for attestation information requesters, and for interfacing with different sources of integrity measurements. These are trust APIs, designed to encourage multiple interoperable attestation solutions from a variety of security-management independent software vendors. The interoperability and diversity minimize the occurrence of vendor lock-in.

- Develop the attestation platform as a true extensible and pluggable framework providing fertile ground for the deployment of innovative third-party attestation techniques and models. Initially, the solution supports a TPM-based static attestation model, and is already being extended to support dynamic attestation techniques for asserting the boot integrity of virtual machines, as well as the run-time integrity of operating systems and hypervisors.

Figure 4-3 captures the high-level architecture of the Intel Trust Attestation Platform. Consistent with the cloud approach, the Intel Trust Attestation Platform features a loosely coupled architecture with a flexible software backplane and fabric with core capabilities and services, including a set of slots to plug in various attestation blades for different types of attestation provided by Intel and third-party independent software vendors. Here are the key aspects of the architecture:

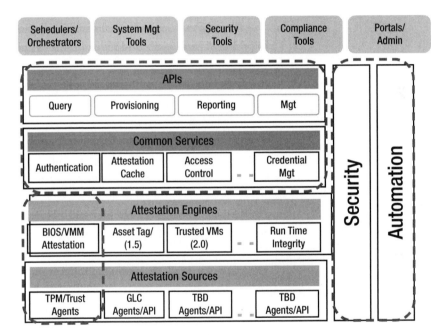

Figure 4-3. *Intel Trust Attestation Platform*

- An *API layer* acting as primary interface for:

    - Endpoint devices needing to carry out an attestation before a request for services

    - Entities requesting integrity verification for policy enforcement and visibility into the trust of the infrastructure

    - Access to compliance and security monitoring tools

- A *common services layer* for the attestation service and platform
  to enable authentication, authorization, and access control (AAA)
  for the API calls, and *a* flexible and extensible data model for the
  attestation platform repository accessible via APIs.

- An *attestation blade* supporting a variety of attestation types
  implemented as plug-ins. The attestation blade is an element
  of a set of pluggable components integrated into the attestation
  platform taking advantage of the fabric and core functionality of
  the platform, including interfaces, security, and common services.
  As shown in Figure 4-3, each blade has two distinct components:

  - A measurement and attestation agent capable of collecting
    measurements from an endpoint device or server.

  - A verification module that uses the attestation platform
    services, and provides custom verification logic for an
    attestation capability instance, using the northbound APIs
    of the attestation platform, thereby exposing an assertion
    function and making it available to policy enforcers and
    other requesting entities.

Mt. Wilson Platform

Mt. Wilson is the code name for the Intel Trust Attestation platform that has the TPM-based boot attestation functionality. It is the first attestation blade that was released as part of the attestation platform. Mt. Wilson provides a secure mechanism for customers and data center operators to attest the integrity of Intel-based systems enabled with Intel's Trusted Execution Technology (TXT) for RTM, along with third-party trusted platform modules (TPMs). The TPM stores and reports the platform measurements, including BIOS firmware and hypervisor software on servers. The architecture of the blade, described in more detail later in this chapter, is applicable to any TPM-based integrity measurement and reporting architecture.

We have assembled proof of existence working prototypes of a boot integrity attestation blade with Microsoft Windows 8, and corresponding TPM using a BIOS boot block as the RTM. We also have constructed a proof point with Citrix XenClient XT using Intel TXT on the client. A subset of the Mt. Wilson functionality has been shared with the open-source community under the name Open Attestation (OAT).

Mt. Wilson is a fast-evolving platform with new features and capabilities developed and released as the community gains experience with the technology. Here is a snapshot of key capabilities in the current Mt. Wilson solution.

Table 4-1. *Mt. Wilson Key Capabilities*

Attestation Support	PCR and module-based attestation and verification for VMware ESXi 5.1 and above, and for Xen, KVM with RHEL, SuSE, and Ubuntu Linux
APIs	REST interfaces for query, reporting, management, and provisioning functions;
	REST interfaces for whitelist definition and management
Security	Digest-style API authentication and validation using RSA keys (<signed http authorization header >)
	SAML-based API responses with signed SAML assertions
	SSL communication and mutual authentication of communication endpoints
Auditability	Secure logging of requests, responses, transactions for auditability, forensics including logging APIs, and support for CEF format for consumption into SIEM tools
Deployability	Automated installation of host trust agents and all Mt.Wilson components
	Solution validation with Hewlett Packard, Dell, Cisco hardware, etc.
Availability	Deployed as Xen/KVM/VMW, virtual machines including high availability and fault tolerance for key components for VMware
Automation and Productivity Tools	API client: utility wrapper code for API invocation and response processing
	Reference integration with OpenStack extensions to flavors, dashboard, scheduler
	Reference trust dashboard with API integration with Mt. Wilson

The rest of this chapter will provide a comprehensive view of this attestation blade, starting with the architecture and design components to support server operating systems and virtual machine monitors, followed by the core attestation related API definitions and security considerations. Sample source code examples are provided in the last section of this chapter to show how to:

- Register the servers with Mt. Wilson

- Request the trust assertions (using the trust APIs)

- Whitelist the golden measurements that are used in the appraisal and verification

Mt. Wilson Architecture

Mt. Wilson, as shown in Figure 4-4, has two main components: the *trust agent* (TA) and the *trust attestation authority* (TAA.)

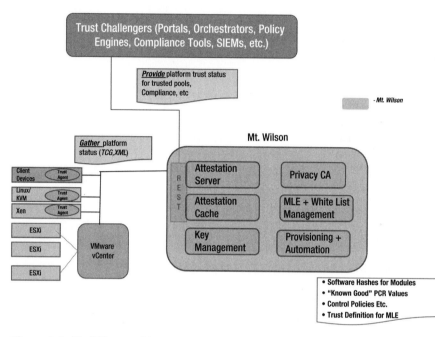

Figure 4-4. *Mt. Wilson architecture*

The trust agent runs on the device or host that is attesting with the trust attestation authority. The trust agent is the collector, and securely uploads the integrity measurements (fetched using the TPMQuote command) and the integrity event log from the TPM. The trust agent is not required in a VMWare environment, since vCenter provides specific APIs (called TrustAttestationReport) and capabilities that provide the functionality. More specifically, vCenter Agent and VMWare vCenter Server enable the necessary handshake, verification of the platform certificates, and invocation of the TPM commands, in response to any entity invoking the TrustAttestationReport web services API.

The trust attestation authority is the core attestation and assessor with a number of key services:

- **Attestation Server:** This is the primary service providing the APIs for the trust attestation authority. It has the function of interfacing with the attesting hosts, requesting the specific host for its measurements following the remote attestation protocol, and verifying certificates, signatures, and logs requests and responses for tracking and auditability. A key role of the attesation server is to appraise the measurements from the device/host, which involves comparing these measurements against golden measurements, whitelists, and known-good values. The whitelists are the final TPM PCR extensions for each of the PCRs of the TPM and granular SHA-1 hashes of the various loadable modules of the measured launch environment (MLE). The appraisal includes verifying the individual module hashes from the SML (event log) against the whitelists of the module hashes and recomputing the PCR values from the event log entries. The recomputed PCR value has to match the value sent from the device (which shows that the log is not compromised) and match the whitelist/known-good. In today's implementation across hypervisor and operating system vendors, there are variations in approaches to measuring the TCB. For instance, VMware has made great strides in measuring a high percentage of their TCB. Open-source operating system and hypervisor providers have, for the most part, reused the Intel reference tboot implementation, and consequently measure a small part of the TCB, mostly the kernels. As the need for trust increases in the cloud data centers, vendors have been expressing a willingness to broaden the amount of measured TCB.

- **Whitelist Management:** This service provides APIs to define the various MLEs in the environment, their attributes, policy-driven trust definition, and the whitelists for the modules or PCRs. Whitelist measurements are usually retrieved from hosts built and configured in an isolated environment/enclave, or provided by the OEM and VMV/OS vendors. The MLEs and the corresponding whitelist measurements need to be configured to specific versions of BIOS and hypervisor.

- **Host Management:** This service provides APIs to register the hosts to be attested with the system. For successful attestation, the whitelists for the BIOS and hypervisor running on the host need to be preconfigured in the Mt. Wilson system, prior to registration of the host that would attest.

- **Privacy CA:** Provides the attestation certificate for the open-source hypervisor hosts and validation of the same. The certificate authority needs to support the OCSP protocol for certificate validation. This capability is subsumed by VMware vCenter Server in the VMWare environment. Management of Citrix XenServer does not need privacy CA since it supports direct anonymous attestation (DAA).

In the next section, we drill into the attestation server and understand the functions and the attestation process flows.

The Mt. Wilson Attestation Process

Figure 4-5 illustrates the attestation architecture in Mt. Wilson, with a drilldown of the attestation server component described in the previous session and depicted in Figure 4-4. The Mt. Wilson attestation process comprises three flows:

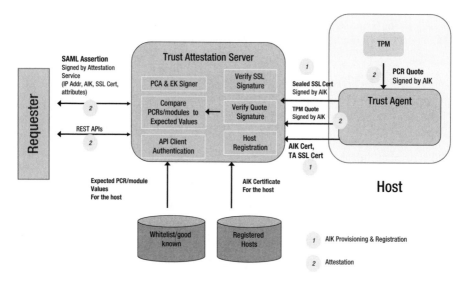

Figure 4-5. *The Mt. Wilson attestation architecture*

1. Provisioning the attestation identity keys (AIKs) and ensuring successful validation of the host

2. Registration of the host with Mt. Wilson

3. Actual attestation request and response

Attestation Identity Key Provisioning

The attestation identity key provisioning process is done in four steps.

1. *TPM on the host is validated.* According to the TCG specifications, compliant systems should contain an endorsement credential and a platform credential. These two credentials are installed by the OEM to certify that the TPM's endorsement key and the entire TCG subsystem are genuine. However, in practice these credentials are often missing. As a workaround, system administrators may inspect a system and generate equivalent credentials locally after being satisfied that the system is genuine. The trust agent software provides a password-protected mechanism in conjunction with the privacy CA service for the system administrator to easily generate and install the equivalent credentials. Additional credentials, known as the conformance credential and validation credential, are also possible but are seen even less in practice, and are not covered during the attestation identity key provisioning and host registration.

2. *The AIK is created by the platform and certified by the privacy CA.* This transforms the platform verification problem into an RSA encryption problem. It is critical for the system administrator to conduct an adequate inspection to ensure that the TPM is genuine and that Intel TXT is properly enabled on platforms that are missing the endorsement credential and the platform credential because, once the AIK is certified by the privacy CA, remote attestation services will trust TPM quotes signed with the corresponding AIK private key. The AIK certificate is imported into Mt. Wilson when the host is registered.

3. *An RSA key pair and transport layer security (TLS) certificate are generated.* These are for the trust agent to use for incoming attestation requests. Mt. Wilson provides a mechanism to import the trust agent TLS certificate on a per-host basis and verifies all attestation connections to that host using the same certificate.

4. *A second RSA key pair and TLS certificate are generated on the platform.* The private key bound to the TPM and the TLS certificate indicates the specifics of the TPM binding. This key pair facilitates applications of the trusted compute pool relying on attestation of the platform to authorize certain actions by providing a mechanism assure a third party that, when it connects to the attested platform, it is the same platform in the same trusted state as was attested. Mt. Wilson provides a mechanism to import the bound or sealed TLS certificate after a host is registered and to provide that certificate to its clients.

Host Registration and Attestation Identity Key Certificate Provisioning

Figure 4-6 depicts the sequence diagram showing the steps for host registration and the management of attestation identity key certificates. As mentioned earlier, these steps are applicable only for hosts running on Xen or KVM.

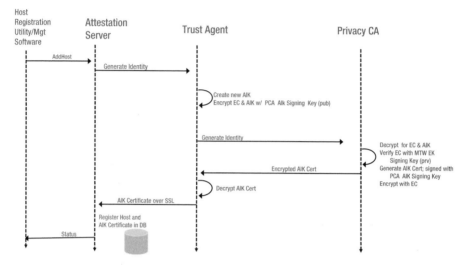

Figure 4-6. *Flow of authority identity key certificate provisioning*

- The host registration process begins with an API request to the attestation server. This request may come from a system administrator using a management portal, or from an automated system in charge of managing hosts in the data center.

- The attestation server sends an attestation identity key provisioning request to the trust agent on the host using a TLS connection secured by the trust agent TLS certificate.

- The trust agent uses the TPM to create a new AIK private and public key pair. It sends the AIK public key and the endorsement credential to the privacy CA, encrypted using the privacy CA's public key to ensure privacy.

- The privacy CA decrypts the AIK public key and endorsement credential using its private key. It then generates a random challenge and encrypts it using the public key certified by the endorsement credential. It sends this challenge to the host.

- The host decrypts the challenge using the endorsement key, a private key corresponding to the endorsement credential. It re-encrypts the challenge using the privacy CA's public key for privacy and sends the re-encrypted challenge to the privacy CA.

- The privacy CA decrypts the challenge to verify it is correct, then certifies the host's AIK public key. The privacy CA sends the AIK certificate to the host, encrypted using the public key in the host's endorsement credential.

- The host decrypts the AIK certificate using its endorsement key.

- The host sends the AIK certificate to the attestation server over the trust agent TLS connection.

- The attestation server registers the host and stores the AIK certificate in the database.

- The attestation server responds to the system administrator or automated system, indicating the success or failure of the registration process.

Requesting Platform Trust

This is the invocation of the trust APIs by an entity requesting trust information. The API request is authenticated and the input parameters are validated and then handed to the appraiser component of the attestation server. The appraiser follows the remote attestation protocol to challenge the platform for the integrity measurements. Once the verification is done, Mt. Wilson summarizes all these steps by generating a SAML assertion of the platform compliance with its trust policy. Details of the SAML assertion and the security and integrity of the exchange are covered later in this chapter.

Security of Mt. Wilson

Security is integral to the Mt. Wilson platform. The ultimate objective of an adversary of Mt. Wilson would be to subvert and control the outcome of the attestation by:

- Spoofing the trust agent to attain a fake TPM quote

- Compromising the Mt. Wilson attestation server to subvert signed content

- Spoofing the Mt. Wilson attestation server to fake a signed content

- Hacking the whitelists

- Compromising the data on the network and repositories

Figure 4-7 shows the threat model considered during the design of Mt. Wilson, with articulation of the consequences when the adversary accomplishes the attack and possible mitigations implemented. We summarize the mitigating actions against the threats listed above.

#	Threat Type	Attack / Rating	Concerns / Consequences	Mitigation
1	Spoof Mt. Wilson to fake signed content	MTW Server "Man in the middle " attack	MITM between Requester and MTW, to provide alternate SAML cert	Mutual certificate validation
		High	Wrong trust status of the hosts to calling application	
2	Compromise Mt.Wilson to affect signed content	Protection of Critical Assets (keys, certs..)	Malicious user with access to Server SSL key, SAML signing key, Mt. Wilson endorsement key	In web servers, critical files stored on file system encrypted but password also must be stored on file system and marked readable only to root. In desktop applications & tools, critical files stored encrypted on file system and user supplies password to decrypt
		High	Fake attestation reports	
3	Spoof Trust Agent to fake TPM quote	Trust agent "Man in the middle " attack	Malware replacing the trust agent and providing wrong trust information	Mutual certificate validation. EK provisioning, Nonce, TCG protocol
		High	Wrong trust status of the hosts to calling application	
4	Redefine white list	DB compromise (tampering with whitelist)	If malware gets access to the database	Least privileged database access levels, RBAC, IP address based database access and strong passwords, encryption of sensitive data in the database audit logging
		High	Host information, manifest related data and white list data	
5	Data compromise	SQL injection	API input data which inserts a parameter into an SQL query and have the server execute it with the rights of the Web Service	Data validation and use of JPA for data access
		Medium	Command execution, data theft and deletion, schema poisoning	
6	Data compromise	Over the network data sniffing	Networking sniffing	Use of HTTPS and SSL for all over the network communication
		Medium	Networking sniffing for host and Whitelist data	

Figure 4-7. Mt. Wilson threat analysis

- Registered API client calls (signed with their private key) can be verified by the Mt. Wilson attestation server using the corresponding public key. These keys get generated and stored by the API client during the registration process. Users are encouraged to secure their private keys using a password-based mechanism, at minimum. The Mt. Wilson Java API Client Library includes convenient functions for this purpose, using the Java Key store format to secure the private keys.

- The communication channels between the hosts and the users are encrypted using SSL. When a new user registers with Mt. Wilson, the Mt. Wilson SSL TLS certificate is verified and stored by the user to secure subsequent communication between the user and Mt. Wilson. The trust agent stores its SSL TLS certificate with Mt. Wilson upon registration of a new host to secure all future communication between Mt. Wilson and the trust agent.

- Trust agents store their TLS private keys in a password-protected Java Keystore file.

- Users are allowed to call into APIs based on their existing roles. Users request roles during registration with Mt. Wilson and these are approved by the Mt. Wilson administrator.

- The attestation status of the hosts is returned as signed SAML assertions that can be verified by the end consumer. The Mt. Wilson SAML certificate is stored by users when they register with Mt. Wilson in order to later verify SAML assertions.

- A public and private key pair is the preferred authentication mechanism for management of the whitelist and host trust policies.

Mt. Wilson Trust, Whitelisting, and Management APIs

Mt. Wilson provides a rich set of APIs for all interactions with it. In fact, the primary communication with the Mt. Wilson attestation authority is via authenticated APIs. There are five categories of APIs:

1. *Provisioning APIs,* for registering hosts and requesting AIKs.

2. *Query APIs,* the trust APIs that requesting entities (requesters/ API clients) invoke to get a trust assertion.

3. *Reporting APIs,* providing details about hosts registered with Mt. Wilson, including the current measurements and the whitelists.

4. *Automation APIs,* allowing an administrator to easily register all hosts within a VMware cluster or create an MLE using a known-good host in a trusted environment.

5. *Management APIs,* enabling registering users, managing their authorized roles, and downloading various certificates managed by Mt. Wilson.

Calls to the API must be sent over SSL TLS. All APIs are REST-based. Mt. Wilson APIs use a client-server model without third-party intervention to provide authentication. The authentication model is very similar to OAuth 1.0 and HTTP Digest, and it provides a stateless scheme for use with clusters and load balancers. However, it does not work with URL-rewriting proxies because the URL is covered by the client's signature. Every API client—that is, any entity invoking the APIs, such as portals, schedulers, other subsystems or policy engines—needs two RSA keys, as follows:

- *API signing key.* The public portion of the API signing key is stored in the Mt. Wilson keystore. The API client retains the private portion of this key in an encrypted and secure keystore

- *SAML assertion validation key.* This is the public portion of the Mt. Wilson SAML signing key and is stored with the API client

- An API client registers with Mt.Wilson via a credential management server to acquire the RSA keys. A Mt.Wilson instance can register a number of API clients.

Mt. Wilson APIs

Figures 4-8 and 4-9 show the core APIs for the Mt. Wilson provisioning and trust query API and the management and whitelisting API.

API Type	Method	Method Name	Description
Provisioning	POST	/hosts	Adds/Registers a new host
	PUT	/hosts	Updates the configuration of an existing host
	DELETE	/hosts?Hostname	Deletes the specified configured host
Query	GET	/saml/assertions/host?Hostname	Provides the current trust status of the host as a SAML assertion.
	GET	/host/trust?Hostname	Provides the Non-SAML trust status of the host specified.
	GET	/hosts/bulk/trust/saml?HostNames&Force_Verify_Flag	Provides SAML assertion for the trust status of all the hosts specified. If the Force_Verify_Flag is set to true, the cached status would be ignored and actual attestation would be done.
	GET	/hosts/bulk/trust?Hostnames&Force_Verify_Flag	Provides Non-SAML trust status for the list of hosts specified. If the Force_Verify_Flag is set to false, then the cached status would be returned back.
	POST	/PollHosts	Gets the current trust status of all the hosts requested.
	GET	/hosts/location?Hostname	Gets the geo location of the host if exists.
Report	GET	/hosts/reports/trust?Hostnames	Retrieves the last 5 attestation status for the hosts specified.
	GET	/hosts/reports/manifest?Hostname	Retrieves the last set of manifest got from the host and the trust status of the same.

Figure 4-8. *Provisioning and trust query API*

API Type	Method	Method Name	Description
Provisioning	POST	/apiclient /apiclient/register	Adds/Registers a new client that would be using the Mt.Wilson APIs. (Client can be portal, tools etc.)
	PUT	/apiclient	Updates the API client with a new keys or roles
	DELETE	/apiclient?Fingerprint	Deletes a currently configured API Client information which would prevent the API client from making future calls into Mt.Wilson
Query	GET	/apiclient?Fingerprint	Provides the details of the API client along with the status, roles, key expiration details etc.
	GET	/apiclient/availableRoles	Lists all the possible roles a client can request for.
	GET	/apiclient/search?searchCriteria	Get the list of API Clients based on the search criteria.
Automation	POST	/host	Registers the specified host with Mt.Wilson by automating all the required white list configurations.
	POST	/host/whitelist	Configures the White list for the MLE associated with the host using the white list measurements from the specified host.
	GET	/saml/certificate	Get the Attestation Service's SAML public key. This would be used to verify the trust status of the host which would be sent as SAML assertions.
OEM Provisioning	POST	/OEM	Adds a new OEM & associated BIOS whitelist
	PUT	/OEM	Updates the existing OEM
	DELETE	/OEM?Name	Deletes the specified OEM
	GET	/OEM	Retrieves the list of all OEMs
OS Provisioning	POST	/OS	Adds a new OS/VMM information into the DB & whitelist

Figure 4-9. *Management and whitelisting API*

To facilitate interoperability, consistency, and seamless integration, we expect the industry to converge toward a standardized set of APIs related to attestation. We offer these as a starting point for the industry to help drive interoperability across different attestation solution implementations.

The API Request Specification

All API calls are http requests with one required header: "Authorization: X509 <authentication-info>". Any unauthorized request is challenged with a standard header: "WWW-Authenticate: X509 <challenge-info>".

Each API request includes the following parameters:

- Fingerprint (base64-encoded SHA-256 digest of the client API certificate)

- Signature method (RSA-SHA256)

- Time stamp from standard http Date header (RFC 822 date format)

- Client nonce (base64-encoded) in http X-Nonce header

- http request method

- Signature over the above and also:

- Original request URL including query string

- http message body (required, use empty string if not applicable)

- Any other custom headers specified besides Date and X-Nonce in the "headers" field of the Authorization line, in the order specified

- Signature created using client's RSA private key, and it is base64-encoded

- Strongest method is RSA-SHA256

Figure 4-10 is an example of a sample API request using authentication.

```
WWW-Authenticate: X509 realm="Attestation"
```

```
GET /reports/trust?hostname=example
Host: attestationservice.example.com
Authorization: X509
  realm="Attestation",
  algorithm="SHA256withRSA",
  fingerprint="0685bd9184jfhq2bafweK...",
  headers="Date,X-Nonce"
  signature="wOJIO9A2W5mFwDgiDvZbTSMK%2FPY%3D"
X-Nonce: 0123456789abcdef
Date: Sun, 06 Nov 1994 08:49:37 GMT
```

Figure 4-10. *API request including authentication*

API Response

Mt. Wilson asserts all API responses. Responses are signed SAML assertions. Assertions are signed with the Mt.Wilson RSA SAML signing key. There is one SAML signing key for each installation of Mt.Wilson. An API client validates the signature with the SAML public key and uses the trust information. Here is an example of an API invocation with a SAML assertion. This Java example uses the Apache HttpClient library to obtain the SAML assertion for "192.168.1.121" by sending a *GET* request to Mt. Wilson:

```
ApiClient api = KeystoreUtil.clientForUserInDirectory(directory, username,
password, server);
String samlForHost = api.getSamlForHost(new Hostname("192.168.1.121"));
```

Here's how to interpret the SAML response:

```
TrustAssertion trustAssertion = api.verifyTrustAssertion(samlForHost);
if( trustAssertion.isValid() )
      for(String attr : trustAssertion.getAttributeNames())
            System.out.println("Attr: "+attr+":"+trustAssertion.
getStringAttribute(attr));
```

Attributes for subject's trust status in the SAML response are:

- *Trusted*: True if both *Trusted_BIOS* and *Trusted_VMM* are true.

- *Trusted_BIOS:* True if the BIOS measurements on the subject match the whitelist (known-good values)

- *Trusted_VMM*: True if the VMM measurements on the subject match the whitelist (known-good values)

Attributes for subject's measured launch environment in the SAML response are:

BIOS_Name, BIOS_Version, BIOS_OEM, VMM_Name, VMM_Version, VMM_OSName, VMM_OSVersion

Mt. Wilson API Usage

There are two options for the requesters of attestation information to call into Mt. Wilson APIs. A direct invocation of the REST APIs is the most basic approach to use and integrate with Mt. Wilson. The user is required to implement the complete API request specifications. This would mean pre-processing the creation and handling of keys and authentication, and post-processing of information for a successful API invocation, and the correct processing of the responses. An API toolkit (called API Client Library) is available to simplify the invocation of the APIs, with bindings for different languages like Java, C#, and Python. This toolkit encapsulates multiple API calls, creation and handling of RSA keys and certificates, and authentication and processing of API responses (which are SAML signed assertions). Using this toolkit, the users can make Java (or C# or Python) function calls to communicate with the system. The sample code and examples that are used in this chapter use the Java binding of the API toolkit.

There are three different options for the *.jar* file:

1. Zip file containing the *api-client .jar* and related dependencies

2. Single *.jar* with dependencies

3. Single *.jar* with dependencies shaded to prevent conflicts with other libraries

Deploying Mt. Wilson

There are multiple models for deploying attestation components in a data center. Ideally, attestation is transparent to applications, carrying its function quietly in the background. In practice, it's far from that. How unobtrusive attestation technology is depends upon the deployment method. Some of the possible models include:

- Dedicated virtual appliances

- Dedicated physical appliances

- Integrated as a function in security application software

- Integrated in cloud and virtualization management software

- Offered as a component of a cloud service

- Integrated as a attestation of a service

Mt. Wilson is delivered today as a virtual appliance, and it is being integrated into security software applications such as HyTrust's Cloud Control, as well as cloud management software such as Virtustream's xStream. An initial approach for adoption is to package and deliver Mt. Wilson software as a separate appliance with cloud management and security management independent software vendor offerings. As the usage and experiences increase with increased design and development of attestation-based solutions, other models with tighter integration will become possible.

As attestation APIs become standardized and integral to the interactions and operations of a trusted cloud infrastructure, there is opportunity for providing value-added services on top of the core attestation APIs. This could lead security management and cloud service providers to offer attestation as a service, with granular control to the usage and evolution of the APIs.

Mt. Wilson Programming Examples

In this section, we look at how to invoke the attestation APIs to get trust information about a server in a data center. Figure 4-11 shows the high-level steps involved in setting up the system and configuring it for use.

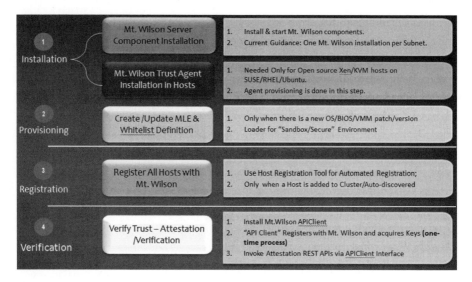

Figure 4-11. *Mt. Wilson high-level programming steps*

After the installation of the Mt.Wilson server and trust agent on the hosts, required only for Xen or KVM hosts, users need to include the *.jar* file provided as part of the API toolkit in their project and import the following packages:

```
import com.intel.mtwilson.*;
import com.intel.mtwilson.crypto.*;
import com.intel.mtwilson.datatypes.*;
import java.io.File;
import java.net.URL;
```

API Client Registration Process

Before the user can make any API calls into the system, the user has to register and the access has to be approved. Below are steps for how to register with Mt. Wilson and how to make API calls after the registration has been accepted. The following code creates a keystore "test1.jks" in the home directory. The keystore contains an RSA keypair that is used to authenticate the API calls to the system. The keystore would also contain the Mt. Wilson SSL certificate and SAML signing certificate, which are downloaded from the server.

```
File directory = new File(System.getProperty("user.home", "."));
String username = "test1"; // you choose a username
String password = "changeit"; // you choose a password
URL server = new URL("https://mtwilson.example.com:8181"); // attestation server
String[] roles = new String[] { "Attestation", "Whitelist" };
KeystoreUtil.createUserInDirectory(directory, username, password, server,
roles);
```

After the request is created, the user has to contact the system administrator to approve the access request (offline step). After the request is approved, based upon the roles the user has, appropriate APIs can be executed, such as maintaining a whitelist, adding hosts, and obtaining a trust assertion on one or more hosts.

To use the API, the user needs first to create an ApiClient object configured with the credentials and the attestation server. Notice that the variables directory, username, password, and servers are the same as what was used during registration.

```
File directory = new File(System.getProperty("user.home", "."));
String username = "test1"; // username created during registration
String password = "changeit"; // password created during registration
URL server = new URL("https://mtwilson.example.com:8181");
ApiClient apiClientObj = KeystoreUtil.clientForUserInDirectory(directory,
username, password, server);
```

Once an APIClient object is created, the user can use that to configure whitelists and also to register the hosts with Mt. Wilson so that they attest when challenged.

Whitelisting and Host Registration

Here's some sample code for how to create a whitelist and register the host with Mt. Wilson—for VMware ESXi hosts:

```
TxtHostRecord gkvHostObj = new TxtHostRecord();
gkvHostObj.HostName = "hostname-in-vcenter";
gkvHostObj.AddOn_Connection_String =
"vmware:https://vcenter.example.com:443/sdk;Username;Password";
boolean configureWhiteList = apiClientObj.configureWhiteList(gkvHostObj);

boolean registerHost = apiClientObj.registerHost(gkvHostObj);
```

Verify Trust: Trust Attestation

Once hosts are registered with Mt Wilson, it is now possible to request a trust assertion in SAML format using getSamlForHost. You can verify the signature on the assertion and get easy access to the details using verifyTrustAssertion.

■ **Note** If you are directly calling into the REST APIs, you have to implement the verification of the SAML assertion using the SAML certificate that needs to be downloaded explicity. The API toolkit downloads this certificate as part of the registration itself.

```
String samlForHost = apiClientObj.getSamlForHost(new Hostname("hostname-in-
vcenter"));
TrustAssertion trustAssertion = apiClientObj.verifyTrustAssertion(samlForHost);
if(trustAssertion.isValid()) {
for(String attr : trustAssertion.getAttributeNames())
        System.out.println("Attr:"+attr+":"+trustAssertion.
getStringAttribute(attr));
}
```

As shown in this above example, using the API Client Library is a very simple way of using the Mt. Wilson attestation mechanism. The Mt. Wilson software is being licensed by many ISV and CSPs to integrate trust into the software and service offerings. More and more organizations are moving to clouds, and they are asking for assurance of trust of the platform on which their workloads are running; they are also asking the CSPs to provide proof of a chain of trust. The attestation solution is fast becoming a critical security component in the security toolset. For developers favoring a DIY approach, the open-source OpenAttestation (OAT) is a good starting point for attestation.

> ■ **Note**   OAT is the open-source version of Mt. Wilson code, and is provided and maintained by Intel Corporation. You can download the documentation, code, and installation/deployment scripts from the OAT website.

Summary

In this chapter we covered attestation as a foundational function of trusted computing environments that provides proof of trustability and auditability of trust for various computing devices. We covered the TCG remote attestation protocol, and we described the vision and architecture of Intel's Trust Attestation Platform, followed by a detailed look one of the first attestation solutions, called Mt. Wilson. The chapter reviewed the security architecture and the attestation APIs, and explained how requesters of trust and attestation information can invoke these APIs and process the assertions for decision making. There are many usages in data centers that would utilize the attestation information. As shown in the previous chapter, attestation is used in the creation of trusted compute pools and the attestation-based policy enforcement in these pools. Thus, attestation can be used to provide granular trust-based access control to consumer and BYOD devices, and the kind of services they can access within the cloud data centers. Attestation as a security management component will become an integral component of virtualization and cloud management, and it's becoming a critical requirement in cloud data centers to assert the integrity and compliance of platforms and systems. ISVs and security management vendors may also start offering it as a SaaS offering. We believe that, over time, value-added capabilities will emerge around the attestation function and will enable monetization possibilities.

Chapter 5 will introduce a new concept and control, called hardware-assisted *asset tag*, which can be used to provide isolation, segregation, placement, and migration control of workload execution in multi-tenant cloud environments. Additionally, as a specialization of asset tags, geolocation/geo-tagging can be enabled to definitively provide increased visibility to the physical geolocation of the server, which may enable many controls that require hardware-based roots of trust to assert the location of workloads and data. These attributes and the associated controls are dependent on the boot integrity assertion of the platform; hence, they become a great adjacency to trusted compute pools and boot integrity.

CHAPTER 5

▣ ▣ ▣

Boundary Control in the Cloud: Geo-Tagging and Asset Tagging

Chapters 3 and 4 focused on platform boot integrity, trusted compute pools, and the attestation architecture. They covered the reference architecture for how organizations and service providers can deploy trusted pools as the enabler for trusted clouds. Data and workload locality and data sovereignty are top-line issues for organizations considering migrating their workloads and data into the cloud. A fundamental capability that is needed is to reliably identify the location of physical servers on which the data and workloads reside. Additionally, organizations would need to produce audit trails of data and workload movement, as well as carry out effective forensics when the occasion demands it. In particular, the asset location identification and attestation capability needs to be verifiable, auditable, and preferably anchored in hardware. These capabilities enable workload and data boundary control in the cloud, effectively conferring users control over where workloads and data are created, where they are run, and where they migrate to for performance, optimization, reliability, and high-availability purposes.

Geolocation and geo-fencing, and the higher level concept of asset tagging, are technology components and associated usages that enable monitoring and control of data processing and workload movement, and they are the subject of this chapter. Geolocation and geo-fencing constitute fitting adjacencies to trusted compute pools usages, and provide a critical security control point to assess and enforce in a data center. Asset tagging is still an emergent industry practice. So, we'll start with some definitions to provide the context, followed by a discussion of enabling the logical control points. The next step is to link asset tagging with the trusted compute pools usages discussed in the earlier chapters. Asset tagging is highly synergistic with trusted compute pools, and the capability adds significant value to any trusted data center operations and compute pools deployment. We will elaborate on this idea as we describe a reference implementation in the last part of this chapter.

Geolocation

As the NIST Interagency Report 7904 clearly delineates, shared cloud computing technologies, designed to be agile and flexible, transparently use geographically distributed resources to process workloads for their customers.[1] However, there are security and privacy considerations in allowing workloads—namely data and applications—to run in geographically dispersed locations with unrestricted workload migration. Even with controls governing the location of the launch of a workload, without additional controls and restrictions in place that workload could move from cloud servers located in one geographic location to servers located in another geographic location. Each country has laws protecting data security, privacy, and other aspects of information technology (IT). An organization may decide that it needs to restrict which cloud service providers and servers it uses based on their locations so as to ensure compliance. An example of such a requirement is to use only cloud servers physically located within the same country as the organization.

Determining the physical location of an object, such as a cloud computing server, is generally known as *geolocation.* It can be a logical description of geographic information, such as country or city, or it can be GPS-based latitude and longitude information. Geolocation can be accomplished in many ways, with varying degrees of accuracy, but traditional geolocation methods are not secure and they are presently enforced through management and operational controls not easily automated and scaled; therefore, traditional geolocation methods cannot be trusted to meet cloud security needs. NIST IR 7904 describes geolocation as follows:

> *Geolocation enables identification of a cloud server's approximate location by adding that information to the server's root of trust. The hardware root of trust is seeded by the organization with the host's unique identifier and platform metadata stored in tamperproof hardware. This information is accessed using secure protocols to assert the integrity of the platform and confirm the location of the host.*[2]

Geo-tagging constitutes the process of defining, creating, and provisioning a set of geolocation objects to a computing device securely. An interesting and very relevant application of the geo-tag is the enforcement of boundary control based on geo-tags; the concept is called *geo-fencing.*

Geo-fencing

The concept of geo-fencing is not new. It has been applied successfully in industries such as mobile computing, supply chain management, and transportation logistics. Geo-fencing is about defining geographical or virtual boundaries using a variety of GPS,

---

[1] Erin K. Banks et al., "Trusted Geolocation in the Cloud: Proof of Concept Implementation" (draft), NIST Interagency Report 7904, U.S. Dept. of Commerce, December 2012.
[2] http://nist.gov\publications\drafts\ir7904\draft_nistir_7904.pdf

RFID technologies, and geolocation attributes. Geo-fencing is also about ensuring that the boundaries are not violated; but if they are violated, that appropriate remediations are enforced. Applications supporting geo-fencing allow an administrator to set rules and apply triggers so that when a device, or workload, or data attempts to cross a boundary so defined by the administrator, the action is blocked and appropriate alerts are sent out for further investigation. Many geo-fencing applications employ mashup concepts, such as incorporating Google Earth, thus allowing administrators to define their boundaries using a satellite view of a specific geographic area. Other applications define the boundaries by longitude and latitude or through user-created and web-based maps.

In traditional data centers, workloads and data are pretty static and have a hard binding to the physical information systems on which they reside and execute. However, with virtualization and cloud computing, this is clearly no longer the case. Geolocation can be an attribute for a virtual machine. The ease with which a virtual machine can move has created intense interest in instituting mechanisms to track and control these movements, however. The power and appeal of cloud computing for IT is its agility, efficiency, and mobility of workloads in order to meet the service-level agreements for customers, and also to improve total cost of ownership for service operators. The mobility and agility are possible because of the abstraction and decoupling of the physical hardware from the virtual machines running on top. However, the mobility that allows workloads and data to move in an unrestricted fashion also brings concerns about violating security and privacy policies. Geo-fencing thus becomes an extremely useful capability in cloud computing environments. Geo-fencing usages in cloud computing environments take advantage of the geolocation attribute as described above. (We define and describe geolocation in exhaustive detail in the later sections.) This expanded usage involves attaching geolocation attributes to workloads or data. With the attributes in place, it is possible to create desired geo-fencing policies and set up the associated monitoring and control mechanisms at multiple levels in the cloud infrastructure.

Here are some potential use cases for geo-fencing, in virtualization and cloud computing:

- *Government security requirements.* Many countries and their governments require that data and workloads stay within designated country and geographic boundaries. For instance, certain data may not be allowed to leave the sovereign territory, with exceptions being made for embassies and safe-harbor countries.

- *E-commerce.* Retailers may want to optimize their business processes to improve taxation outcomes—for instance, in the United States, for interstate commerce where tax rates vary by state or to gain special tax benefits, such as hosting sites in export only zone. Geo-fencing allows restrictions where workloads and data are stored in the cloud and provides audit trails detailing where those workloads and data have been. Retail applications go beyond the brick-and-mortar stores when the consumables are digital, such as video, audio, images, software, books, and more. Banking is another regulated industry, and customer data sometimes enjoys greater privileges owing to international agreements.

- *Research.* Companies may restrict what categories of research are carried out in particular geographic locations, so as to be compliant with local regulations or for intellectual property management purposes. For example, stem cell research and pharmacological research fall into this category.

There are many other examples of situations in which geo-fencing is applicable, such as in finance, health care, and other regulated industries. An expansion of the geo-tagging concept is that of asset tagging, whereby the attribute associated with the device or a server is a functional asset descriptor.

Asset Tagging

Geo-tagging can be generalized to be any arbitrary datum about a server. Given a trusted source of information about a server, trusted compute pools with asset tagging enable organizations to enforce running workloads only on trusted servers tagged with specific attributes. For example, an organization might be willing to pay a premium for dedicated trusted servers with bonus points for a capability to segregate workloads by department, each of which may have different policies regarding trusted platforms. The organization can provision an asset tag to each server, indicating the department to which that server is assigned. The organization can then extend its overall trusted computing policy to restrict workload execution to servers carrying a specific asset tag. There are many such potential usage models for asset tagging:

- *SLA-based zoning of data center assets.* This would include tagging compute, storage, and network devices serving specific SLA zones, as in "bronze," "platinum," and "gold." The partitioning can be linked to security, performance, availability, or reliability goals, in any combination.

- *Sarbanes-Oxley audits.* The visibility and verifiability of asset tags augmented by the assurance from hardware-based roots of trust for any Sarbanes-Oxley–related audits can save IT operations a significant amount of time and resources.

- *Workload segregation.* This is useful where tenants request segregation of workloads from other tenants or workloads or workload types.

■ **Note**   An asset tag is a geo-tag when the attributes of the tag represent geolocation. For the rest of this chapter, we will use *geo-tag* to represent an asset tag with geolocation attributes. *Asset tagging* and *geo-tagging* are terms used interchangeably, from an architecture and provisioning process perspective.

Trusted Compute Pools Usage with Geo-Tagging

Cloud service providers who implement trusted compute pools (TCP) and their customers are requiring additional boundaries beyond platform trust to assure control of their workloads. A high-priority boundary condition to enforce is one based on the specific physical location of a host, such that workload placement can be:

- Monitored and enforced based on customer policies for boundary controls

- Verified and provided in audit and compliance reports to tenants to meet their internal and regulatory needs for data security reporting

There are a few ways of attaching geolocation attributes to a platform. For instance, geolocation can be arranged through a trusted platform module (TPM) security chip based on a Trusted Computing Group standard. This approach aligns naturally with trusted compute pools as the foundation for use case capabilities requiring established platform trust status and physical location with verification and reporting. That is exactly what trusted compute pools provide. Cloud service providers are expected to extend their current trusted compute pools solutions with trusted location controls to provide additional granularity of control above platform trust.

Trusted compute pools with geo-tagging enable organizations to ensure their workloads are executed only on trusted servers located in authorized geographical areas. For example, as depicted in Figure 5-1, an organization like U.S. government with multiple geographically distributed data centers, might require that certain virtual servers be located in U.S. data centers. Such controls are specified or supported by a growing body of customer requests and regulatory mandates, such as the ability to separate customers or workload types to address region-specific data protection requirements, as defined in FISMA SP800-53 and NIST IR 7409. The controls also support expected needs for eased auditability and verifiability pursuant to compliance mandates.

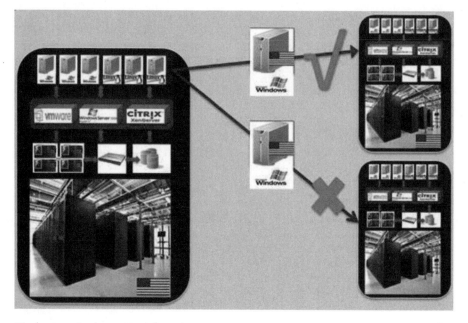

Figure 5-1. *Geolocation and geo-fencing*

NIST, in partnership with industry participants, published an interagency report, NIST IR 7904, documenting trusted compute pool usages with geolocation descriptors, as well as the geo-fencing policy enforcement in multi-tenant cloud computing environments. Figure 5-2 illustrates the IR 7904.

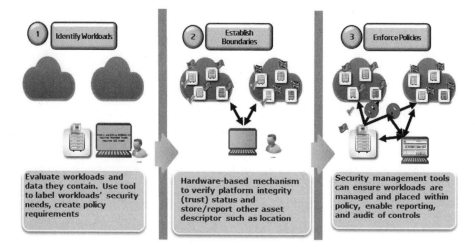

Figure 5-2. *NIST IR 7904 – trusted geolocation in the cloud*

Establishing a trusted compute pool with a trusted geolocation in a cloud comprises three main stages, as shown in Figure 5-3. First, each compute platform must be attested as trustworthy, enabling a safe hypervisor. Second, the cloud system must ensure that workload migration occurs only between trusted resources. And third, trusted geolocation is ensured with continuous monitoring and enforcement of geolocation restrictions. Let's look closer at each of these stages.

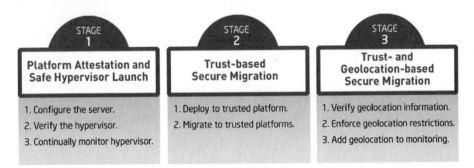

Figure 5-3. *The three stages for establishing a trusted compute pool with trusted geolocation*

Stage 1: Platform Attestation and Safe Hypervisor Launch

This initial stage provides a basic assurance of platform trustworthiness and enables faster detection of security issues. There are three steps to this stage:

1. *Configure the server.* Set up the cloud server platform as being trusted, including configuring the hardware, BIOS, and hypervisor.

2. *Verify the hypervisor.* Before each hypervisor launch, verify the trustworthiness of the cloud server platform set up in the previous step. Remote attestation is the way the integrity of the launch of the platform is verified.

3. *Continually monitor the hypervisor.* During execution, frequently repeat the measurements done in step 2 to continually ensure trustworthiness. These measurements should then become an ongoing part of a continuous monitoring process.

Stage 2: Trust-Based Secure Migration

Ensure that workloads are deployed and then are migrated only among trusted server platforms within the cloud. There are two steps to this stage:

1. *Deploy to trusted platforms.* Apply the verification tests established in stage 1, step 3 and only deploy a workload to those platforms deemed trustworthy.

2. *Migrate to trusted platforms.* Once a workload is deployed, ensure that it migrates only to hosts with comparable trust levels. This is determined by applying the verification tests from stage 1, step 3 on both the workload's current server and the server to migrate the workload to. Migration is allowed only if both servers pass their audits.

Stage 3: Trust- and Geolocation-Based Secure Migration

Build on previous stage by ensuring that workloads migrate only to trusted server platforms while also taking geolocation restrictions into consideration. There are three steps to this stage:

1. *Verify geolocation information.* Ensure that any platform to be included in the trusted geolocation pool has its geolocation set as part of its initial configuration in stage 1, step 1. This is a cryptographic hash within the hardware cryptographic module in BIOS. Ensure that the geolocation information can be verified and audited readily.

2. *Enforce geolocation restrictions.* Add a geolocation check to the pre-deployment and pre-migration verification in stage 2, steps 2 and 3 before deploying or migrating a workload.

3. *Add geolocation to monitoring.* Add geolocation checks to the continuous monitoring put in place in stage 1, step 3 to ensure trustworthiness of the platforms. This process should audit the geolocation of the cloud server platform against geolocation policy restrictions.

Adding Geo-Tagging to the Trusted Compute Pools Solution

As we discussed in the introduction to this chapter, geo-tagging and asset tagging will deliver increased value to trusted compute pools usages in data center operations and for customers. Geo-tagging and asset tagging bring valuable additional security controls to the data center, as well. Supporting geo-tagging and asset tagging, and implementing geo-fencing require some functional changes to the original trusted compute pools architecture that was introduced in Chapter 3. Figure 5-4 provides a summary of these changes, and in the next sections we explain the changes at each layer of the architecture.

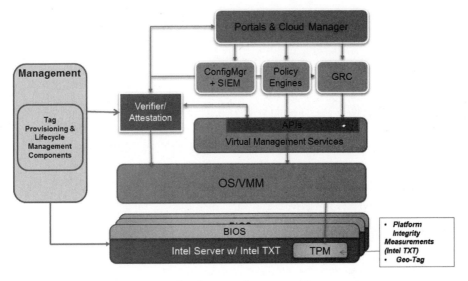

Figure 5-4. *Trusted compute pools solution architecture with geo-tagging*

Hardware Layer (Servers)

There are no changes required at this layer; the trusted platform module (TPM) takes care of secure storage for the geo-tags. Through a secure provisioning process, the geo-tag is provisioned into a nonvolatile index (NVRAM index) in the TPM, and the trusted boot process extends the contents of the specific index into a PCR in the TPM. PCR22 has been selected to capture the geo-tag attributes. As per the TCG client specifications, PCR22 is allocated for OS/VMM use, and in the case of VMWare ESX, Citrix XenServer, open-source Xen, and KVM implementations, it is not used for any other function, hence it was a logical choice to extend the geo-tag attributes. (Geo-tag provisioning and management will be covered in the following sections.) Entities above the stack use the TPMQuote process to fetch this PCR value for attestation and decision making, and this was covered in Chapter 4.

■ **Note** Re the NVRAM index for geo-tagging: For TPM 1.2 compliant devices, the NVRAM index is 20 bytes to accommodate a SHA-1 hash value. The current index used for storing the geo-tag is index 0x40000010, and is created with AUTHWRITE permissions. As TPM 2.0 begins to deploy, the geo-tag index will need to accommodate a SHA-256 hash value of 32 bytes in length. The same NVRAM index cannot be used for the SHA-256 value and hence the solution will require a different index. The trusted boot process (tboot) might require modification for TPM2.0 implementation to extend PCR22 from the new 32-byte index location.

Hypervisor and Operating System Layer

As we discussed in Chapter 3, operating systems and hypervisors participating in a trusted compute pool require servers provisioned with Intel TXT. Tboot is by far the most widely used mechanism to serve as a foundation for software vendors enabling their operating system or hypervisor. The tboot code extends PCR22 from the NVRAM index during the measured boot process. VMware ESX has been supporting tboot extensions to read the NVRAM index and extend PCR22 since ESX 5.1. As of this writing, the open-source tboot code has also been extended to extend PCR22 from the NVRAM index. This is the only incremental change at this layer to support these usages.

Virtualization, Cloud Management, and the Verification and Attestation Layer

To recap, the key functions of this layer are:

- Providing a *secure interface* to the measured launch measurements on each of the servers.

- Providing an *attestation mechanism* to evaluate platform trust and assert its integrity.

- Consuming the *trust information*, essentially helping to identify which platforms are trusted and which ones are not.

- Making use of this information to establish an *enhanced security capability* through policy definition and enforcement linked to platform trust.

The main functional change needed to extend TCP with geo-tagging support involves the attestation capability. The attestation server verifies the platform geo-tag and geolocation by comparing the attributes and the geo-tag certificate against a known-good geo-tag fingerprint for that server or device in addition to evaluating platform trust and verifying the integrity measurements of the launch in the original TCP. The attestation subsystem comprises additional APIs for geo-tag attestation, and the capture and storage of known-good geo-tags for the host. The SAML assertion for the attestation subsystem provided to the requester now includes geolocation assertion. We will dig deeper into this and also explain the additional APIs in Mt. Wilson to accommodate geo-tagging.

The resource scheduler in this layer makes decisions on the placement and migration of virtual machines and workloads. The location policy for data and virtual machines is evaluated and enforced at the security management layer, and the results are provided to the resource scheduler to make security decisions.

■ **Note** The functionality of trusted compute pools (TCP) as described in Chapter 3 has been implemented in OpenStack as scheduler filters. These extensions, and the Horizon dashboard and API extensions to tag Flavors with "Trust" policies, have been part of OpenStack since the Folsom release. As of this writing, a reference implementation demonstrating OpenStack TCP filter extensions to use the geo-tag or asset tag attributes is available. Extensions to Horizon and Flavor attributes are also provided as reference implementations. The expectation is that these will become part of core OpenStack distribution in the near future.

Security Management Layer

Policy managers, security monitoring tools, and compliance and risk management tools make their security decisions based on platform trust and geolocation assertions from the layers below. Policy tools use the geolocation assertions to control the creation, launching, and migration of the workloads and data to carry out geo-fencing policies. Policy management tools need to implement mechanisms to tag virtual machines and data with specific geolocation policies. For instance, the tags identify a virtual machine as *run only on data centers within the continental United States* or as *belongs to the Finance Department*.

The actual mechanisms for policy enforcement depend on how the orchestrator and scheduler software are architected. In OpenStack, policy management is integrated into the orchestrator as pluggable filters. These filters consume the attestation assertion from the attestation service and make decisions to identify and select the appropriate target platforms to instantiate virtual machines. With VMware, a HyTrust Appliance functions as a gateway between VMware VCenter and VMware ESXi hosts. The HyTrust Appliance evaluates the policy against the attestation information, including the geo-tag descriptor for a potential target ESXi host.

The outcome of a policy evaluation is either to proceed with the launch or migration of the virtual machine on the target host, or to deny the request to launch owing to a geolocation policy violation. Policy enforcement and control information is passed on to a security information and event management (SIEM) or governance and to risk compliance (GRC) solutions for reporting and audit compliance. If the solutions used already support trusted compute pool controls, simple extensions will suffice to read, understand, and display the compliance with geo-tagging security controls.

Provisioning and Lifecycle Management for Geo-Tags

The main capabilities needed to support geo-tagging in trusted compute pools are tag provisioning and lifecycle management. The capabilities allow securely creating, selecting, provisioning, and lifecycle management of geo-tags that enables the layers above to make decisions, carry out reporting, and evaluate tags against security controls. The associated process defines the geo-tag workflow lifecycle, covered in the next two sections, including architectural considerations.

Intel Corporation provides reference implementation for tag provisioning and lifecycle management. The reference implementation doesn't dictate what the contents for geo-tags or asset-tags should be. Cloud service providers or enterprise end users have the option of determining the appropriate tag taxonomy for their customers. The lifecycle of geo-tag provisioning and management is covered in the next section.

Geo-Tag Workflow and Lifecycle

The geo-tagging lifecycle consists of seven discrete steps, as depicted in Figure 5-5: tag creation, whitelisting, re-provisioning and deployment, in-validation, validation, attestation, and re-provisioning. Let's go over each.

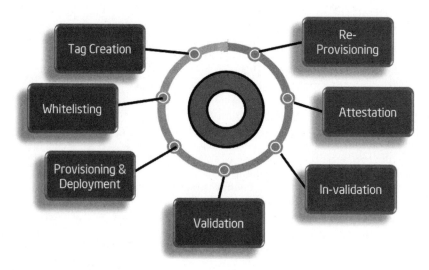

Figure 5-5. *The geo-tagging management lifecycle*

Tag Creation

A tag, as shown in Figure 5-6, is an attribute that has a name and one or more values. The values can be "user-defined," like *united states*, or *san jose* or *Finance*. Values can be "pre-defined," like country or state or postal codes from USG/NIST databases. Values can be dynamic, like latitude/longitude/altitude from a GPS system. The dynamic values would be fetched during the actual provisioning of the tag onto an asset. The tags can be geolocation objects or asset descriptors as well. In this context, an asset is a compute node like a server, end-user device, storage, or network device. The tag creation step involves creating a taxonomy of tags—a set of acceptable name-value pairs applicable to an organization.

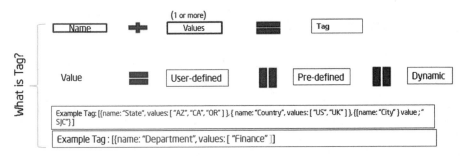

Figure 5-6. *Tags defined*

Tag Whitelisting

Typically, a business analyst at an organization or a suborganization creates this taxonomy of acceptable tags at the corporate level. A subset of tags is then selected for a particular business function. The subset defines the *whitelist* of the tags for that business function, and compliance is evaluated and enforced against that whitelist. A policy creation and definition tool uses this whitelist to associate the geo-tags with the VMs or workloads, and also to enforce the policy.

Tag Provisioning

There are two distinct steps in tag provisioning:

Tag selection

This is the process of selecting one or more tags from the whitelist that would be bound to an asset. In most cases, a selection is applied to many assets. The selection has a name that is a unique descriptor of the purpose of those tags and the list of associated tags. This construct becomes the unit of deployment of these tags onto various computing assets. The binding of this selection to a specific asset (a computing device) is an *asset tag*. To ensure that the tags in the selection are associated with an unique physical asset, the selection is bound to a unique hardware attribute of the asset that is usable as a *universally unique identifier* (UUID), such as a motherboard identifier. As dicussed in the earlier sections, an asset tag that has geolocation attributes is a geo-tag.

To ensure cryptographically secure binding associated to the intended asset, we define the concept of an *asset certificate*. An asset certificate is a document containing a digital signature of the tags in the selection, with the binding to the asset with the UUID. The certificate is digitally signed by a trusted authority and maintained for verification and attestation as X.509 attribute certificate or SAML certificate. A SHA-1 Hash (SHA-2 in the future with TPM2.0) of the asset certificate is what that gets provisioned into a secure location on the asset as the asset tag or a geo-tag (the latter, if the attributes are geolocation attributes). Figure 5-7 illustrates how the asset tag is created from an asset certificate, which in turn is created with the tag selection and the UUID of the asset.

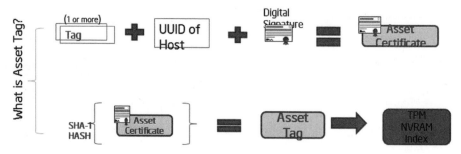

Figure 5-7. *Asset tags*

Tag deployment

This encompasses the secure deployment of that asset tag onto the asset. We recommend using the trusted platform module (TPM) for securely storing the geo-tags and asset tags on the platform, taking advantage of the hardware roots of trust with attestation.
Figure 5-8 shows the template of what an asset certificate looks like. A SH1-hash of this is written in the TPM NVRAM index during the provisioning process. At the end of a successful provisioning process, the asset certificate and the geo-tag (the fingerprint) are securely imported into the attestation authority (like a Mt. Wilson) for attestation during policy execution and enforcement.

UUID: Motherboard ID..

Validity:

Owner:

Issue Date:

Tags

- Country: USA
- State: CA, NV
- City: SJC, Fremont

Digital Signature of all of this

Signing Algorithm

Public Key

Figure 5-8. *Asset tag certificate fields*

Figure 5-9 illustrates the tag creation and provisioning steps. It shows the two actors and the functions they perform to define, select, and provision the asset tag and/or geo-tag to the TPM. Tag re-provisioning essentially follows the same process as provisioning. It is triggered by an invalidation event, where the asset tag on the asset is invalidated. (Invalidation is covered in the next section.)

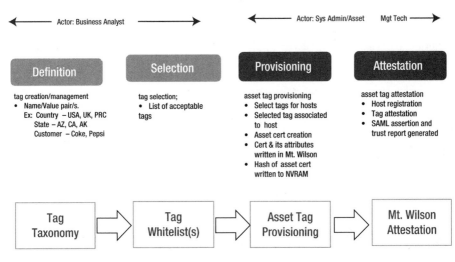

Figure 5-9. *Steps for tag creation and provisioning*

Validation and Invalidation of Asset Tags and Geo-Tags

This is a mandatory step in the geo-tagging lifecycle to prevent misuse and spoofing of the geo-tags, either accidentally or maliciously. Validation can be carried as a manual process, but ideally it should be intelligent, proactive, and automated. Automated processes enable deployment scaling and security automation, offering an extra backstop against provisioning and deployment errors or even malfeasance. Local and remote methods allow automated and auditable validation and invalidation, as well as modification of tags, on individual and groups of assets. Here are some automation mechanisms that have been considered in the development of the reference architecture:

- Heuristic analysis models using external comparison, such as near-neighbor tag analysis, GPS inputs

- Marking geo-tag certificates signed by an unknown authority as untrusted

- Marking expired geo-tags as untrusted and expired

- Marking geo-tags with UUID mismatches as untrusted

- Automated hardware-based mechanisms to monitor power cable connections to the device, or network heartbeat or deadman mechanisms to assess the validity of the geo-tags

Validation and invalidation capabilities would be pretty rudimentary in the initial implementations of the geo-tagging solutions, and they can support one or all of the first four mechanisms listed above. The expectation is that over time the automated hardware-based mechanisms would be broadly supported so the geo-tags become highly tamper resistant and can enable automated compliance with policy controls.

Attestation of Geo-Tags

Attestation of geo-tags involves ensuring that the geo-tag fingerprint that is reported from the server or device is what is expected for that server or device. When a geo-tag is provisioned to the server, it is also stored in the attestation server as the golden fingerprint. During operation of the data center environment, the geo-tag fingerprint as reported by the server is verified against the golden one, and an assertion is generated about the trustability of the geo-tag. The orchestration, policy, and compliance tools use this assertion to make decisions in the cloud. The geo-tag attestation process piggybacks on the platform boot integrity attestation architecture that was covered in Chapter 4. Two new APIs have been added to the attestation authority to address the needs for geo-tagging and asset tagging. These attestation server changes and extensions are covered in the attestation service section later in the chapter.

Architecture for Geo-Tag Provisioning

Figure 5-10 shows an abstract architecture for defining, provisioning, monitoring, and enforcing geo-tags in a trusted compute pools host.

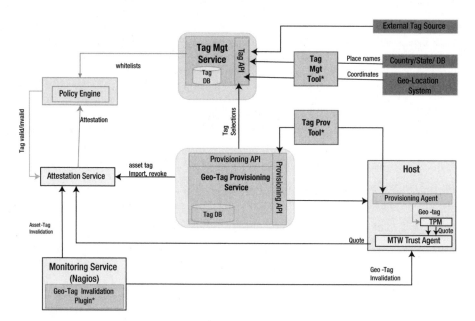

Figure 5-10. *Geo-tag solution architecture*

There are four key components of the solution architecture:

1. Tag provisioning service

2. Tag provisioning agent

3. Tag management service and management tool

4. Attestation service

Let's cover each in sequence.

Tag Provisioning Service

The tag provisioning service implements tag creation—creating asset tag certificates when tags are bound to the UUID of a host—and communicates with the tag provisioning agent on the host to securely deploy and write the geo-tag to the TPM. An asset tag authority (ATA) can be part of the tag provisioning service for automatic approval of certificate requests, or it may reside in external software, polling the tag provisioning service for pending requests and posting certificates for approved requests back to the tag provisioning service. There must be at least one asset tag authority in a working asset tag system. The public key certificates of external authorities must be imported to verify the certificates they create.

The tag provisioning service exposes a set of RESTful APIs for the various entities to interface and integrate with it. Callers are fully authenticated to ensure that legitimate entities are invoking these APIs.

There are two set of APIs for this service:

- *Tag provisioning APIs,* for the tag selection tool and provisioning agent to request and create an asset certificate, and to search existing certificate requests or provisioned certificates.

- *Invalidation APIs,* for monitoring and policy enforcement engines in the data center to invalidate existing asset certificates.

Table 5-1 shows the tag provisioning API. These APIs include functions to create, fetch, delete, search, and revoke asset certificates.

Table 5-1. *RESTful Tag Provisioning APIs*

API Name	Parameters	Description
POST /certificate-requests	{tags[{ uuid|url|name, value }+], authority? }	Create certificate
GET /certificate-requests/{id}	{id, url, tags[ ], status, certificate-url? + }	Read one or more certificate
DELETE /certificate-request/{id}	{id}	Delete certificate

(*continued*)

Table 5-1. (*continued*)

API Name	Parameters	Description
GET /certificate-requests?criteria	{id}	Search certificate id={id} id={id},{id},... tagNameEqualTo={name} tagNameContains={text} tagValueEqualTo={name} tagValueContains={text}
POST /certificate-revocations	{id}	Revoke certificate
GET /certificate-revocations/{id}	{id}	View revoked certificate

Tag Provisioning Agent

The tag provisioning agent provides an API for deploying asset tags to the TPM on the asset. This API is only available on systems where the provisioning agent can run to accept asset tags in push mode. For systems where that is not possible or desirable, the provisioning agent can be activated whenever the administrator needs to provision and deploy an asset tag and request the asset tag from the tag provisioning service in pull mode.

The tag provisioning agent needs authorization to interact with the TPM and write the geo-tag into the NVRAM index. This means it needs the ownership password to acquire ownership of the TPM and write the index. The security of the ownership password, the authentication of the provisioning agent to get access to the ownership password, and the authentication of the provisioning agent with the tag provisioning service is a critical design element of the solution. In the Intel reference implementation, the ownership password is in a configuration file on the host with root access, and the configuration file is encrypted with a symmetric password used by the system administration during provisioning.

Tag Management Service and Management Tool

The tag management service and management tool are primarily required to create the tags—the name-value pairs of the tag taxonomy selected and used to create the asset certificates and the geo-tags and asset tags. These components are an optional part of the geo-tagging architecture; the architecture and workflows do not depend on the existence of these two components. The architecture allows integration of third-party tag-creation tools, such as the HyTrust Appliance. The architecture also provides a well-defined

XML file to codify the tag selection to be used with the provisioning. Provisioning tools can take the file as input to complete the geo-tag provisioning. Alternative tag creation and management tools provide the selected tags in the XML configuration file for the provisioning tools to import and create the asset certificates and the geo-tags with binding to the individual hosts.

The reference tag management service provides the APIs and functionality to store the tag taxonomy and allow other software to access it to create and store the tags. The tag management service provides APIs for creating attribute definitions (the attribute name and possible values for the attribute); for searching the taxonomy for attributes having a specific name or possible value; for managing relationships between attributes; and for managing any local policies associated with the provisioning of attributes.

The relationship between attributes may be hierarchical, such as country-state-city or datacenter-room-aisle-rack, or flat, such as price and location. A policy associated with provisioning the attributes could be that an asset certificate containing the customer attribute *Coca-Cola* cannot also contain the customer attribute *Pepsi* at the same time; or that an asset certificate containing the department attribute *Finance Server* must also contain the country attribute *United States*. Table 5-2 shows the tag management service API in its reference implementation.

Table 5-2. *RESTful Tag Management API*

API Name	Parameters	Description
POST /tags	{ oid?, name, values[ ]? }	Create single or multiple tag definition
POST /tags/{id}/ values	[value+]	Add values to existing tag definition
PUT /tags/{id}/ values	[value+]	Update values for existing tag definition; [ ] empty array deletes all values for existing tag definition
GET /tags/	{id}	Read/load tag contents by ID
GET /tags?criteria	criteria	Search tag definitions Examples: Id = {id}; nameEqualTo{name};nameContains= {text};valueEqualTo={name};valueContains={text}
POST /rdf-triples	{subject, predicate, object}	Create relationship between tags Example: { subject: *Country*, predicate: *contains*, object: *State* }

Attestation Service

The attestation service is an extension of the trust attestation service code-named Mt. Wilson, covered in Chapter 4. These extensions effectively add another plank to the attestation platform providing the geo-tag and asset tag attestation capabilities. That is, the attestation service adds asset tag verification information to its security assertions. It keeps an audit log of asset tag certificates associated with specific compute nodes, and it maintains copies of the asset tag certificates. This allows the attestation service to log not just when an asset tag is updated in an asset but also any changes made to the set of attributes associated with that asset from one asset tag to the next. Thus, the attestation service must apply integrity protection to its repository of trusted asset tag authorities to prevent tampering.

The Mt. Wilson attestation service adds two new APIs that support the geo-tag implementation.

API: importAssetTagCertificate

This API is invoked by the tag provisioning service when a new asset tag certificate is created and is provisioned into the TPM. The certificate is mapped to the host information in Mt. Wilson during the host registration step.

API: revokeAssetTagCertificate

This is also invoked by the tag provisioning services when a geo-tag or asset tag certificate is revoked (expired, invalidated, decommissioned). On the Mt. Wilson side, it is disassociated from the host and is also deprecated in the certificate store.

From the attestation side, the SAML security assertion from a trust attestation request adds one additional assertion section, as shown here. In this example, the security assertion is asserting that the geo-tag or asset tag has been verified for a specific server, host, or device as indicated by the UUID of the host, carrying highlighted attributes (name-value pairs). Note the multiple types of attributes from the tag definitions, geo-tags, and tenant descriptors. This SAML assertion is digitally signed by the Mt. Wilson attestation authority to guarantee the integrity of the assertion. (Chapter 4 covered the attestation components and the SAML assertion contents and its integrity.)

```
<saml2:Attribute Name="Asset_Tag">
        <saml2:AttributeValue xmlns:xs="http://www.w3.org/2001/XMLSchema"
xmlns:xsi="http://www.w3.org/2001/XMLSchema-instance" xsi:type=
"xs:anyType">attested(true)</saml2:AttributeValue>
    </saml2:Attribute>
    <saml2:Attribute Name="ATAG :Country ">
        <saml2:AttributeValue xmlns:xs="http://www.w3.org/2001/
XMLSchema" xmlns:xsi="http://www.w3.org/2001/XMLSchema-instance"
xsi:type="xs:string">US</saml2:AttributeValue>
    </saml2:Attribute>
    <saml2:Attribute Name="ATAG :State">
        <saml2:AttributeValue xmlns:xs="http://www.w3.org/2001/
XMLSchema" xmlns:xsi="http://www.w3.org/2001/XMLSchema-instance"
```

```
xsi:type="xs:string">CA</saml2:AttributeValue>
      </saml2:Attribute>
      <saml2:Attribute Name="ATAG :City">
            <saml2:AttributeValue xmlns:xs="http://www.w3.org/2001/
XMLSchema" xmlns:xsi="http://www.w3.org/2001/XMLSchema-instance"
xsi:type="xs:string">Folsom</saml2:AttributeValue>
      </saml2:Attribute>
      <saml2:Attribute Name="ATAG :Tenant">
            <saml2:AttributeValue xmlns:xs="http://www.w3.org/2001/
XMLSchema" xmlns:xsi="http://www.w3.org/2001/XMLSchema-instance"
xsi:type="xs:string">Coke</saml2:AttributeValue>
      </saml2:Attribute>
      <saml2:Attribute Name="ATAG :Tenant">
            <saml2:AttributeValue xmlns:xs="http://www.w3.org/2001/
XMLSchema" xmlns:xsi="http://www.w3.org/2001/XMLSchema-instance"
xsi:type="xs:string">Pepsi</saml2:AttributeValue>
      </saml2:Attribute>
      <saml2:Attribute Name="ATAG :UUID">
            <saml2:AttributeValue xmlns:xs="http://www.w3.org/2001/
XMLSchema" xmlns:xsi="http://www.w3.org/2001/XMLSchema-instance"
xsi:type="xs:string">e64d9248-59d9-e111-b527-001e67576c61</
saml2:AttributeValue>
      </saml2:Attribute>
```

The first attribute section of the example SAML code above asserts that the geo-tag fingerprint on the host has been verified against the expected/known-good fingerprint in the attestation authority. The next set of attribute sections of the SAML provides the various attributes and the descriptors that are asserted by this SAML certificate. These are the various geo-tags and/or asset tags presented by the host and verified against the attestation authority. The last section in the example is the assertion of the UUID of the host. This SAML certificate is provided to any entity or component that would make decisions about VM and data placement, migration, and access decisions.

Now that we have covered the various architectural components of the geo-tagging architecture, let's look at the tag provisioning models and process.

Geo-Tag Provisioning Process

We envision two models for geo-tag provisioning in virtualized data center environments. As indicated in Table 5-3, depending on the type of operating system or virtual machine monitor, one or both options are available.

Table 5-3. *Geo-Tag Provisioning Model*

Provisioning Mode	KVM	Xen	ESXi	Hyper-V
"push" tags to running host	Yes, requires provisioning agent	Yes, using XenAPI	No	?
PXE Boot	Yes	Yes	Yes	Yes

Push Model

Provisioning under the push model, shown in Figure 5-11, is initiated remotely by a provisioning tool. After mutual authentication between the provisioning agent and the provisioning tool, the geo-tag, which is the SHA-1 hash of the host's asset certificate, is pushed to the running host and the geo-tag is written (or updated) in the NVRAM index. A reboot of the host or server is needed to complete provisioning. This option is available for Xen, KVM, and Citrix XenServer hypervisor environments, but not for VMware. VMWare ESXi takes exclusive ownership of the TPM once it is installed and running, and no other entity can manipulate the TPM thereafter.

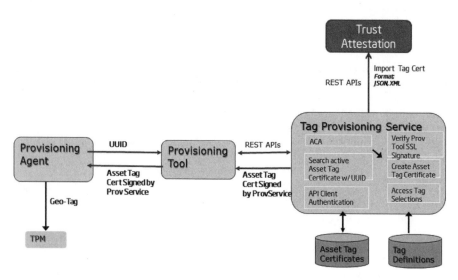

Figure 5-11. *Push mode for geo-tag provisioning*

Pull Model

Pull provisioning, shown in Figure 5-12, is initiated by modifying the boot order on the host and launching a custom PXE boot image to provision the geo-tag. For hosts with VMware ESX, the action needs to be carried out prior to installing or running ESX on the host. The PXE script is built to launch the provisioning agent to interact with the tag provisioning service for creating the asset certificate and the geo-tag, and their storage to the TPM. The location of the tags is provided to the PXE script to allow the tag provisioning service to create certificates for the geo-tags. The PXE script can then initiate a reboot to start running the hypervisor on the host or start installing the operating system or hypervisor. Figure 5-12 shows the PXE-based pull model for provisioning geo-tags.

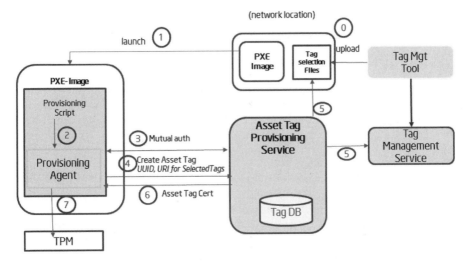

Figure 5-12. *Pull mode for geo-tag provisioning*

Table 5-4 summarizes the key steps of the pull model.

Table 5-4. *Steps for Geo-Tag Provisioning*

Step	Geo-Tag Provisioning with PXE
0	With the tag management tool, the business analyst selects tags to be associated with hosts and uploads them in the form of a pre-defined XML tag specification file format to the network location as the PXE image, or stores them in the repository of the tag management service. This is referred to as "tag selections." The XML is optional encrypted and the keys are provided to the tag provisioning service with appropriate authentication.
1	The system administrator launches the PXE image for provisioning the geo-tag on the targeted host.
2	The PXE image is launched and it then starts the provisioning script, which starts the provisioning agent.
3	The provisioning agent and the tag provisioning service mutually authenticate each other using SSL/TLS certificates.

(continued)

Table 5-4. (*continued*)

Step	Geo-Tag Provisioning with PXE
4	The provisioning agent requests the asset tag from the tag provisioning service. The UUID of the host and URI for tag selections is passed to it.
5	Depending on the policy at the tag provisioning service, if a valid and latest asset certificate is available for that host, it is returned to the provisioning agent , or else the provisioning service creates an asset certificate for the host using the URI for the "selected tag" and the UUID of the host.
6	The asset certificate is downloaded to the tag provisioning agent, and the SHA-1 hash of the certificate, which is the asset tag, is created by the provisioning agent. Alternatively, the asset tag is downloaded to the provisioning agent. This depends on implementation of the provisioning service.
7	The provisioning agent writes (or over-writes) the geo-tag to NVRAM index of the TPM, after the appropriate ownership of the TPM has been acquired.

As we have seen in this section, there are two models supported for provisioning geo-tags to assets. The two provisioning models have very different deployment considerations, however. The pull model requires changes to the boot options on the hosts, with modified PXE configuration options to launch the tag PXE boot image. This PXE image is used with iPXE (or equivalent) on a provisioning network to boot to the provisioning image remotely. The model requires the hosts to be on a provisioning network prior to installation, configuration, and launch of the OS/VMM, and they are moved later to the production management network. On the other hand, the push model can happen on the production management network with appropriate authentication of the provisioning tools. Both of these models have a place in a virtual environment and in cloud data centers. The pull model is applicable to all the OS/VMM platforms, but the push model is not available for VMWare ESXi hosts, owing to the way ESXi handles TPMs on the compute platforms.

In the next section, we will look at reference implementation of a complete geo-tag solution, including the definition of tags, selection, and attestation.

Reference Implementation

This section describes a reference implementation highlighting the tag provisioning, management, and attestation steps. The purpose of this implementation is to facilitate knowledge sharing and also to demonstrate the possible visualization of the functionality to partners. The expectation is that ISVs and CSPs will provide their specific implementation for tag provisioning and management in a way that seamlessly integrates with their respective solution environments and interfaces. Key screenshots from the reference implementation are included to illustrate the various steps in the geo-tag solution.

Step 1

This is the tag definition step, where organizations create the tag taxonomy and a tag whitelist to be used for geo-tagging or asset tagging purposes.

Tag creation is the core function of the asset tag service. A tag is an arbitrary name for a classification, which has one or more potential values. For example, a tag named *State* might have values like *California* or *New York*, while a tag named *Department* might have values like *Accounting, Sales,* and so on. As shown in Figure 5-13, a set of tags forms a tag taxonomy. The whitelist for a given domain or function is drawn from this taxonomy, to be provisioned to a host or an asset (generically). For example, you might have a server tagged with a selection like *State: California; Department: Accounting.*

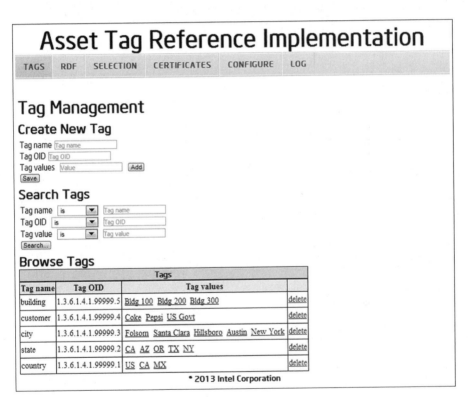

Figure 5-13. *Tag taxanomy*

Step 2

This is the selection step, whereby a specific set of tags for a business function are picked from the whitelist, as shown in Figure 5-14. In this example, the selection is named "default" and has six tags selected that would be provisioned to one or more hosts. As part of the tag provisioning service and API design, automation and scalability have been given deliberate attention. There are well-documented configuration options provided for the tag provisioning service that fully automate the asset certificate creation, geo-tag and/or asset tag generation, provision the tag to the TPM, and register it with Mt. Wilson.

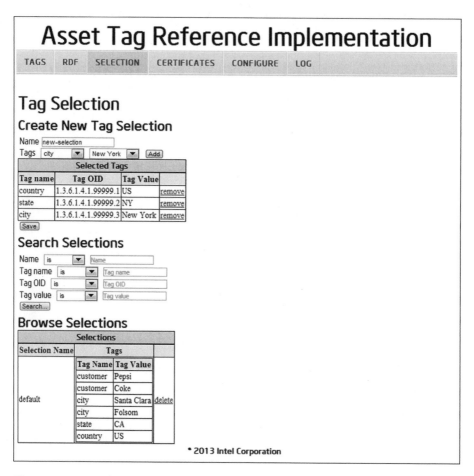

Figure 5-14. *Tag whitelist selection*

Step 3

This is the provisioning step, whereby an asset tag or geo-tag is created by associating one or more of the selection attributes with the asset's UUID, as shown in Figure 5-15; this could be either the push or the pull model for provisioning. As shown in Figure 5-15, the tag provisioning service creates the asset certificate, and the provisioning agent in either of the two models writes the tag to the specific TPM NVRAM index.

Figure 5-15. *Asset certificate, asset tag and geo-tag creation and provisioning*

Step 4

The last step is to provide visibility and attestation for the tags and certificates, as shown in Figure 5-16. Once the host is registered with Mt. Wilson (after the host has been provisioned with asset tags), the Mt. Wilson trust dashboard displays the tags provisioned to the host and allows Mt. Wilson to attest to the validity of the asset certificate, as well as assert the geo-tag. Essentially, the geo-tag and/or asset tag fingerprint reported by the host is compared and verified to be the same as the expected fingerprint stored in the Mt. Wilson environment. If they are the same, the location attestation is affirmed; if not, it is marked as untrusted. As described in the attestation section, there are multiple reasons for failing the attestation: bad certificate, different fingerprint compared to the expected, and so on. Figure 5-16 also shows the current PCR22 value (where the tag is extended) and the expected value of the PCR22, as well as the SAML assertion that indicates the results of the verification.

Mt. Wilson Extensions for Asset-Tag Verification & SAML Assertion

```
</saml2:Attribute>
  <saml2:Attribute Name="Asset_Tag">
    <saml2:AttributeValue xmlns:xs="http://www.w3.org/2001/XMLSchema" xmlns:xsi="http://www.w3.org/2001/XMLSchema-instance" xsi:type="xs:anyType"
  </saml2:Attribute>
  <saml2:Attribute Name="ATAG :1.3.6.1.4.1.99999.1">
    <saml2:AttributeValue xmlns:xs="http://www.w3.org/2001/XMLSchema" xmlns:xsi="http://www.w3.org/2001/XMLSchema-instance" xsi:type="xs:string">
  </saml2:Attribute>
  <saml2:Attribute Name="ATAG :UUID">
    <saml2:AttributeValue xmlns:xs="http://www.w3.org/2001/XMLSchema" xmlns:xsi="http://www.w3.org/2001/XMLSchema-instance" xsi:type="xs:string">
  </saml2:Attribute>
  </saml2:AttributeStatement>
</saml2:Assertion>
```

Figure 5-16. *Asset tag verification and example of SAML assertion for asset tag—Mt. Wilson extensions*

As of this writing, the geo-tag provisioning and management solution, as well as the reference implementation, have been provided to many Intel ISVs and CSP partners to enable geo-fencing, workload segregation, and other interesting solutions for cloud computing usage models. Given the significant interest in these uses, the expectation is that many ISVs and CSPs will complete the eventual enablement and integration of these capabilities into their services and product offerings, and they begin to offer them as core services to their customers.

Summary

Boundary control of workloads and data in the cloud through asset tagging and geo-tagging constitutes a critical requirement for organizations as they consider moving their business-critical applications and data to the cloud. Capabilities with trusted compute pools usage models take organizations a long way toward attaining the visibility and transparency they need for confirming the integrity of their cloud infrastructure through a hardware roots of trust. Organizations also gain control of the placement and migration of their workloads. Asset tagging and geo-tagging as described in this chapter are highly complementary to the trusted pool usages, because they enable organizations to securely provision an asset and geolocation descriptors to platforms with desired location properties. Cloud service providers and IT organizations building private clouds can provide the boundary control for workloads and data in their clouds with extensions to the trusted compute pools solution architecture, as described in this chapter. The controls are rooted in hardware, and are auditable and enforceable. The trusted compute pools solution architecture, with tag provisioning and lifecycle management of the constituent services, provides significant additional capabilities to address customer needs. In this chapter we presented a reference architecture and an implementation for these asset tag provisioning and lifecycle management components, with details on tag definition and specification, APIs for tag management and provisioning, and extensions to the Mt. Wilson attestation service to attest the geo-tags.

Geo-fencing is just one and the most obvious many possible usages that can be enabled with a hardware roots of trust-based asset tag or geo-tag information. Usages like SLA-based zoning of data center assets, Sarbanes-Oxley audits, and workload segregation can be enabled by this tagging mechanism, resulting in better compliance and higher quality of service that is rooted in hardware. As the solution stack becomes pervasive in the data center, the expectation is that many such usages of this tagging could be explored to provide proof of locality, of both physical and virtual data center assets.

In the next chapter, we shift gears a bit and focus attention on network security, the synergy of trusted infrastructure, and how it is essential to have hardware-assisted security in network devices to provide network security in the cloud.

■ ■ ■

CHAPTER 6

Network Security in the Cloud

The cloud can't exist without a network. It is the network that glues cloud-based applications to its users. It is the network that connects applications to the Internet, making them widely available. It is also the network that provides redundant paths between cloud-based applications and users, which makes them business worthy and reliable. Finally, the network can provide a number of security functions that further enable end-to-end security in the cloud.

Boot integrity of the network infrastructure is a prerequisite to trust and enables security functions in the network. The concepts, architecture, and technology components we discussed in the previous chapters on platform trust, attestation, and asset tagging are all equally applicable to the network infrastructure. In this chapter, we look beyond the integrity of the server platforms, and cover concepts relating to network security functions and their essential role in enabling trusted clouds. We look at how companies like M2Mi are automating the many steps required to enable the network security functions via high-level programmatic APIs, and we show how this automation is having a direct impact on the security, scale, and automation of clouds. We will also briefly examine software-defined networks (SDN), an emerging technology bringing solutions that seem to address some of key requirements of cloud computing and that has implications for network security.

As mentioned in previous chapters, cloud computing provides an on-demand virtual infrastructure enabling consumers of the cloud to easily manage their applications. One of the goals of cloud computing is to provide services that abstract the complexity of the cloud and make it simple to manage applications contained within the cloud. Application owners should be able to easily manage their applications without having to know the complexity or the details of the cloud and how is constructed. One of the most important components of the cloud is the network, so we begin with that.

The Cloud Network

The network can be thought of as the glue that holds cloud applications and users together. If the network is the glue, then one might ask how it works. What would a cloud-based network look like? Let's address these questions by examining what a basic network is and work our way to some complex examples found in modern cloud-based networks.

Network Security Components

The most basic network consists of computers connected to a switch, as shown in Figure 6-1. In this case the computers' network port has a cable that connects to a switch. The network switch is the device that enables communications between computers in the network. This simple type of network is commonly found in homes and/or small offices.

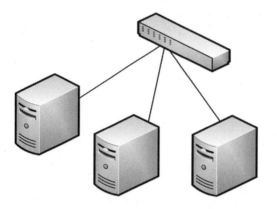

Figure 6-1. *Computers connect to the network through a switch*

If we wish to connect this network to the Internet, then we need to add possibly two network devices. The first device is a firewall, which is used to protect the network from malicious attacks. The second device is a router, used to forward network traffic from the local network to the Internet. Quite often the functions of the firewall and router are consolidated in one device. This scheme is depicted in Figure 6-2.

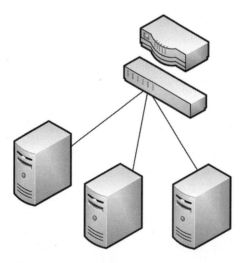

Figure 6-2. *Simple network with a switch and a firewall*

The main concerns and functions of networks are to allow communication between devices connected to the network. In a modern data center hosting a cloud computing environment, the network is much more complex. Nonetheless, it is composed of many of the devices found in a simpler network, except they are in greater numbers and have increased functionality. For example, in a data center there would be a large number of racks housing servers. The servers are connected to switches contained at the top of each rack. These are commonly referred to as *access switches*, or top of rack (TOR) switches; see Figure 6-3. These switches are normally deployed in pairs to provide failover capability and redundancy.

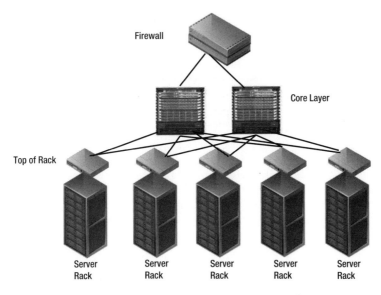

Figure 6-3. *Network racks connected to distribution switches*

There could be tens, hundreds, and even thousands of these racks distributed in a data center. The access switches are connected in turn to *distribution switches*, otherwise known as aggregation switches. These switches aggregate the access switch connections and provide the pathway out of the network into a firewall or a router.

There are a number of optional, but commonly found components in cloud-centric networks, such as load balancers, intrusion detection devices, and application delivery controllers (ADCs). The idea behind these components is to inspect network traffic and perform a function upon it. Let's look at each of these briefly.

Load Balancers

The main function of load balancers is to balance traffic between web servers and application clients. For example, a website could be composed of several web servers in order to handle a high number of client requests and provide redundancy in case one fails. The load balancer distributes the client requests among the web servers, based on a distribution algorithm such as a round robin or web server load.

Intrusion Detection Devices

These devices monitor the network by looking for malicious malware such as viruses or cyber-attacks attempting to penetrate sensitive systems. When these attacks are discovered, an intrusion detection system can log the event and notify network administrators, or it could possibly take an action to prevent the attack, such as creating a firewall policy rule to block attacks.

Application Delivery Controllers

These devices can be considered an evolution of load balancers. They can load balance network traffic and perform advanced tasks such as inspecting traffic to detect and avoid IP fragmentation, data rate shaping, SSL offloading, and analyzing data and transactions in real time. They can also protect against targeted attacks like cross-site scripting, SQL injection, cookie poisoning, forceful browsing and invalid input.

End-to-End Security in a Cloud

When an architect designs a data center to host a public, private, or hybrid cloud, a primary consideration is end-to-end security. The architect analyzes security all the way from application clients, such as a laptops and hand-held devices, to the data center, where applications are housed. The path of the client requests is noted, and how the data traverses the devices, hosts, virtual machines, and backend storage is studied.

For example, a typical web application could flow as follows: From a web browser through a firewall over the Internet, it arrives at a data center's router, passes through a firewall and distribution switch, to reach a load balancer and application delivery controller. The load balancer redirects the traffic to an application server or web server running in a virtual machine; the application receiving the traffic may then access backend data based on the nature of the traffic. This flow is shown in Figure 6-4.

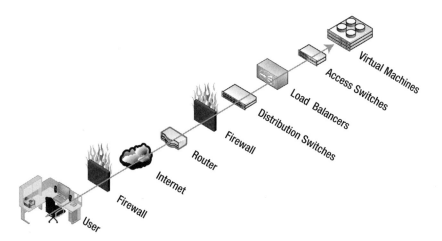

Figure 6-4. *Trajectory of a user request*

While this chain may seem excessively lengthy, it is actually just one of many traffic flows to consider. An architect will diagram and note all possible network and data flows and track them. The architect then looks at each participant of the end-to-end flow and considers how each step needs to be secured, as well as thinks about what would happen to the others if its security were compromised. For example, a security architect may consider how to secure the backend block storage used by databases and virtual machines. Backup, application, and administrative access to the block storage are examined. After analyzing the network flow, the architect may decide to encrypt selected data and apply enhanced firewall rules to restrict access.

Network security: End-to-End security: Firewalls

In the example above, we have explored the components of a network. The network in which an application resides must be secure if that application is to be secure. There are a number of means by which this is accomplished.

Firewalls and routers are the front-line defense in a network. Most modern routers have firewall capabilities, such as screening for malformed packets and blocking inappropriate protocols and ports. Modern firewalls can filter inbound traffic and sessions, and apply policies that block unwanted traffic.

Firewalls can also support dedicated virtual private networks (VPNs) for remote office connectivity and encrypt traffic between branch offices.

Network security: End-to-End security: VLANs

Virtual local area networks, otherwise known as VLANs, allow the segmentation of network traffic over a network. VLANs are typically assigned based on requirements such as application, bandwidth, or user access. For example, in a private cloud there could be VLANs for the engineering, human resources, and accounting divisions. Another example is a dedicated VLAN that is used by system and network administrators for managing servers and network devices.

There are a number of ways to lock down and secure VLANs so they don't become compromised:

- Strictly controllling physical security, physical access to network, and server hardware.

- Not using VLAN1 as the primary network data VLAN; this is the default VLAN, therefore it is easily compromised.

- Disabling high-risk protocols on any switch or firewall network port that does not require them; for example, protocols such as CDP and PAgP do not need to be enabled on all ports.

- Pruning VLANs not in use; this will prevent unwanted access from a rogue computer on the network.

- Controlling inter-VLAN routing by using firewall policies.

End-to-End Security for Site-to-Site VPNs

Many companies use public clouds to achieve certain cloud benefits or they consolidate IT resources into a private cloud. Both require that companies be able to connect private and public clouds. The secure and logical way to do this is by using virtual private networks (VPNs). These connections are commonly referred to as site-to-site VPNs.

The basic concept of a site-to-site VPN is that it extends a private network across a public network such as the Internet. In the case of cloud computing, a VPN can connect to a remote cloud located in a remote corporate data center, or to a publicly hosted cloud provider such as Rackspace, Amazon, or Softlayer, as shown in Figure 6-5.

Figure 6-5. *Joining remote network into the local network using a VPN*

A VPN provides a tunnel connection between specified VPN endpoints, usually firewalls. These connections are typically authenticated and then secured using encryption techniques. This prevents networked traffic from being analyzed via sniffing techniques. For example, an attacker could possibly see the traffic at the packet level, but after analyzing it, would only see encrypted traffic.

The legacy methods to establish VPNs were to use hardware-based firewalls or routers. In cloud computing environments, it is now becoming more common to use software-based appliances to establish VPNs, which allows greater flexibility, fine-grained security, and quick configuration and provisioning times, as shown in Figure 6-6.

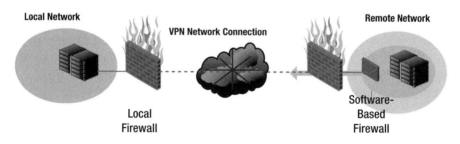

Figure 6-6. *Joining a remote network to the local network using a software VPN*

The two most common site-to-site VPNs used for connecting to remote clouds are IPSEC and SSL/TLSEC. IPSEC is a Layer 3 VPN with an encrypted Layer 3 tunnel between the peers. SSL is a higher layer security protocol than IPSEC, working at the application layer rather than at the network layer.

Site-to-site VPNs were typically built using IPSEC, but now SSL-based VPNs are becoming popular. Major vendors such as Citrix and VMWare provide SSL VPN products to enable remote cloud access. Also, firewall vendors such as Vyatta and Juniper offer software appliances that can be used to enable VPNs and provide a higher level of security through advanced firewall features.

Network security:End-to-End security: Hypervisors and Virtual Machines

One concern within modern data centers is that of securing virtual machines. In public and private clouds, these virtual machines may share the same network and compute resources, not only between company departments but also between separate companies in a public/hybrid cloud environment.

Hypervisor Security

In a cloud, each server has a hypervisor virtualization layer installed, such as Xen, VMWare, KVM, and Hyper-V. As discussed in Chapter 3, an important component for securing a cloud is to establish trust across virtual machines. This is accomplished by using servers that have trusted platform hardware modules that allow the server to verify the boot process of the server's management domain virtual machine. The objective is to protect virtual machines against attacks such as kernel rootkits or viruses. Boot integrity and attestation have been covered in Chapter 3 and Chapter 4.

Another important way to secure the hypervisor is by locking down management access to the hypervisor. A best practice is to reserve a VLAN to isolate access to the management interface. This separates management traffic from data or application traffic.

The same could be said for all the guest virtual machines: traffic is isolated from other guest virtual machines. If one of the guests is compromised by an attacker, it may inject malicious traffic into the network. Inter-VLAN routing should not be performed by the virtual switch in the hypervisor. Best practice is to force traffic up to the firewall and allow the firewall to control inter-VLAN routing. This protects guests from one another in a multitenant cloud, as shown in Figure 6-7.

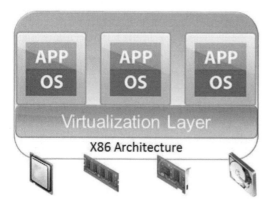

Figure 6-7. Virtualization layer managing guest virtual machines

Resources shared by the hypervisor and guests should be removed or restricted. Features such as shared folders can be exploited by attackers, moving from a virtual machine guest to gain access to the hypervisor by placing executable files on the shared resource and then executing them.

Virtual Machine Guest Security

Virtual machine guest security is similar to hardening an operating system. Accounts need to be restricted, and the operating system is maintained up to date and patched. The main concern with virtual machine guests is that virtual machines live in a shared environment. Therefore, extra steps should be taken to protect them from potentially nosy guests. A virtual machine guest, for instance, should restrict traffic from other virtual machine guests and only allow traffic from intended sources. Virtual machine guests should carry internal firewalls configurable to allow only the protocols necessary for the applications installed to function correctly. For example, this includes HTTP or HTTPs traffic from the Internet, SQL traffic to a backend database, and management traffic via SSH from an administrative VLAN.

Secure Storage: Mission-critical applications used in public or hybrid clouds require a higher level of security to comply with corporate security policies or to meet other compliance requirements. For instance, data in shared networked storage environments needs to be encrypted. Users need to know where data is before figuring out how to protect it. Therefore, a complete and accurate inventory of systems, software, and data located in the cloud is necessary at all times. Encrypted data is intrinsically protected, so policies should enforce automatic encryption of data before it is stored or moved to the cloud. In the case of a hybrid cloud, connections between the internal network and the cloud should also be encrypted.

Virtual Appliances: Network security devices such as firewalls, switches, and load balancers at one time could be found only in hardware. Now vendors have started to supply appliances in prepackaged virtual machines. This allows users to spin up instances of their software when specific capabilities are needed. For example, if a new group of applications is deployed, a new load balancer may need to be created along with it. If a new network segment is created dynamically, a new firewall may need to be created to support that. In the opposite case, if a network segment is deprovisioned, then the firewall could be spun down.

Software-Defined Security in the Cloud

Another concept that has evolved in association with cloud computing is the software-defined networks (SDN). Applications in the cloud can be dynamic in size, location, and lifetime. This puts increased pressure on coming up with the means to secure the cloud in this challenging environment. Software-defined security was conceived to address these concerns.

The term *software defined security* evolved from *software defined networking* (SDN). SDN was conceived to solve similar problems found in dynamic, challenging networks like those in cloud computing. So there is a bit of overlap between the two, since both address matters of security in the network space.

Initially, software-defined networking focused on making the network control plane programmable through application programing interfaces (APIs) and protocols. The concept evolved to meet the needs of a dynamic IT infrastructure. Provisioning storage, virtual machines, switches, load balancers, and firewalls in such environments required APIs so they could be automated through workflows and orchestration engines.

SDN OVERVIEW

SDN is an approach to computer networking in which the control plane for network switches is extracted and centralized on one or more servers. Figure 6-8 illustrates this concept. The data plane is illustrated in the figure by API and switch Silicon, whereas the control plane is illustrated by Network Intelligence and OS. In traditional networking, every switch has both a data plane and a control plane. In SDN, switches only have a data plane and support for communicating with a remote (and centralized) control plane. The original protocol defined for this communication is called OpenFlow, although recently other protocols have been introduced by certain networking vendors.

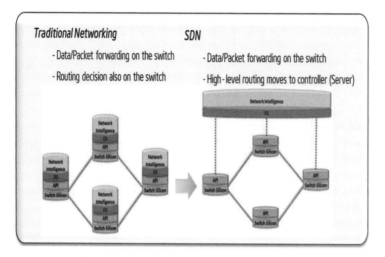

Figure 6-8. *Traditional Networking vs. SDN*

The software representing the centralized control plane is known as the SDN controller and runs on a server platform, illustrated in Figure 6-8.

SDN provides the following advantages:

Unmatched Network Agility: Programmability and automation provide dramatic improvements in service agility and provisioning time.

Choice in Networking Hardware: Standards-based OpenFlow switches provide choice in networking hardware for the first time ever.

Optimized Network Operations: Automation of network provisioning tasks and integration with data center resource orchestration platforms drives dramatic reduction in network operation tasks and requirements.

Centralized view of the network

Figure 6-9 illustrates usage models that have been identified as getting significant benefits from SDN.

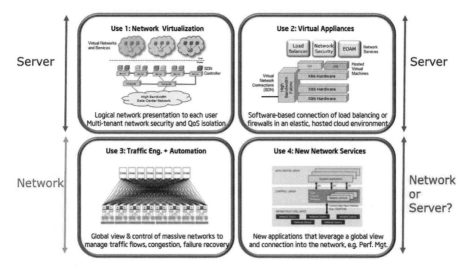

Figure 6-9. *SDN use cases*

The SDN network virtualization usage model provides tenants with their own virtual (and isolated) networks while running on top of a common physical network infrastructure. The virtual appliance usage model enables the instantiation of security on demand in order to fulfill the specific needs of a virtual machines or group of virtual machines.

Specific advantages of these two usage models in cloud multitenant (IaaS) data centers include:

- A VPN would be created support for unrestricted VM migration (i.e., VM migration across subnets)

- Improved visibility (for network management software) of intra-node traffic (i.e., VM to VM running on the same node)

- Improved virtual network management by allowing tenants to manage their virtual networks without interfering with the cloud provider or other tenants

- Improved flexibility to deploy virtual security appliances (e.g., firewalls, intrusion detection/prevention systems, etc.)

Taking advantage of SDN in cloud multi-tenant (IaaS) data centers does not require changing physical network switches. All of the advantages mentioned above can be obtained by adding SDN support to virtual switches (software switches that allow virtual machines to communicate inside and outside the physical server) and putting in place an SDN controller that communicates with the virtual switches and that provides interfaces for a virtualization management infrastructure to create and manage virtual networks.

SDN makes it easier to intercept traffic directed to a virtual machine and redirect it to a security appliance such as a firewall or an intrusion detection and prevention system. Given that trusted compute pools prescribe and enable higher levels of protection for critical workloads, a tenant's security personnel might like:

- Tenant-defined and specified IPS/IDS/firewalls security appliances for their workloads and applications, rather than the generic ones that the Cloud Service Provider supplies.

- Security appliances run on trusted compute pools to ensure integrity, protections, and control policies.

There are two major concepts for security and software-defined networks. The first is APIs, used to make changes to network and hardware elements found in a data center. The second is orchestration, namely taking these APIs and putting them to use in a logical manner.

- *APIs.* There are a number of APIs and software solutions that support the notion of SDN. Vendors such as Juniper, Cisco, and VMWare all supply pre-packaged APIs to enable the control and management of their hardware and software. The APIs can be used by developers to manage, orchestrate, and automate their cloud resources.

- *Orchestration.* Security tasks in the cloud typically require the invocation of a number of APIs to fulfill a set of tasks. For example, when a new virtual machine instance is created, a security policy will need to be provisioned in order to allow traffic to flow to it. The following is an example orchestration initiated after the new virtual machine instance is created:

  - A load balancer may need to be created or updated to accommodate the new virtual machine instance.

  - VLANs may need to be created to allow traffic to the virtual machine.

  - The firewall's rules are updated to regulate traffic to it.

  - Monitoring rules can be added to observe traffic and user access.

Ideally, orchestration should be atomic in the sense of transactions: if the task fails at any point during the orchestration, a smooth rollback of the API executions that did manage to complete in the chain of API invocations would be completed transparently.

All of these concepts and network technology elements play a critical role in real-world cloud computing environments built on cloud management software like OpenStack, Eucalyptus, Amazon AWS, Virtustream xStream, and so on. OpenStack, discussed in the next section, will be introducing a first-order mapping to the network security primitives and components we have discussed in the previous sections.

OpenStack

OpenStack is the leading open-source package for managing cloud environments. Knowledge of the basics of OpenStack provides understanding of what's needed to manage and secure a cloud computing environment.

OpenStack is a Python-based cloud computing management application developed collaboratively by Rackspace and NASA. Later, as the technology grew in popularity, companies such as Dell, Red Hat, HP, Intel, IBM, and Citrix got involved and started contributing to the project. OpenStack is a collection of open-source components delivering a massively scalable cloud operating system. It can be thought of as a service (IaaS) software package designed to manage end-to-end cloud infrastructure.

The management of cloud infrastructure can be quite complicated, since it is composed of a number of different resources: servers, hypervisors, storage, hard drives, network, and racks. OpenStack was designed to manage all these resources in a modular fashion.

OpenStack consists of a set of inter-related projects that address the various resources of a cloud computing platform. Its services are interoperable with existing cloud services like AWS, which heightens its appeal. As of this writing, there are seven projects: Nova, Swift, Glance, Cinder, Neutron, Horizon and Keystone, with a few more in proposal and blueprint development:

- *Nova* provides the ability to provision virtual servers on demand.

- *Swift* is similar to Amazon's S3, a highly scalable and durable object storage system used to store data accessible through RESTful HTTP APIs.

- *Glance Image Service* provides services for discovering, registering, and retrieving virtual machine images.

- *Cinder* provides block storage for virtual environments. This is similar to Amazons EC2's Elastic Block storage, where the block storage volumes are network-attached and can persist independently from the life of an instance.

- *Neutron* provides networking as a service functionality to OpenStack. This involves configuring network components such as virtual switches, firewalls, hardware switches, load balancers, and more.

- *Horizon Dashboard* is the web-based dashboard for exposing the cloud management capabilities of OpenStack.

- *Keystone* provides identity, token, catalog, and policy services for projects in the OpenStack family. For example, before a Glance call is made, authentication is processed by Keystone. Glance depends on Keystone and the OpenStack Identity API to handle authentication of client requests.

- *Ceilometer* was created to allow the metering of cloud environments. Metering includes virtual machine instances, CPU and RAM usage, network data I/O, and block storage hourly usage.

OpenStack Network Security

OpenStack has essential security features. For example, OpenStack's APIs allows exposing firewall, load balancer, switch, and intrusion detection system (IDS) capabilities as infrastructure services. Specifically:

- *LB-aaS* or *load balancing* is an important capability. For example, if an additional virtual machine instance is spun up to meet increased load, then it can be added to an application pool on a load balancer through an API.

- *VPN-aaS* or *VPN* is another popular feature. Picture a new network segment provisioned for a tenant at a remote cloud. A VPN needs to be created after provisioning to enable a secure connection from the tenant's data center to the network segment at the cloud provider.

- *Firewall-aaS* or *firewall* allows tenants to customize firewall rules to meet their application security needs and match corporate security and compliance requirements.

- *VLAN-aaS* or *VLAN* offers tenants the ability to expand their cloud network resources. Often, more IP addresses are needed and logical separation of network resources is required. In this case, a new network segment and VLAN need to be provisioned on demand. VLAN as a service exposes this functionality as an API.

Furthermore, each of these services can be exposed to tenants under a cloud security model. For example, a tenant may be able to create a VPN to its network segment, but not allowed to see VPN resources of other tenants. An administrator may have the ability to see created VPNs, but would be unable to delete it unless special permissions were in place. OpenStack's architecture was designed to provide fine-grained management of cloud resources. It allows cloud administrators and architects to apply role-based controls to network functions and services, as shown in Figure 6-10.

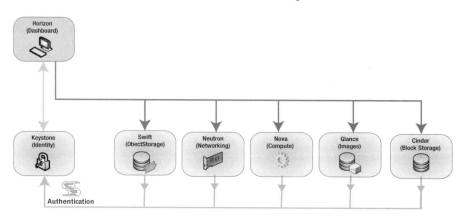

Figure 6-10. *Access to cloud services are managed using roles and privileges*

This gives OpenStack the capability to virtualize network functions. In the case of network security, items such as switch, NAT, DHCP, load balancing, network interface configuration, and firewall security policies can be quickly and securely instantiated.

Network Security Capabilities and Examples

M2Mi Corporation provides cloud network services. The company offers a set of appliances callable by applications like OpenStack through its APIs, providing higher level management, workflow, and analytics tools. The API allows engineers to request specific actions, make changes, or request data without having to have knowledge of vendor-specific capabilities. For example, suppose a new network segment is needed to be provisioned for a new set of applications. Tasks such as segment allocation, DNS provisioning, VLAN provisioning, and network security policy creation are carried out in an orderly manner. The APIs can autodetect device types and perform the above actions as necessary. The API relationships are shown in Figure 6-11.

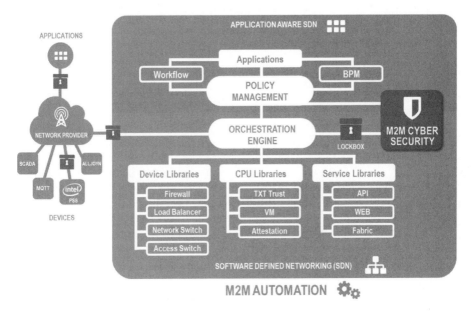

Figure 6-11. *Protecting the cloud using M2M automation from M2Mi*

For example, perhaps a new virtual machine is about to be provisioned and will use VLAN 150. A network administrator typically checks on whether the VLAN already exists on the switch, and if so, on the customers or applications using it. If it isn't there, then the administrator can create it in the switch's VLAN database. The next step enables the VLAN on the physical port connecting the switch to the virtual machine's server. In a data center, this is typically a trunked port, which means the network port can support multiple VLANs with the same physical port. Also, the switch will likely have multiple connections to the physical server using an 802.3ad link aggregated channel. See Figure 6-12.

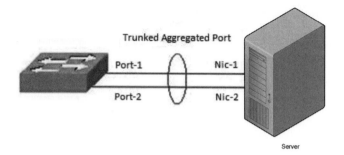

Figure 6-12. *VLAN trunking*

Let's take a look at the commands that would enable the VLAN on the switch. The following commands will illustrate the simplest use case, where there is only one cable connecting the server to the switch. The first command to be sent to a switch will check to see which VLANs have been created on the switch:

```
switch# show vlan brief
VLAN Name                       Status    Ports
---- ----------------------- --------- ----------------------------
                                          Gi1/46, Gi1/48
1    default                  active    Gi1/23, Gi1/24, Gi1/25
137  VLAN0139                 active
140  VLAN0140                 active
141  VLAN0141                 active
142  VLAN0142                 active
```

This command shows that the VLANs 139 through 142 have previously been created. VLAN 143 would need to be added to VLAN database on the switch:

```
switch# configure terminal
switch(config)# vlan 143
switch(config-vlan)# name CustomerA
```

Note that a name can be used for the VLAN. This is used as a tracking mechanism to associate the VLAN with a logical name. Often, data centers will use an application's name or owner as the VLANs name. The next step is to create the VLAN on the port. In this case, the port on the switch that connects to the server is Gi1/5:

```
switch# configure terminal
switch(config)# interface Gi1/5
switch(config-if)# switchport trunk allowed vlan 143
switch(config-if)#
```

The final step is to check the interface to make sure the VLAN was added.

```
Switch# Show interface Gi1/5
Name: Gi1/5
Switchport: Enabled
Administrative Mode: trunk
Operational Mode: trunk
    ...
```

Trunking VLANs enabled: 140-143. If adding and removing VLANs is a regular occurrence, then it is desirable to automate the process. The M2Mi APIs provide a VLAN orchestration call that allows all the previous steps to be accomplished in one simple one call:

```
addVLAN("143","Customer A","cisco10.example.com");
```

This call sends the following request to the server:

```
<soapenv:Envelope xmlns:soapenv="http://schemas.xmlsoap.org/soap/envelope/"
xmlns:jax="http://jaxws.switches.cisco.m2mi.com/">
    <soapenv:Header/>
    <soapenv:Body>
        <jax:VLANOrchestration>
            <!--Optional:-->
            <vlanID>143</vla8nID>
            <!--Optional:-->
            <vlanName>Customer A</vlanName>
            <!--Optional:-->
            <port>Gi1/5</port>
            <!--Optional:-->
            <hostname>cisco10.example.com</hostname>
        </jax:VLANOrchestration>
    </soapenv:Body>
</soapenv:Envelope>
```

The idea is to automate several of the manual steps and remove the element of human error from the configuration. There are other advantages to using APIs. For instance, invocation of the APIs can be limited by users or groups, providing a complete audit trail of all commands that were sent to a device.

Summary

Implementing network security in the cloud requires an in-depth analysis of the hardware and software found in the data center hosting the cloud. There are additional considerations for hybrid cloud or public clouds, with more factors to consider involved in an analysis, such as security issues when traversing the Internet and the quality of the security in the remote data center hosting the cloud.

Security in the cloud is based on best practices evolved over years in order to meet new threats and adapt to new hacking technologies. These best practices can be applied to cloud computing, and a number of companies provide services out of the box to enhance cloud computing security. While many see cloud computing as a technical revolution, the security applied to it is based on hard experience, evolved from known protective measures and standard operating practices. Practices include encrypting data at rest, separation of concerns through delegated administration, application fingerprinting, secure logging, secure backups, auditing, and threat identification.

CHAPTER 7

■ ■ ■

Identity Management and Control for Clouds

In the last few chapters we covered the technologies, usage models, and capabilities that are required to enable trusted infrastructure in the cloud–one of the foundation pillars for trusted clouds. We looked at the concepts, solution architectures, and ISV components that establish and propagate platform trust, attestation, and boundary control, all of which are required to enable the trusted clouds. The other foundational pillar to enable them is identity management, and that is the focus on this chapter.

Identity management encompasses the management of individual identities and their authentication, authorization, roles, and privileges and permissions within or across system and enterprise boundaries, with the goal of increasing security and productivity while decreasing cost, downtime, and repetitive tasks. Identity management thus constitutes an essential capability for attaining trusted clouds. From a cloud security perspective, and given the distributed nature of the cloud, questions like, "How do I control passwords and access tokens in the cloud?" and "How do I federate identity in the cloud?" are very real and thorny ones for cloud providers and subscribers. In this chapter, we will provide a broad introduction to identity, survey the challenges and requirements for identity management systems, and describe a set of technologies from Intel and McAfee that address identity requirements.

The emerging cloud infrastructure connects remote parties worldwide through the use of large-scale networks and through a diverse and complex set of hardware and software technologies. Activities in various domains, such as e-commerce, entertainment, social networking, collaboration, and health care are increasingly being implemented by diverse sets of resources and services. These resources and services are engaged at various levels within those domains. The interactions between different parties at remote locations may be (and sometimes should be) based on the information that's needed to carry out specific transactions with little knowledge about each other beyond that.

To better support these activities and collaborations, it is essential there be an information technology infrastructure with a simple-to-use identity management system. We expect, for example, that personal preferences and profiles of individuals be readily available as a cloud service when shopping over the Internet or with the use of mobile devices. Extensive use of cloud services involving sensitive computation and storage should be done without the need for individuals to repeatedly enter user credentials. In this scenario, the technology for *digital identity management* (IdM) is fundamental in customizing the user experience, underpinning accountability in the transactions, and complying with regulatory controls. For this technology to fully deploy its potential, it is crucial we investigate and understand the concept of digital identity. This in turn helps in developing solutions for the protection of digital identity in IdM systems, solutions that ensure such information is not misused and individuals' privacy is guaranteed. Moreover, several strong authentication techniques aimed at protecting digital identity from misuse and access control rely on multi-factor identity verification and strong identity factors.

Phillip Windley defines digital identity as "the data that uniquely describes a person or a thing and contains information about the subject's relationships."[1] We like this definition because it allows for practical ways to assert identity. Identity may simply be a collection of attributes that together disambiguates someone, or it may be a digital identifier with known unique properties.

Note that identity plays a role in many contexts, interactions, and transactions of everyday life. Examples of "contexts" include personal, social, work, government and e-commerce. The interpretation and view of the same identity information may vary based on other contextual information, thus increasing the complexity of the problem of managing such identities. Moreover, the policies, control, and management of the same identity information may differ based on:

- Identities owned and controlled by users or data subjects

- Identities controlled by third parties or cloud service providers but known to data subjects

- Identities controlled by third parties, such as credit rating agencies and unknown to data subjects

Analysis of the multi-dimensional aspects of the management of identity information and other related details regarding IdM components is important while assessing which identity solution best fits consumers' or business users' interaction with cloud services. In this chapter we focus on methodologies of IdM, and especially Intel technologies. We will not explore why users submit or share information in the various mentioned ways and for what purposes. That limitation notwithstanding, such legal, social, and behavioral contexts may be important when considering the management and use of identity information.

Identity Challenges

There are a number of obligatory considerations in the architecture of almost any identity system. These include issue identity, identity usage, identity modification, and identity revocation. Based on the simple identity credential lifecycle illustrated in Figure 7-1, we can identify some general shortcomings in current approaches to managing identity information.

---

[1]Phillip J. Windley, *Digital Identity* O'Reilly Media, 2005), 8–9.

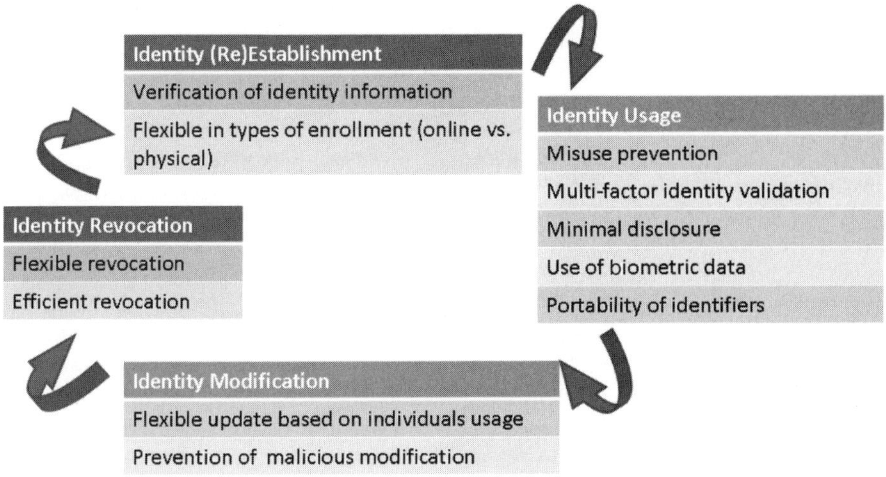

Figure 7-1. *Shortcomings of current federated IdM approaches in the credential lifecycle*

A limitation of current systems is that no information is provided about whether the strong and weak identifiers being enrolled and stored at the identity provider (IdPs) have been verified to be correct with respect to validity and ownership, as well as any indication of the strength of this verification. If an IdP has such information, then service providers are in a position to make a more accurate judgment concerning the trustworthiness of such identity information.

Furthermore, most IdM systems lack flexible enrollment mechanisms for the individuals who want to enroll in their systems. Enrollment can be in person at a physical location of an IdP or online. Current systems, however, do not provide alternative mechanisms for individuals to enroll. Moreover, the types of identity attributes that can be enrolled in most systems are restricted, based upon the nature of the IdP organization.

Identity Usages

A major drawback of current systems is that no specific techniques are provided to protect against the misuse of identity attributes stored at the IdPs and service providers. Even the notion of misuse is still being investigated and the solutions are in early stage of maturity. By "misuse" we refer to when dishonest individuals register fake attributes or impersonate other individuals of the federation, leading to the threat of identity theft.

To mitigate this threat, an upcoming trend is to require strong authentication. *Strong authentication* often refers to systems that require multiple factors, possibly issued by different sources, to identify users when they access certain services and applications. However, current approaches to strong authentication, such as those deployed by banks, enterprises, and government institutions, are neither flexible nor fine-grained. In many cases, strong authentication simply means requiring two forms of identity tokens—for example, password and biometric. Through prior knowledge of these token requirements, an adversary can steal and compromise that required identity information. Moreover, if the same tokens are repeatedly used for strong authentication at various service providers, then the chances of these tokens being compromised increase. Yet, individuals should be able to choose any combination of identity attributes to perform strong authentication, provided the authentication policies defined by the verifying party are satisfied.

A recurrent issue in identity usage is the inability of some individuals to disclose minimal identity data about themselves to the service provider and IdPs, as per required to obtain the service requested. Digital identifiers have uniqueness properties that disambiguate someone or something within some domain of reference. For example, virtually every average-size company has two or more people with the same first and last names. Smaller companies have fewer name–space collisions; larger companies have more. To minimize the occurrence of these name–space collisions, identity management systems typically create unique digital identifiers. Interestingly, the identity management system could create a digital identifier that is globally unique, meaning that the identifier is not only unique within the company, but also may be unique at every other organization. This suggests that globally unique identifiers can be used to track and correlate activities between multiple organizations. Of course, such identifiers would be more than minimal, able to disambiguate individuals beyond what is required for the employer's use.

There are, likewise, several security and privacy concerns related to the extraneous identity information of the individuals stored at service providers and IdPs. Moreover, such data may be aggregated or used in a manner that could potentially violate the privacy requirements of those individuals.

Approaches need to be developed to address how biometric data can be used in an IdM system. Use of biometrics as an integral part of individual identity is gaining importance. At the same time, because of the nature of biometric data, it is not easy to use such data in a way similar to the traditional attributes. In theory, it should be possible to use biometric data together with other identity attributes to provide greater protection against identity attribute misuse. Biometric identifiers are designed to be globally unique. DNA biometrics are universally unique—it is believed that no human being has exactly the same DNA sequence as any other human who has ever lived or who will ever live.[2]

Another type of identity data becoming increasingly important in current systems is that related to individuals' histories of online activity. If this history can be verified and used for evaluating properties about an individual—for example, his or her reputation—then this data becomes part of that individual's identity. Consider a scenario in which an individual frequently buys books from an online store. This purchasing history can be encoded as an identity attribute of that individual, which in turn can be used to evaluate the person's reputation as a buyer. This history-based data needs to be better supported in current IdM systems. Companies like Amazon, Netflix, and Apple are using these types of attributes to classify customer buying habits and nature, in order to present a customized shopping experience.

Identity Modification

There are different approaches to take when it comes to finding mechanisms for the notification of changes in attributes. However, further investigation is required to develop flexible mechanisms for updating or modifying user-controlled enrolled identity

---

[2]*Encyclopedia of Espionage, Intelligence, and Security* Internet service. http://www.faqs.org/espionage/De-Eb/DNA-Sequences-Unique.html#b.

attributes. As the information is shared within the federation, updates performed on one system do not ensure consistency across the federation. Additionally, systems may fail to prevent malicious updates by attackers impersonating honest individuals.

Identity Revocation

Current federated IdM systems lack practical and effective revocation mechanisms. To enable consistency and maintain correctness of identity information, revocation should be feasible. Revocation feasibility for biometrics can be problematic, though. People can't simply change their fingerprints, irises, or DNA. Revocation in provider-centric systems, in which the IdP provides the required credential to the user each time, is relatively simple to achieve, however. A cryptographic digital identity can be mapped to a biometric identifier to create a credential with a manageable lifecycle. Such credentials are typically short term, and cannot be used without consulting the issuer again. If, however, the credentials are stored with the user, such as a long-term credential issued by the appropriate authority, then building a revocation system becomes more challenging and critical.

Identity Management System Requirements

In emerging paradigms of identity systems (such as user-centric identity) there are several distinct properties of the identity attributes that must be maintained. A key property is that of user control. While reasoning about the security and privacy properties of user control, we refer to the OECD countries. The OECD guidelines are widely accepted and they are the cornerstone of fair information practices and regulations designed to protect personal information around the world. In addition, Cameron's Laws of Identity are a recent set of prevalent guidelines regarding digital identity management.[3] They both aim at explaining the successes and failures of digital identity systems. In addition, design principles and rules to achieve several security and dependability properties are included. Figure 7-2 shows the properties of our taxonomy related to user control, illustrated as nodes. Taken together, these basic properties define what we mean by security and privacy in our solution.

---

[3]http://msdn.microsoft.com/en-us/library/ms996456.aspx.

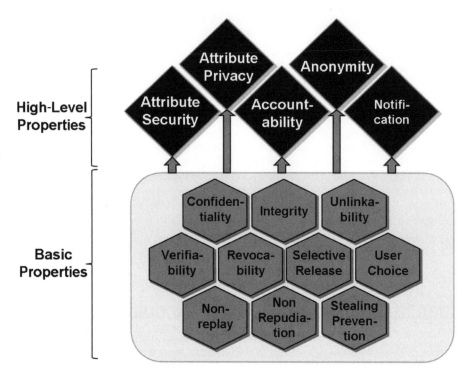

Figure 7-2. Taxonomy of user control properties for identity attributes

Basic User Control Properties

The basic properties related to the identity attributes either apply to the entire IdM system, to transactions in the system, or to the identity information and credentials of the entities involved. Although this classification is not exclusive, the semantics of the properties highlight which of the three they are relevant to. Table 7-1 briefly describes these properties.

Table 7-1. *Basic Properties Achieving Security and Privacy*

Property	Description
Confidentiality	This deals with the protection of information from unauthorized disclosure. This property applies to identity information and transactions in the system. Identity information should be accessible only by the intended recipients.
Revocation	Revocation of identity information is required to maintain the validity of information in the system. It should ensure that once invalid information is recognized, it is not used for identity verification purposes.
Integrity	This requires data not be altered in an unauthorized way.
Unlinkability	Ability to unlink two or more users or transactions so that an attacker, after having observed the transactions, cannot gain additional information by linking onto those transactions. Unlinkability prevents (illegitimate) merging of user profiles.
User Choice	The individual can choose among multiple IdPs and determine which attributes to release.
Verifiability	The individual can verify that the IdP provides the correct identity data about him or herself and according to that individual's intention. As such, an individual giving consent for what data is revealed, for what purpose, and to whom means that the individual's view of the transaction corresponds to the actual transaction and that the individual has agreed to execution of the transaction.
Non-replay	This prevents unauthorized parties from successfully using an individual's identity data to conduct new transactions. Non-replay is one prerequisite for obtaining the non-repudiation property.
Non-repudiation	The sending of non-repudiatable identity data cannot be denied by its sender and the ownership of the identity data cannot be denied.
Stealing Protection	This concerns the protection against unauthorized entities illegitimately retrieving an individual's data items. Stealing protection is required to achieve properties such as non-repudiation.
Selective release	Identity information can be released at a fine-granular level, as controlled by the individual. In this way, an individual can provide only the identity information that needs to be released for a service, without having to release additional information.

Key Requirements for an Identity Management Solution

The key requirements for an identity management system to ensure security and privacy of the identity data are as follows.

Accountability

Accountability refers to an ability to hold entities responsible for their actions in user transactions and for their use of identity information at the service provider and IdP. IdM systems have typically been focused on underpinning the accountability in business relationships and checking adherence to regulatory controls. In user-centric systems, the identity information of a user may be provided via the user's client. Therefore, it is required that, in addition to guaranteeing the integrity of the identity data, there should be accountability in providing such data. Accountability also becomes a significant issue if the user is to stay anonymous, as accountability and anonymity are, per se, contradictory properties. Nevertheless, conditional release of identity information can help in obtaining accountability in anonymous transactions. The eighth OECD accountability principle is devoted to understanding accountability, especially as it relates to privacy.

Notification

Notification Identity management (IdM):notification is desirable as a means for improving security by enhanced user control. Users should be able to receive and retrieve notifications regarding the usage of their credentials, so as to identify security breaches, and to estimate the extent of their compromised user identity information previously shared with external entities. It is desirable to allow users to collect data, whether under receive (push model) or retrieve (pull model) notifications regarding the usage of identity data. The sixth and seventh OECD principles of openness and individual participation can potentially be satisfied using comprehensive notification mechanisms.

■ **Note**　Privacy legislation often requires notification of individuals impacted by release of privacy-sensitive *personally identifiable information* (PII). Identity credentials may be considered PII. Notification also helps individuals manage their privacy.

Anonymity

In transactions, *anonymity* deals with subjects remaining anonymous within an anonymity set—that is, with not being identifiable within some context or "set." In this context, something is more anonymous when it can be hidden in a population of otherwise indistinguishable members. A white sheep in a herd of white sheep is more anonymous than a black sheep in that same herd of white sheep. Thus, anonymity is a specific notion related to data minimization, obtainable when the released attributes are not identifying the user.

Anonymity is supported by unlinkable transactions. Without such unlinkability, the anonymity set shrinks quickly when executing several transactions. *Pseudonymity*, or the use of pseudonyms as user identifiers, is a concept related to anonymity.[4] It plays a critical role in providing unlinkability and data minimization. There has been extensive work on the concept of pseudonymity, from both conceptual and implementation perspectives.

Note that conditional anonymity—that is, anonymity that holds only as long as a well-defined condition has not been fulfilled—can be based on conditional release of the identity information. In this way, the mechanisms providing for anonymity remain useful, as they are complemented by mechanisms for realizing accountability.

Data Minimization

Data minimization deals with minimal data release within a transaction. This can be achieved by having appropriate policy system support, by having unlinkable transactions, and by having a data release system that allows for selective and conditional release of identity information. This approach corresponds to the first OECD principle relating to collection limitation. It is also reflected in the European Data Protection Directive 95/46/EC and the national data protection laws within the European Union.

Attribute Security

The attribute *security property* reflects a comprehensive view of the security of a user's attributes. The main focus is on the correctness of attributes in the view of a service provider, meaning that the attributes belong to the person executing the transactions. This requires the attribute information to be integrity protected. Additionally, protections against stealing, and mechanisms to prevent sharing must be in place in order to stop another person from maliciously impersonating a user's identity. Furthermore, revocation of identity information must be feasible. Attributes in certain cases must be kept confidential with respect to parties other than the ones involved in the transaction.

Attribute Privacy

Attribute privacy refers to giving the user control over the attribute data. This is supported by system assurance and by allowing for user-chosen IdPs. Both those properties account for user-centric decisions regarding which IdP to trust. Anonymity and dependent properties very likely contribute to attribute privacy in that they help avoid the unnecessary release of (identifying) information. Data minimization also directly provides privacy.

---

[4]http://en.wikipedia.org/wiki/Pseudonymity.

An orthogonal property essential for reaching attribute privacy is support of privacy policy management, enforcement, and agreement. User control over attributed data helps the user remain anonymous outside the context or domain in which the identity is being used. Preventing disclosure of privacy sensitive information outside the context where it is needed is important; once this information is disclosed, it can't be reclaimed. Confidentiality measures ensure that privacy-sensitive attributes are not unintentionally disclosed to any party.

Identity Representations and Case Studies

There are various types of identity tokens used for device and user identification and for access control. Key examples are illustrated in Figure 7-3. From a security perspective, the prevalent method of conveying identity information that is certified by a trusted third party is through certificates.

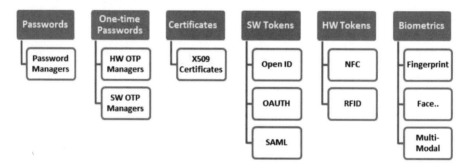

Figure 7-3. *Types of identity tokens*

Based upon the representation of certified digital identity information, the resulting system may or may not satisfy one or more of the properties covered in the previous section. In the following, we discuss technical mechanisms that can be used to obtain an identity management system with the properties described in our taxonomy. We refer to three different core mechanisms. Note that what follows is not a complete survey of mechanisms but, rather, focuses on the more interesting properties relevant to the representation of certified digital identity information.

PKI Certificates

Standard certificates, like X.509, allow, in conjunction with a private signing key, a user to prove that attributes have been issued to him or her. The certificate contains attributes and a public key signed by the IdP (the issuer of the certificate). Note that in a typical IT enterprise, such certificates are used for managing users and client machines in order to establish secure channels between two enterprise entities, for provisioning, and for updating user machines or profiles.

To assert the attributes of a certificate to a relying party, the user engages in a challenge-response protocol with the relying party. This protocol requires the certificate to be sent to the relying party and a signature made with the private key. The step reveals all attributes of the certificate to the recipient. Technically, certificates are based on standard digital signature schemes such as RSA and are represented by standards like X.509,[5] which define the formats of the certificates.

Traditional certificate-based technologies allow for constructing systems in which a certificate is issued once and can be used repeatedly by users to reveal the attributes contained in the certificate. Thus, this technology allows for off-line IdPs. The tokens are generated by the user without involvement of the IdP, making this method flexible with respect to this aspect. This technology is, for example, used in multiple ID card proposals and public key infrastructure-based systems.

Security and Privacy Discussion

In the discussion of security requirements, note that the integrity of such schemes is accounted for by the user attributes being included in the certificate signed by the IdP, using standard signature schemes, and e being provided each time the attributes are asserted to a relying party. Confidentiality of attribute information is achieved by using encryption schemes in conjunction with public key infrastructure (PKI). Stealing prevention methods for standard certificate systems target protection of the master private key, as the certificates are made available to relying parties anyway. The following mechanisms can be used, also in a combined fashion:

- Binding all certificates to one master private key of the user and mandating appropriate protection of this key—for example, in a hardware token. As this requires the hardware token be used in each transaction, the portability of such tokens becomes important.

- Applying operating system mechanisms to prevent a user from sharing his or her key.

- Using multi-factor authentication makes it harder to share the token—for example, if it is derived from the biometrics of the user.

Finally, revocability can be achieved by the prominent mechanism of certificate revocation lists (CRLs) and associated protocols. This requires an additional protocol to be run in order to obtain the latest revocation list.

With respect to the privacy requirements, verifiability holds as a user can inspect the certificate and thus has control over the attribute information being revealed. Conditional release cannot be realized in the setting in which the protocols operate, as an IdP is not involved in the transactions. Technically, of course, protocols could be conceived that involve the IdP in a transaction to obtain the conditional release property, but by discussing this we would leave the basic paradigm of the system.

---

[5]http://en.wikipedia.org/wiki/X.509.

Selective disclosure is not possible in a setting that uses standard certificates, as these certificates always have to be revealed as a whole and no subset of their attributes can be revealed because of the properties of the employed standard signature schemes like RSA or DSA. Finally, unlinkability may not be achievable in this setting. This is because transactions done with multiple IdPs, or multiple transactions with one IdP, are linkable, as the same certificate bit string is being provided in every transaction.

Limitations

The main problem with using standard user-side certificates is the lack of overall privacy properties, and thus the strong trust assumptions that we have to make on the relying parties. Assuming stronger trust in a relying party may not be realistic, relying parties may benefit from gathering extraneous users identity information. The U.S. National Institute of Science and Technology (NIST) has defined comprehensive criteria for understanding and evaluating identity management systems.[6] Those criteria demonstrate how the principles of identity management may be applied when evaluating identity management systems for purchase or use.

Identity Federation

There are several enterprise identity usages that require nonemployee accounts, business-to-business (B2B) interactions, and interaction and use of data from multiple applications that may exist across different networks. *Identity federation* is a term used when organizations form trust relationships whereby identities or assertions of an identity can be shared by all applications within the federation. It is critical that business partners involved in a federation build a trust relationship with one another. This trust relationship, defined by business, technical, and legal agreements, describes the applications that are involved, the user profile information that is to be shared, and the responsibilities of all parties to manage and protect user identities.[7]

Several standardization initiatives for identity federation are being developed across the world. Among them, Kantara Initiative (http://kantarainitiative.org/) and WS-Federation (http://en.wikipedia.org/wiki/WS-Federation) are two significant efforts. These initiatives define an identity federation framework that allows assurance-levels mapping for various service providers. For example, the Kantara Identity Assurance Accreditation and Certification Program assesses applicants against its assessment criteria, including alignment with the NIST 800-63 Levels of Assurance (http://csrc.nist.gov/publications/nistpubs/800-63/SP800-63V1_0_2.pdf) and it grants successful candidates of the program the right to use the Kantara Initiative Mark, a symbol of trustworthy identity and credential management services at specified assurance levels. It also collaborates with Open Identity Exchange (OIX) and other related initiatives to allow an interoperable digital trust framework to promote adoption of a robust online trust ecosystem. Similarly, WS-Federation was created with goal

---

[6]csrc.**nist**.gov/publications/**nist**pubs/800-63-1/**SP-800-63**-1.pdf.
[7]http://assets1.csc.com/cybersecurity/downloads/FIM_White_Paper_Identity_ Federation_Concepts.pdf.

of standardizing the way companies share principals and machine identities among disparate authentication and authorization systems that cross corporate boundaries. This translates to mechanisms and specifications that enable federation of identity attributes, authentication, and authorization information, but it does not include trust establishment and verification protocols.

The common objectives for federation proposals have been primarily to reduce the number of user-business interactions and exchanges of information such that critical private information is used only by appropriate parties. There is a need to ensure that user information is available to the SPs on demand, online and with low delay. Thus, user data is more up to date and consistent compared to the situation where each principal has to maintain its data in multiple places. Federations reduce costs and redundancy because the member organizations do not have to acquire, store, and maintain authorization information about all their partners' users. Also, both the federation initiatives try to preserve privacy, as only data required to use a service is transmitted to a business partner.

Single Sign-On

Single sign-on (SSO) improves security and usability. With SSO, user accounts and passwords are not reused across multiple sites or servers. SSO also improves usability by limiting the number of times the user must re-authenticate. Popular SSO systems include Kerberos, ActiveDirectory, SAML, and OpenID. The SSO systems work by converting the user authentication event into an access credential that is cryptographically protected. An access manager located at a remote server or within the same platform verifies the credential, rather than performing an authentication challenge with the user. The SSO credentials grant access for a period of time; that access is rescinded upon credential expiry. These systems make security and usability trade-offs that can be undesirable, however. If the credential timeout value is too long, malware can reuse the credential to prolong access that is otherwise unauthorized. If the timeout value is too short, the user must re-authenticate to continue the session.

An example of an SSO system is the McAfee Cloud SSO. It ensures that strong authentication is used for the customer's cloud-based software as a service (SaaS) applications, and helps allow SSO access to the cloud-based applications while complying with enterprise security policies. This solution is flexible and permits for an on-premises as well as SaaS-based solution, or both (hybrid model).

Intel Identity Technologies

Intel Corporation has developed several technologies useful for implementing identity management systems. Hardware support is often beneficial because it presents physical boundaries that can inhibit or prevent compromise of the identity management system by malware.

Hardware Support

Intel provides hardware support to enable hardened identity technologies on Intel platforms. Some basic underlying capabilities as of 2013 are as follows.

Virtualization Technology (VT)

Intel's Virtualization Technology (VT; see Figure 7-4) creates an additional layer of protection between physical memory and devices beneath the operating system.[8] Virtualization can be used as a security mechanism by isolating the operating system and applications from hardware using a small, and therefore well-understood software layer, that's also known as the hypervisor, ensures that hardware access follows some prescribed rules of behavior. The hypervisor implements a security policy designed to protect the integrity of information in memory, in peripheral devices, and in the CPU.

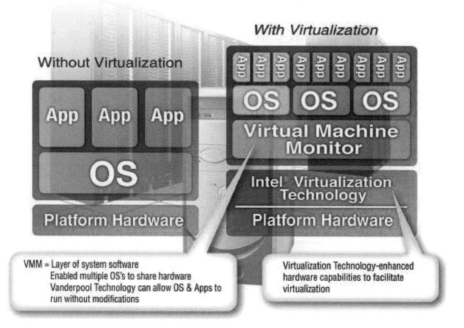

Figure 7-4. *Intel Virtualization Technology*

Intel Identity Protection Technology (IPT)

Intel's Identity Protection Technology (IPT; see Figure 7-5) consists of several credentialing and credential management capabilities for client platforms.[9] They are implemented in a security engine in hardware and offer an additional layer of security hardening and isolation from malware.

---

[8]For information about Intel Virtualization Technology, http://ark.intel.com/products/ virtualizationtechnology.

[9]http://www.intel.com/content/www/us/en/architecture-and-technology/identity- protection/identity-protection-technology-general.html.

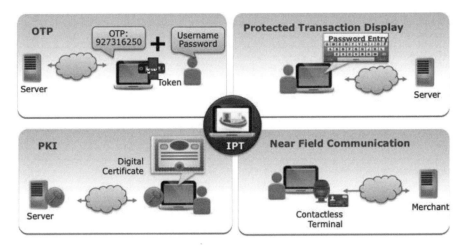

Figure 7-5. *Intel Identity Protection Technology*

- **IPT-OTP.** One-time passwords are single-use identifiers that cannot be anticipated or replayed by an attacker. Typically, the user and service provider agree to use a common "seed" from which a sequence of one-time passwords is generated. Keeping the seed secret is essential to security. IPT-OTP protects seeds in a hardware security engine.

- **IPT-PKI.** Public key infrastructure (PKI) is a set of hardware, software, people, policies, and procedures designed to create, manage, distribute, use, store, and revoke digital certificates.[10] Certificates are identity credentials that associate an asymmetric key[11] with an identifier. IPT-PKI is a cryptographic service provider that protects private asymmetric keys in a hardware security engine.

- **IPT-PTD.** In many cases, use of a credential requires user approval. Malware attacks that fake user approval may be a sufficient form of compromise to achieve the attacker's objective. IPT-PTD protects the output path between the hardware security engine and the graphics controller. Malware may not observe information displayed to a user. Protected output may be used to protect PIN input by rearranging a PIN pad display in a random order. When a user inputs the PIN using the randomized PIN pad, malware observing the mouse clicks cannot determine which (X,Y) coordinates map to which PIN digit. PINs are used by IPT-PKI and IPT-OTP to authorize use of a credential by a specific person.

---

[10]See Wikipedia, "Public Key Infrastructure." http://en.wikipedia.org/wiki/Public-key_infrastructure.

[11]See Wikipedia, "Public Key Cryptography." http://en.wikipedia.org/wiki/Public-key_cryptography.

- **IPT-DeviceID.** Use cases involving the computing platform when no user is present may require authentication. IPT-DeviceID associates a platform identifier with a credential. IPT-DeviceID protects the device credential in hardware.

Intel Security Engine

The security engine used to implement Intel's Identity Protection Technology has several capabilities that may be useful for enhanced privacy protections.

- **Enhanced Privacy ID (EPID).** The EPID is an asymmetric key provisioned at platform manufacturing time by Intel. It can be used to authenticate that an Intel platform security engine is performing a function securely. For example, the EPID key may be used to digitally sign the applet running on the security engine to prove its integrity and validity. EPID may also be used to prove an Intel security engine protects an IPT-PKI key. As the name suggests, EPID is privacy enhanced. This means the verifier can tell that the endpoint is an Intel security engine, but can't tell which one–even when the same platform returns a second time, the verifier can't correlate the second session with the first session.

- **Sigma.** The Intel security engine also implements a SIGn-and-MAc protocol (Sigma) based on a Diffie-Hellman key exchange that is signed using the EPID key. Sigma produces symmetric session keys for encryption and mac-ing of bulk data. Sigma allows a stream of data originating from the security engine to be transferred to a remote service provider. Sigma is useful for protecting logged event data, sensor input values, and configuring of policies.

The use of EPID and Sigma building blocks allows a client platform to interact securely without disclosing privacy sensitive information unnecessarily.

Intel's Manageability Engine (ME) implements security primitives for encryption, key exchange, and identity protection. It is integrated into Intel's chipsets. The ME (Figure 7-6) is isolated from the host operating environment and memory.

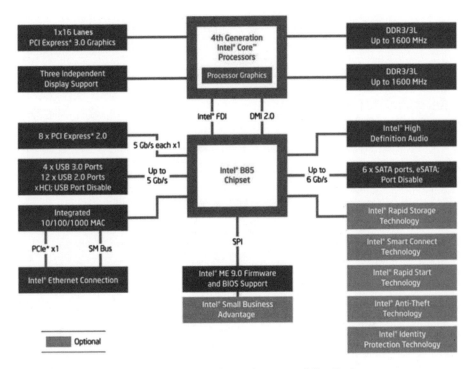

Figure 7-6. Intel B85 chipset containing the Intel Manageability Engine

Cloud Identity Solutions

Security services vendors such as McAfee provide a suite of security solutions for a wide range of enterprise and cloud-hosted services. Identity management is part of a comprehensive solution. Identity management services implement the credential lifecycle and ensure interoperability with a wide variety of services and applications.

The McAfee Cloud Ecosystem (see Figure 7-7) includes unified management, policy, reporting, and enterprise integration of pluggable security capabilities ranging from data loss prevention to web security. These capabilities are built upon an infrastructure that supports global threat intelligence monitoring and response, cloud-aware security, and enterprise-orchestrated policies. Such cloud-based security solutions offer dynamic protections that adjust as situational awareness changes. Cooperation among thousands of nodes participating in building a clearer picture of the threat landscape ensures that security incidents are processed and countermeasures are applied.

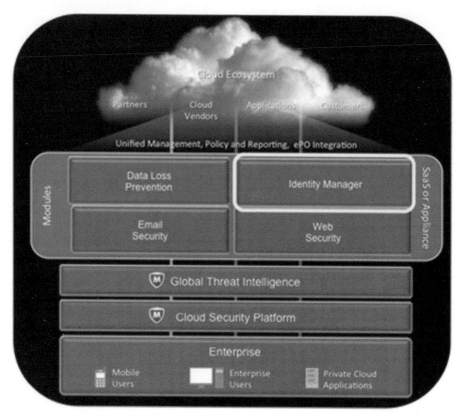

Figure 7-7. *McAfee cloud identity solution*

A cloud-based approach to security that includes identity management ensures that the known trusted users can be distinguished from the unknown and less trusted. Selection of a security services provider that implements such identity management comes with the implication that the provider is protecting the user's privacy in addition to ensuring computing security.

Summary

Identity management is an important component of a comprehensive cloud security infrastructure. This infrastructure must be rooted in sound identity management principles that not only ensure robust control of the identity credential lifecycle but also satisfies users' privacy desires. The identity management landscape is complicated by constant innovation and the evolution of authentication factor technology, identity credentials, and infrastructure investments. Complexity isn't necessarily good for security and privacy protection, but it appears to be an unavoidable reality. Taking the time to select a competent identity management provider can be an effective strategy for managing this complexity.

Computers that have deeply integrated identity protection technologies can be very effective in protecting user privacy and identity, while also delivering identity management solutions that interoperate with an already complex ecosystem of cloud services and that can promise continued support for an emerging Internet-of-things.

Identity management in the future holds many interesting challenges, especially when the Internet-of-things (IOT) is factored in.[12] The IOT promises Internet connectivity to a host of embedded systems, building automation control, smart appliances, and vehicles of all kinds. Technology advances make it practical to build wireless self-contained sensors that link directly to the Internet, feeding databases that analyze and infer new knowledge about the world. As people interact ever more widely with the world, sensors may be able to identify their unique properties using kinematics.[13] In an IOT world, devices will come equipped with device IDs to ensure they can be managed and controlled by authorized servers. They will have privacy-preserving capabilities that respect their user's right to privacy by filtering biometric data locally and translating it into digital credentials that more easily support credential lifecycle management.

In the next chapter, we focus on building and extending security, integrity, and confidentiality to applications and workloads that run in the cloud. As you would expect, the applications and workloads, which are typically packaged as virtual machines, anchor their integrity and trust in the chain of trust that is built with trusted compute pools and associated concepts and technologies that have been discussed in preceeding chapters.

---

[12]Intel adds Intelligence to Cloud for Internet of Things. http://iotinternetofthingsconference.com/2013/10/09/intel-adds-intelligence-to-cloud-for-internet-of-things/.
[13]See Wikipedia, "Gait Analysis Using Kinematics." http://en.wikipedia.org/wiki/Gait_analysis.

■ ■ ■

CHAPTER 8

Trusted Virtual Machines: Ensuring the Integrity of Virtual Machines in the Cloud

In Chapters 3 and 4, we described how a service provider can ensure that the infrastructure on which the workloads and applications are instantiated has boot integrity, and how these workloads can be placed in trusted pools with compute assets exhibiting demonstrated trust that is rooted in hardware. This model provides an excellent framework for a trusted compute infrastructure, but it's not sufficient for the cloud. Cloud data centers today almost invariably run virtualized. Stopping the chain of trust at the bare hypervisor is clearly insufficient; that is but the proverbial tip of the iceberg. Protection needs to be extended to support the multi-tenancy and virtualized networks of the cloud. Extending the chain of trust described to encompass these virtualized resources, embodied in the concept of *trusted virtual machines,* is what this chapter is about.

Critical concerns for cloud users are for protecting workloads and data *in* the cloud and *from* the cloud, and for ensuring trust and integrity for virtual machine images launched on a service provider's cloud. For virtual machine and workload data protection, cloud-user organizations need a method to securely place and use their workloads and data in the cloud.

Current provisioning and deployment models include either storing the virtual machine and application images and data in the clear—in other words, unencrypted—or having these images and data encrypted by the keys controlled by the service provider, which are likely applied uniformly to all the tenants. Increasingly, however, virtual machine images—effectively containers for operating system and application images, configuration files, data, and other entities—need confidentiality protection in a multi-tenant cloud environment. These images need to be encrypted by keys that the tenant controls, and that can be decrypted for provisioning by the keys also under tenant control, all done in a manner that's transparent to the cloud service provider.

Additionally, tenants would like the chain of trust and the boot integrity of these virtual machines assessed by the attestation authority in the infrastructure or the cloud before they are launched and begin participating on the network to satisfy service requests. With the tenant-controlled encryption and decryption, and integrity attestation of virtual machines, there can be clear security statements made about the confidentiality and protection of these application workloads in the cloud.

With interest in these topics driving cloud security considerations, Intel has reached out to the independent software vendor and cloud service provider community to develop a set of technology components and associated solutions architecture built on top of the trusted compute pools foundation to build proof points for these usage models. These are reference and prototype demonstrations that, it is hoped, will light a path to deployable solutions that address the concerns voiced above.

Requirements for Trusted Virtual Machines

Organizations are clearly leveraging the cost-saving (from capX reduction) and flexibility benefits of virtualizing their data centers, as opposed to the traditional deployment model in dedicated, corporate-owned infrastructure resources. The ease with which virtual machines can be created, deployed, and moved brings a multitude of security issues not present in those traditional, physical data centers, however. Protecting data and applications in traditional data centers is fairly well understood. In addition to security appliances and measures like firewalls, intrusion detection, intrusion prevention, anti-malware controls, encryption, access controls, monitoring, and logging, there are physical security measures like locked cabinets and cages, and these all go a long way toward defending sensitive data.

Software-defined virtualized data centers are very different, though. The unit of deployment is a virtual machine, and the entire lifecycle, connectivity, and storage associated with these virtual machines is defined, managed, monitored, and secured using software. The ability of virtual machines holding sensitive and confidential data to be easily moved or replicated in a matter of seconds requires special solutions and protections designed for virtual and cloud computing environments. Most Infrastructure as a Service (IaaS) providers either store the virtual machines in the clear—meaning no encryption—or encrypt them with keys that they control. This may be acceptable for some tenants, but most public or hybrid cloud tenants are concerned about leakage of data and sensitive information stored in some of these virtual machines. For example, insider threats at the service provider constitute legitimate concerns for organizations. Organizations are also concerned about the privacy of data running and processed in the virtual machines, and they must demonstrate the ability to measure and control risk, owing to the significant implications for meeting legal and fiduciary responsibilities.

Another essential aspect of the virtual machine lifecycle is decommissioning. A cloud service provider replicates virtual machines to multiple locations and availability zones as a matter of policy, ensuring later availability and for disaster recovery. While this allows service providers to comply with demanding SLAs, it raises security risks. Geographically dispersed copies of virtual machines can also proliferate sensitive data, credentials, and information, leaving it floating in the cloud. Additionally, a benefit end users get from cloud use is the ability to switch providers. Former customers need to be assured that they can make a clean break when they switch providers. This includes the ability to destroy any virtual machine and associated data left at the former provider, including backups. Most cloud service providers can't promise that, if only because in the current state of the art there are no standards for proving that disks and backup media are properly wiped before disposal or repair.

Standards organizations and compliance regulation bodies have started to acknowledge these needs for requirements. The Payment Card Industry (PCI) Standards Council recently released an information addendum to the latest data security standard (DSS) specification regarding vulnerabilities laid to virtualization, including exposure of personally identifiable information (PII) and credit card information residing in the virtual machines. The addendum also highlights vulnerabilities with regard to snapshot files and virtual machine backups. The dormant virtual machines in these backups can lie there for years, to be spun up anytime and anywhere, exposing the data and sensitive information.

Consequently, in addition to the encryption of application data, new PCI guidelines recommend encrypting virtual machine images with an operating system and applications with keys managed securely to reduce the footprint of any sensitive data left behind. Figure 8-1 illustrates the concept of tenant-controlled virtual machine encryption and decryption.

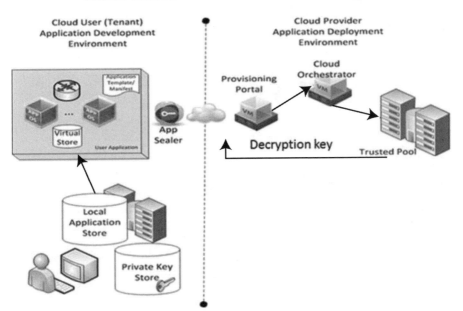

Figure 8-1. Tenant-controlled virtual machine encrytion and decryption

In addition to confidentiality protection, organizations would like to verify the integrity of virtual machines before launching them. For instance, if a hardened Linux virtual machine configuration is available, and a user wants it, the user will want a proof of this machine's being used. Doing so within the cloud model is harder than within a corporate-owned infrastructure, since the tenant organization doesn't own the infrastructure. A chain of trust rooted in hardware, with continuous monitoring of the integrity of infrastructure, the workloads, and virtual machines, can provide the assurance the organization wants.

All of this can be distilled into three key requirements that need to be in place to ensure integrity and confidentiality of these virtual machines in a virtual and cloud environment:

- ***Virtual machines must be launched on servers with provable boot integrity.*** The trusted compute pools usages, platform/host attestation, and geo-fencing solutions described in Chapters 3, 4, and 5 address this requirement. This is foundational.

- ***Virtual machine images must be encrypted in transit, at rest, and during execution.*** This is essential to preserve confidentiality and secrets. The keys are under the control of the tenant, and they are released (key policy management) to the service provider only when they provide attestation that the virtual machine images are being launched on trusted servers.

- ***Launch and provision only qualified and attested virtual machine images***. Virtual machines about to launch must attest their launch integrity with the infrastructure.

In the rest of the chapter we'll cover usages, a conceptual architecture, and a reference implementation that addresses requirements for service providers to offer protection of tenant payloads. Before we jump into details, though, we have to look at the basics of a virtual machine image to understand what needs to be encrypted and what needs to be measured and attested. We will look at the various virtual image formats and also consider virtual machine templates, a standard operating procedure for cloud operators to instantiate virtual machines.

Virtual Machine Images

Virtual machine images come in two different formats: *disk* and *container*. Hypervisor management tools accept both formats, and so do most of the cloud management platforms. However, as of this writing, the OpenStack Image Service (Glance) and other projects do not support the container format. It is possible, however, to associate metadata with images using OpenStack Image Service properties (key/value pairs).

The *disk format* of a virtual machine image is the format of the underlying disk image. Virtual machines can have different formats for laying out the information contained in a virtual machine disk image, as outlined in Table 8-1.

Table 8-1. *Virtual Disk Image Formats*

Type	Description
raw	An unstructured disk image format
vhd	VHD, a common disk format used by virtual machine monitors from VMWare, Xen, Linux/KVM, Microsoft, VirtualBox, and others
vmdk	Common disk format supported by many common virtual machine monitors
vdi	Format supported by VirtualBox virtual machine monitor and the QEMU emulator
ISO	An archive format for the data contents of an optical disc, such as CD-ROM
qcow2	Format supported by the QEMU emulator that can expand dynamically and that supports Copy on Write
AKI	An Amazon kernel image (as used in Amazon Web Services EC2)
ARI	Amazon ramdisk image
AMI	Amazon machine image

A *container format* indicates whether the virtual machine image is in a file format that also contains metadata about the actual virtual machine. The container format for a virtual machine image is a self-contained package with two items:

- Metadata about the virtual machine.

- One or more virtual disks containing the operating system, applications and data. The virtual disk is on the formats as described above.

The image by itself can be a representation of one virtual machine image or could be a composition of multiple related virtual machine images pertaining to a multi-tier service or distributed application workload.

Let's look at the details of the image components. The metadata included in the virtual machine image includes specific information about the operation information about the virtual machines, including:

- Metadata describing server resources needed to run the image: number of CPUs, either dedicated or shared, and memory requirements for the workloads running in the virtual machine.

- Metadata articulating the goals and constraints. This comprehends performance and availability goals and any placement constraints, such as security isolation.

- Metadata describing virtual machine configuration variables like IP addresses and application configuration parameters.

- Metadata describing the package integrity, like SHA1/SHA2 hashes of the virtual disks and modules.

Virtualization management software uses metadata information to create the right type of virtual machine container with the required platform resources. Once the virtual disk image, built as a bootable image, is copied and made accessible to the physical host system, the virtual machine is started from the bootable disk image.

The Open Virtualization Format (OVF)

Virtual machine images can be assembled and delivered in many ways. To ensure interoperability of virtual machines and seamless deployment and management across virtualization platforms, standardization of the virtual machine distribution format is essential. That is exactly what Open Virtualization Format (OVF) is. OVF is a hypervisor agnostic virtual machine packaging and distribution format, standardized by the Distributed Management Task Force (DMTF). It provides a complete description of a single virtual machine or a complex multi-virtual machine software solution package. It is extensible so that DMTF or third parties can add features and extensions to it. OVF goes beyond just the description and virtual hardware attributes.

Open Virtualization Format allows a virtual appliance/ISV vendor to add items like a EULA, comments about the virtual machine, boot parameters, minimum requirements, and a host of other features. OVF specification calls for an OVF descriptor, typically called the OVF envelope, which is an XML file describing the software in the OVF package. The OVF descriptor has ten core sections for metadata, such as the virtual hardware, EULA, product information, and so on. In order to support the extensibility, the OVF specification provides *extension points*. These custom extension points may be used to specify items such as multiple networks, specific firewalls, firewall rules required for the virtual machines, and the setup of a load balancer for multiple instances of virtual machines. A virtual machine author can describe in "levels" the conformance to the OVF specification as part of the OVF envelope. Level 1 indicates that there are no custom extensions, Level 2 indicates that there are custom extensions but they are optional, and Level 3 indicates that the custom extensions are required. This information helps the deployer to figure out the appropriate set of virtualization environments to deploy the virtual machines.

Intel has been working with the industry to deliver a solution architecture and implementations that address security requirements in virtualized environments. The usage models are called *trusted virtual machines* and are code-named *Mystery Hill* (abbreviated MH). The usage models cover the tenant-controlled encryption of virtual machines with tenant-controlled key management , decryption of the virtual machine images and data on servers or hosts with attested integrity and hardware roots of trust, and the attestation of the virtual machines prior to their launch. In this section, we discuss a reference architecture, with details about the key components of the architecture and the workflow. Following this, we present a reference implementation in the OpenStack cloud environment.

A Conceptual Architecture for Trusted Virtual Machines

Figure 8-2 shows the conceptual architecture for trusted virtual machines. There are four key elements needed to enable the usages described in the previous sections:

1. Mystery Hill (MH) client

2. MH key management and policy server (KMS)

3. MH plug-in that runs on the host or server

4. Mt. Wilson trust attestation server technology

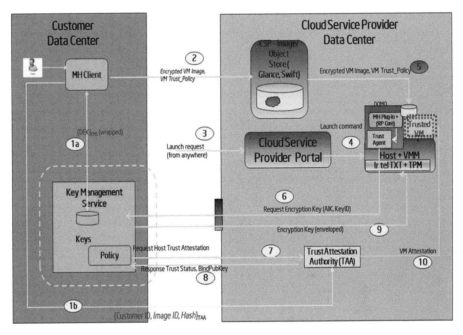

Figure 8-2. *Conceptual architecture for trusted virtual machines*

The conceptual architecture calls for loosely coupled components with well-defined APIs and interfaces. Let's look at each of these in detail.

Mystery Hill (MH) Client

The Mystery Hill (MH) client is an application that runs under tenant or organization control and that carries many functions. It is the primary mechanism by which the service owner (tenant) encrypts the virtual machine images, generates the module manifest for the VMs (list of all files that need to be measured and verified), generates SHA-1/SHA-2 hash values of the modules (whitelist), and specifies the VM trust policies. The MH client interfaces with the key management server (KMS), which is assumed to be a service under tenant or organization control. The MH client also interfaces with the cloud management software, such as Amazon AWS EC2 or OpenStack, to be able to upload the encrypted virtual machine images and the meta-data onto the image server for provisioning and launch.

The VM payload includes one or more encrypted virtual machine images and the metadata. The metadata contains:

- Module manifest and hash of the modules, signed by the trust authority (like Mt. Wilson)

- Key ID (data encryption key ID) to determine the decryption key in the KMS store

- URL for the KMS from where the decryption key can be obtained

- VM trust launch policies

We will cover the trust launch policies in a later section. The MH client generates a new symmetric encryption key for each VM that is being encrypted, wraps the symmetric key using an asymmetric key (provided by the KMS), and posts the wrapped key to the KMS. The metadata is stored in either the OVF envelope for the virtual machine (if the container format of virtual machine image is used) or as additional attributes or properties of the image server (for disk-based virtual machine image formats). Figure 8-3 shows the OVF envelope with the metadata extensions.

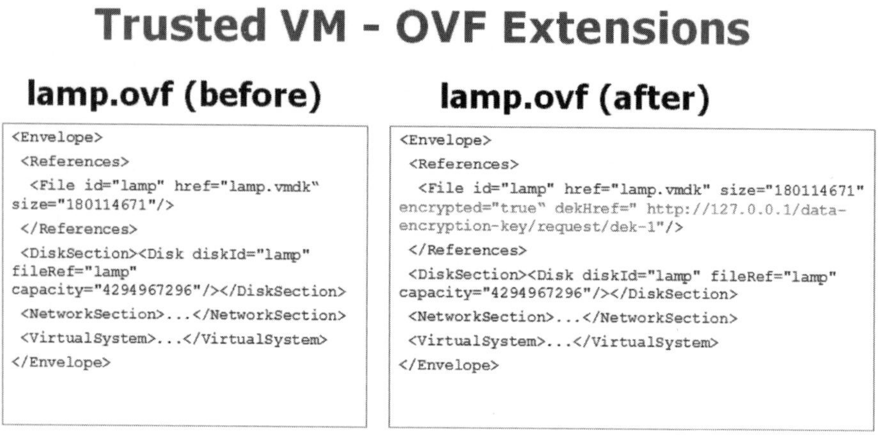

Trusted VM - OVF Extensions

lamp.ovf (before)

```
<Envelope>
 <References>
  <File id="lamp" href="lamp.vmdk"
size="180114671"/>
 </References>
 <DiskSection><Disk diskId="lamp"
fileRef="lamp"
capacity="4294967296"/></DiskSection>
 <NetworkSection>...</NetworkSection>
 <VirtualSystem>...</VirtualSystem>
</Envelope>
```

lamp.ovf (after)

```
<Envelope>
 <References>
  <File id="lamp" href="lamp.vmdk" size="180114671"
encrypted="true" dekHref=" http://127.0.0.1/data-
encryption-key/request/dek-1"/>
 </References>
 <DiskSection><Disk diskId="lamp" fileRef="lamp"
capacity="4294967296"/></DiskSection>
 <NetworkSection>...</NetworkSection>
 <VirtualSystem>...</VirtualSystem>
</Envelope>
```

Figure 8-3. OVF extensions for VM encryption

Mystery Hill Key Management and Policy Server (KMS)

The Mystery Hill key management and policy server (KMS) is the core key generation and management service, designed to allow control of key generation and management functions by the tenant organization. It provides the standard web services interface for generating the keys and delivering those keys to the MH client after successful authentication, to allow an MH client to encrypt virtual machine images. It also provides the decryption key URLs to the MH client to be included in the OVF envelopes. We recommend for the KMS to use a hardware security module (HSM) for the generation, storage, and processing of the keys. The second function of the key management and policy server is to evaluate trust policies before decryption keys are handed to the requesting entity. The trust policies can include user roles, license verification, application certification, server or host platform integrity and attestation, and geolocation or geo-fencing policies, as well as network attributes.

Mystery Hill Plug-in

The Mystery Hill plug-in is a set of two components that reside and run with the hypervisor on the host/server on which the virtual machines are being deployed. These components are:

- *MH Agent.* Part of the platform trust computing base (TCB), it performs the functions for decryption of the tenant virtual machines and integrates with the virtualization and cloud management environment. In OpenStack environments, the MH agent integrates with the Nova compute node service to intercept encrypted virtual machine launch requests to the hypervisor, obtains the decryption key from the MH key management service after the server or node attests to its integrity with a trust attestation authority, and decrypts the virtual machine images. It provides local (and transparent) encryption of the decrypted VM images on the compute node disk prior to the launch, so they are not in the clear, even for a short time prior to launch.

- *MH Measuring and Quoting Agent.* This component, also part of the platform TCB, measures the virtual machine images, verifies the measurements against the whitelist, and also provides a Quote-analogous to the TPMQuote, which is rooted to the physical TPM on the server. The measuring agent runs with the hypervisor on a host server and measures the VM images, per the manifest sent as part of the VM payload metadata. The MH quoting agent has the primitives to Quote, Seal, and Attest. Based on the VM trust policies, once the measurement and attestation of the VM image is completed, the decrypted image is passed on to the hypervisor to continue the normal launch sequence.

Encrypted virtual machine requests are identified using attributes present in an OVF envelope, similar to what is shown in Figure 8-3. The attributes indicate that the VM image is encrypted and show a URL where the decryption key can be obtained. The URL points to the KMS. When the MH plug-in requests the decryption key from the KMS, it provides the compute node's attestation identity key, to request an attestation from Mt. Wilson. The section "Workflows for Trusted Virtual Machines" below describes the complete process.

■ **Note**   The MH measuring agent could get complex, owing to the various virtual machine formats that would need to be comprehended. This would increase the TCB significantly. It is possible to migrate the measuring agent outside the TCB but still ensure its integrity. One way to accomplish this is to keep a hash of the measuring agent as part of the TCB, and to measure/attest the measuring agent before it is launched to perform the measurement of the VM image.

Trust Attestation Server

The trust attestation server is the attestation authority monitoring the compute nodes in the trusted data center, as described in detail in Chapter 4 and shown in Figure 8-4. The attestation server maintains the trust policy for every attested host and evaluates reports from the hardware roots of trust on each node to determine if each node is in compliance with its trust policy. The attestation server tracks the attestation identity key (AIK), public key, and an encryption public key for each compute node, among other information. When the KMS requests an attestation of a compute node that in turn requests a decryption key for an encrypted virtual machine, the MH key management server provides the AIK public key to the attestation server in order to uniquely identify the compute node to attest. The attestation server identifies the compute node to attest based on the provided AIK public key and returns the result to the KMS.

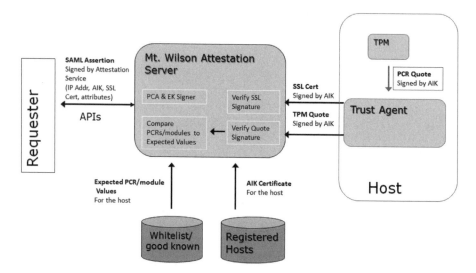

Figure 8-4. *Attestation architecture*

Workflows for Trusted Virtual Machines

Figure 8-5 shows the flow of encryption, decryption, and launch of the virtual machines according to the conceptual architecture. The workflow builds upon the foundation established by the trusted compute pools to support virtualized cloud environments, adding the concept of trusted virtual machines. This is how the security capabilities and benefits of trusted compute pools are extended and become usable in virtualized cloud environments. Note that the elements in the workflow can be implemented in a distributed and scalable fashion under the cloud paradigm, in which Mt. Wilson and the KMS can be delivered through a PaaS provider, the cloud service provider and the hosts with Intel TXT are IaaS instances, and the cloud storage is a SaaS instance. There are nine steps involved in this workflow, noted as follows:

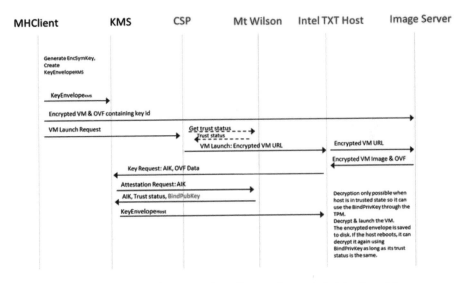

Figure 8-5. *Encryption and decryption flow diagram for trusted virtual machines*

Step 1: The launch of an encrypted virtual machine begins with creating an encryption key. The MH client can automatically generate new encryption keys as needed. Users have the flexibility of using the same key multiple times to protect different virtual machine images, or to create a new key for every virtual machine image. Every key that the MH client generates is wrapped and posted to the KMS so that it can later be retrieved for decryption. The corresponding key URL, provided by the KMS when the encryption key was wrapped and posted, is also stored by the MH client.

Step 2: This involves selection of an encryption key and a plaintext virtual machine image, and subsequent encryption with the key. The encrypted virtual machine image can then be uploaded to servers in the data center. See the upper arrow to "Cloud Storage" in the flow diagram. The MH client attaches metadata to the virtual machine image—in particular for this case, the URL identifying the encryption key.

Step 3: Once the encrypted virtual machine image and associated metadata are posted in the cloud, the virtual machine can be launched using the cloud service provider's existing mechanism for launching virtual machine workloads. This is noted in the diagram as "VM Launch Request."

Step 4: Cloud service providers featuring trusted compute pools can query the trust status of a compute node and ensure that it is trusted before sending a new workload to it. This check is performed by sending an attestation request to the attestation server and inspecting the result. After identifying an available trusted compute node, the cloud service provider sends a launch request to that compute node with the encrypted virtual machine image information. The launch request includes the image metadata, image download URL, and decryption key URL. At this point, if the compute node does not have the MH plug-in, or has not been enabled with Intel TXT and registered with the attestation server, it will not be able to continue with the launch. The system prevents the encrypted image from even reaching the hypervisor.

Step 5: An Intel TXT-enabled trusted compute node with the MH plug-in can detect that the VM image is encrypted by examining the metadata or the OVF plug-in. The MH plug-in connects to the decryption key URL and sends the compute node's AIK public key to that URL to identify the compute node that is requesting the decryption key. The URL points to the KMS, which already has the decryption key, wrapped by MH client.

Step 6: The attestation server looks up the compute node details using the AIK public key, obtains a TPM quote from the compute node, and verifies the compute node's state against its trust policy. The result is reported back to the KMS. In addition, if the attestation server determines the compute node complies with its trust policy, the attestation server will then provide an asymmetric encryption public key for the compute node to the KMS, noted in the diagram as "BindPubKey."

Step 7: The KMS, upon receiving a favorable trust report on the compute node from the attestation server, wraps the requested decryption key and sends it back to the compute node. The key wrapping is done using the public key of the compute node, as provided by the attestation server. The compute node has the corresponding private key. It's possible to bind the private key to the TPM on the compute node such that it can be used only if the host complies with its trust policy.

Steps 8, 9, and 10: The compute node unwraps the decryption key with the TPM, decrypts the encrypted VM, and as an additional step, can measure the virtual machine image and attest with the trust attestation authority before handing control to the compute node to proceed with the launch as usual.

As seen from this flow, the virtual machine image is protected at rest, in motion, and up until execution with protection under tenant control. The decryption keys are released only when the cloud service provider can demonstrate the integrity of the server on which the virtual machine is being provisioned.

Deploying Trusted Virtual Machines with OpenStack

Here, we document a reference implementation constructed to demonstrate trusted virtual machine usages with OpenStack. This proof point provides an opportunity to highlight the finer points of an actual implementation, allowing a more accurate evaluation of the value proposition, its applicability, and its usability. The reference implementation has been demonstrated at a number of industry-wide security conferences, including the OpenStack Summit, with excellent reviews. We expect the independent software vendor and cloud service provider community to scale production implementations of this usage to their own infrastructures—and ultimately to their service offerings—so as to offer a soup-to-nuts chain of trust, running from cloud service offerings all the way down the layers to the underlying host hardware. This implementation is an instantiation of the workflow described in the previous section.

Figure 8-6 shows the reference implementation in OpenStack. It works with OpenStack environments using either KVM or Xen hypervisors. A set of screenshots of the implementation follows, illustrating the flow and the process of integration into OpenStack.

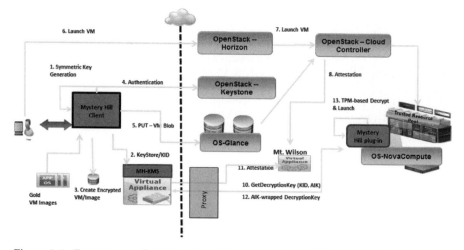

Figure 8-6. *Tenant-controlled virtual machine encryption and decryption with trusted launch in OpenStack*

As shown in Figure 8-6, the process begins with creating the encryption keys to be applied to the virtual machine images. The goal is to implement a secure process under tenant control. The tenant or the service consumer, perhaps DevOps staff, uses the MH client to create keys, store them in the KMS, and encrypt the virtual machine images. In OpenStack, a virtual machine image is assumed to be in disk image format, ISO, vmdk, xva, or vhd. Although it is possible to upload encrypted virtual machine images manually to OpenStack Glance image service, and to use the Glance client to add the encryption metadata, it is far more convenient to let the MH client upload the encrypted virtual machine image and add the encryption flag and decryption key URL to the Glance image metadata using the Glance APIs.

As can be seen in Figure 8-7, there are two steps before an encrypted virtual machine can be uploaded to OpenStack Glance. First, either an existing key is selected or a new key is generated to use for encryption. The new key interfaces with the KMS. (For the reference implementation, no HSM was used with the KMS.) The KMS returns the URL and a decryption key ID (DKID) to be associated with the encrypted target virtual machine. Second, a virtual macine image to encrypt is selected and encrypted using the key just selected or generated. Third, the encrypted VM image is uploaded along with its encryption metadata to Glance, using the Glance client to upload the image and set its metadata in Glance.

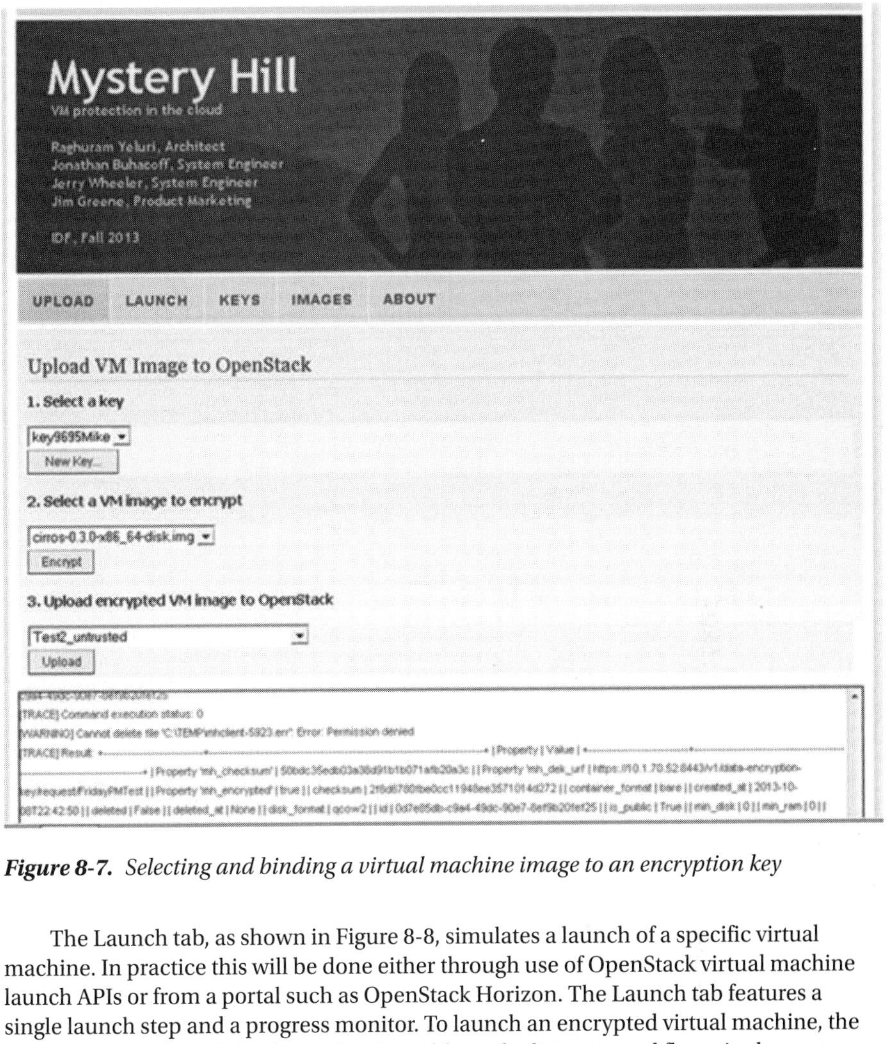

Figure 8-7. Selecting and binding a virtual machine image to an encryption key

The Launch tab, as shown in Figure 8-8, simulates a launch of a specific virtual machine. In practice this will be done either through use of OpenStack virtual machine launch APIs or from a portal such as OpenStack Horizon. The Launch tab features a single launch step and a progress monitor. To launch an encrypted virtual machine, the encrypted virtual machine image is selected from the list, a trusted flavor is chosen to use for the virtual machine instance, and the Launch button is clicked. The MH client reference implementation conveniently preselects the last virtual machine image encrypted in the Upload tab. The flavor list is downloaded from Nova Controller and reflects the same list as is available in the Horizon dashboard.

VM protection in the cloud

Raghuram Yeluri, Architect
Jonathan Buhacoff, System Engineer
Jerry Wheeler, System Engineer
Jim Greene, Product Marketing

IDF, Fall 2013

UPLOAD   LAUNCH   KEYS   IMAGES   ABOUT

Launch a VM Image in OpenStack

Test2_untrusted ▼   m1.tiny.trusted ▼

Launch   Stop   Clear

✓ OpenStack - Initiated launch FMSMYTXT-node2   Tue Oct 8 00:00:00 PDT 2013
✓ Agent - Received VM launch request   Tue Oct 8 15:46:06 PDT 2013
✓ Agent - Detect VM is encrypted   Tue Oct 8 15:46:00 PDT 2013
✓ Agent - Request DEK   Tue Oct 8 15:46:00 PDT 2013
✓ KMS - Received DEK request   Tue Oct 8 15:46:04 PDT 2013
✓ KMS - Request attestation from Mt Wilson   Tue Oct 8 15:46:00 PDT 2013
✓ KMS - Received attestation from Mt Wilson   Tue Oct 8 15:46:14 PDT 2013
✓ KMS - Host is trusted   Tue Oct 8 15:46:14 PDT 2013
✓ KMS - Sending DEK to host (only if trusted)   Tue Oct 8 15:46:14 PDT 2013
✓ Agent - Received DEK   Tue Oct 8 15:46:17 PDT 2013
✓ Agent - Decrypting VM image   Tue Oct 8 15:46:17 PDT 2013
✓ Agent - Launching VM   Tue Oct 8 15:46:17 PDT 2013
✓ OpenStack - Open VNC window   Tue Oct 8 15:46:17 PDT 2013   info VNC

```
[DEBUG] update launch status, event name = AGENT_REQUEST_DEK date: 1381272366000
[DEBUG] update launch status, event name = KMS_DEK_REQUEST date: 1381272364000
[DEBUG] update launch status, event name = KMS_REQUEST_ATTESTATION date: 1381272366000
[DEBUG] update launch status, event name = KMS_RECEIVE_ATTESTATION date: 1381272374000
[DEBUG] update launch status, event name = KMS_HOST_TRUSTED date: 1381272374000
[DEBUG] update launch status, event name = KMS_REPLY_DEK date: 1381272374000
[DEBUG] update launch status, event name = AGENT_RECEIVE_DEK date: 1381272377000
[DEBUG] update launch status, event name = AGENT_DECRYPT_IMAGE date: 1381272377000
[DEBUG] update launch status, event name = AGENT_LAUNCH_VM date: 1381272377000
[DEBUG] update launch status, event name = OPENSTACK_VNC_READY date: 1381272377000
```

Figure 8-8. *Launching a virtual machine image*

■ **Note**   Trusted compute pools (TCP) function, as described in chapter 3, has been implemented in OpenStack as scheduler filters. These extensions, and the Horizon dashboard and API extensions to tag Flavors with trustpolicies, have been part of OpenStack since the Folsom release.

In the screenshot of the Launch tab, the selected flavor is m1.tiny.trusted, which in the reference implementation refers to a single virtual CPU, with 512 MB of memory, no extra disks, and a trust requirement from the attestation server. When a virtual image is launched with a trusted flavor, the trust scheduler in OpenStack Nova queries the attestation server for the trust status of available compute nodes and only selects trusted compute nodes for launching the virtual machine instance. When the Launch button in the Launch tab is clicked, the MH client uses the Nova client to request a launch of the selected encrypted virtual machine image using the selected flavor. The trust scheduler selects a trusted compute node and initiates a launch of the virtual machine image instance on that compute node.

The reference implementation integrates MH plug-in with the Nova compute node for KVM and Xen hypervisors. On KVM, the MH plug-in integrates with the *libvirt* driver (`driver.py`) on the compute node to intercept the launch request of an encrypted image, request the decryption key, and decrypt the image. On Xen, the MH plug-in integrates with the `xapi.d` plug-in for Glance (in *dom0*) to perform the same actions, but integrates the decryption into the image stream downloaded from Citrix into the Xen hypervisor's work area.

When the MH plug-in requests the decryption key from the KMS, it sends an HTTP POST request to the decryption key URL noted in the image metadata. The body of the POST request is simply the AIK public key of the compute node. On KVM nodes, the AIK public key is managed by the trust agent, an additional component required for the attestation server. On Xen nodes, the AIK public key is managed by the Xen API performing the same functions as the trust agent.

The KMS forwards the AIK public key to the attestation server to obtain a report on that compute node. If the compute node is trusted, the report includes a public key that can be used for wrapping keys to be sent to the compute node. The corresponding private key is bound to the TPM on the compute node. The KMS wraps the decryption key using the compute node's public key and sends it to the compute node. This mechanism ensures that the key can be unwrapped only by the compute node that was reported as trusted by the attestation server. This enables some flexibility on the part of the cloud service provider to anonymize, proxy, aggregate, or otherwise manage the decryption key requests without the risk of leaking the decryption key to any intermediate network node.

The MH plug-in receives and unwraps the decryption key, uses it to decrypt the encrypted VM image, measures the virtual machine image with additional primitives in DOM0, and attests to it with the attestation server. The attestation report from the attestation server indicates whether it can be launched. If so, the virtual machine launch continues as usual. In this reference implementation, the sequence of steps is reflected in the checkboxes on the Launch tab.

Summary

Building on the foundation of trusted compute pools, the concept of trusted virtual machines extends the chain of trust in the cloud computing environment to cover guest virtual machines and associated workloads. In this chapter we covered what trusted virtual machines mean, how a tenant can control the encryption and decryption keys, and how to protect the confidentiality and integrity of the virtual machines in transit, at rest, and up to execution, using encryption and decryption and other policy implementation techniques. We presented a reference architecture for realizing the vision of trusted virtual machines, and also reviewed a reference implementation of that architecture as it appears in OpenStack. Clearly, this implementation is very early in the industry's process for realizing the full vision of trusted virtual machines. The need is there: users are demanding cloud providers to offer security for their virtual machines, while permitting cloud customers to retain control over encryption keys. They would also like to see decryption keys released only when the service provider can demonstrate the integrity of the compute nodes on which the virtual machines are going to be deployed and launched. The model for trusted virtual machines showed how it is possible to bind decryption of the keys to the TPM on a server that has demonstrated integrity. This ensures that the virtual machine is decrypted only inside the trusted server and not anywhere else.

Intel has started to work with the community of independent software vendors and cloud service providers to develop the solutions that bring trusted virtual machine usages and associated technical architecture to scalable and production-ready offerings that can be used with private, public, and hybrid cloud deployments. Chapter 9 brings together all the concepts, usages, and technologies that we have reviewed in the first eight chapters, via a compelling usage model called "Secure Cloud Bursting."

CHAPTER 9

■ ■ ■

A Reference Design for Secure Cloud Bursting

In this chapter we'll see how the concepts covered individually in the previous chapters relate to each other. We have been looking at the many concepts and components of the technology solutions needed to enable the trusted infrastructure that moves us toward the goal of delivering trusted clouds. We have covered the foundational elements of platform trust attestation, network virtualization security, and identity management in the cloud. In this chapter, we put all these elements together. Virtustream, a key Intel partner, took a proof of concept implementation, originally developed with Intel, for a key customer and evolved it into a new capability to enable *secure cloud bursting* that is available to all Virtustream customers. We'll explain the nature of this new capability and examine the architecture and reference design for this capability in the next few pages.

Virtustream, then, is a cloud service provider and a cloud management software vendor at the forefront of private and public cloud deployments. Virtustream's flagship cloud management software is xStream. (See sidebar for an overview of Virtustream xStream.) The proof of concept project was designed to demonstrate application workload mobility and "bursting" capabilities between a customer's primary IT facilities and its geographically disperse data centers and application profiles, while simultaneously ensuring policy, security, and performance controls. In addition to addressing the networking, identity management, and cross–data center orchestration, this project validated Intel's TXT as a foundational technology to enable the critical secure cloud bursting features supported by the Virtustream platform.

This infrastructure reference design is a way to highlight the essential elements for secure hybrid cloud services. Virtustream is the first such example in the industry to provide a robust, secure, and elastic cloud management service, intended for managing and controlling bursting and the orchestration of workloads on the virtualization platforms at multiple sites under control by multiple providers. This new reference design addresses the demanding requirements from cloud customers related to personally identifiable information (PII), location enforcement, auditability, infrastructure security, network security, application bandwidth, and service levels and performance.

Cloud Bursting Usage Models

New cloud computing clients envision an application computing environment in which computing capacity can be expanded by what has been termed *cloud bursting*, or switching critical application loads from facilities within a company's headquarters to geographically disperse data centers as demand requires.

An Explanation of Cloud Bursting

Figure 9-1 depicts the basic principles of cloud bursting and how it operates. This technology enables virtualized data centers to expose their excess capacity to other virtual data centers. It enables collaboration in a federated cloud that allows partners to offer capacity and move workloads or parts of workloads on demand between each other, all without compromising security and operational related SLAs.

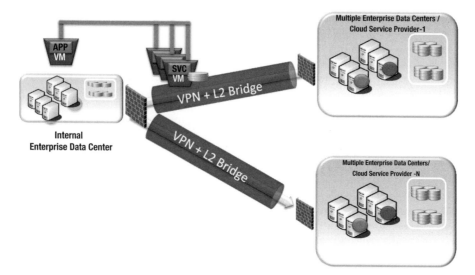

Figure 9-1. *The structure and operation of cloud bursting capability*

With cloud bursting capability, it becomes possible to deploy all or some application components, packaged as virtual machines, that normally run on traditional corporate resources, transferring them to one or more data centers that host pooled resources. This allows enterprises to respond to spikes in demand, to enhance business continuity, manage capacity, and optimize cost. Hence, the general premise of cloud bursting is to use the cloud as an overflow resource—for example, in the event an organization's base infrastructure becomes overloaded. A reduction in total cost of ownership may be possible with this overflow model if extra capacity is needed on a seasonal basis or for only a few minutes per day, or to employ disaster recovery practices. Typical utilization rates for these usages are abysmally low—namely, a few minutes per day for workload peaking or in the unlikely event of a disaster-triggered outage. In contrast, expanding a data center to address those eventualities results in poor capital utilization for the enterprise.

In short, resource utilization should be a tactical, responsive, and transparent operation. Business outcomes for a data center are no longer measured in terms of glacial five-year planning cycles; they now measured as current operational conditions in responding to short-term business demand and they use real-world metrics, such as the quality of experience and service (QoS). Cloud bursting aligns the traditional safe enterprise computing model with that of cloud computing; in essence, it means "bursting" into the cloud when necessary or using the cloud when required temporarily. These practices have the potential of improving, by several orders of magnitude, the data center's agility and operational transparency, such as having server resources allocated in minutes instead of going through a six-month or year-long budgeting and procurement process.

Cloud bursting addresses three basic needs of an enterprise data center:

1. Companies need additional capacity to handle occasional demand spikes, lest they encounter unacceptable server utilization and application response times. Investing internally to handle peak loads leads to unused capacity and stranded investment. Most enterprises want to reduce capital expenditures to the extent that does not impact QoS.

2. Companies are hesitant to delegate all infrastructure to cloud computing providers, owing to serious security and stability concerns. Presently, cloud service providers are used for important but noncritical applications such as human resources and expense reporting. The organization's crown jewels currently need to run on corporate-hosted, dedicated infrastructure and are treated as premium applications, justifying the extra cost involved. Cloud bursting addresses those concerns about migrating workloads to cloud by providing a hybrid model, and the net effect is a reduction in the total cost of ownership.

3. Cloud bursting meets a need to migrate workloads from one cloud to another, based on resource consumption and performance. This involves network bandwidth, storage, management, security, among other considerations. In this scenario, bursting is not triggered by load overflow; rather, it is initiating by a need for workload migration to optimize the resource utilization.

Implementing a cloud bursting strategy brings with it a need for automation in the data center and capabilities to orchestrate the local and remote resources, as well as to globally enforce policies from a specified command point or entity. It requires enterprise service consumers to manage not only the deployment of applications and resources in the enterprise data centers but also those within the cloud platform of the cloud service provider, accomplished through a cloud API using the cloud service provider's self-service portal or by directly manipulating the hypervisor. For ultimate flexibility, operators will want to implement the cloud bursting across heterogeneous hypervisor environments. Doing so brings up issues of virtual machine interoperability.

The Open Data Center Alliance has carried out initial studies on this usage. All demand spikes on a virtualized enterprise data center infrastructure are not the same; the spikes come in different shapes and forms. Today, enterprises handle spikes through the one-size-fits-all approach of overprovisioning the infrastructure. But with cloud bursting, enterprises have another means for handling overflow capacity and delivering the same or better QoS. They get to take the money to the bank that otherwise would have been spent on addressing this occasional demand.

Architectural Considerations for Cloud Bursting

There are key architectural considerations for successfully deploying cloud bursting.

- *Security and isolation.* In the end-to-end view of this deployment model, security and isolattion are extremely critical. Enterprises would be hesitant to trust a third-party service provider to host applications or components thereof, and so they access the enterprise data either by reaching back into the enterprise through long pipelines or by caching the data at the service provider. Service providers need to prove they meet compliance and audit requirements as specified by the enterprise customer. In addition to the primary capability of facilitating migration and use of overflow capacity, they need to address to their customers' satisfaction the security for data in transit, in use, and at rest, as well as the implementation of access control mechanisms. For cloud bursting to be embraced, there needs to be bilateral trust between cloud data centers. The relevant technologies and security standards are still in their infancy at the time of this writing.

- *Network performance and data architecture.* Network latency and bandwidth are logical concerns for bursting applications to handle overflow capacity. The connectivity between the clouds looks like a horizontal hourglass; the Open Data Center Alliance speaks of this as the "trombonning" phenomenon. Even with the best WAN networks and WAN performance optimization, the throughput and latency can have significant impact on application performance. Also, the connectivity of choice for cloud bursting data centers is almost invariably a VPN connection with encryption, which adds to the latency. The challenge is to determine the best way to deal with the data that distributed applications require or generate. There are several strategies for dealing with cloud bursting, each with its different implications for cost, performance, and architecture. Some architectural remedies involve data cache in the overflow capacity and replication, and shadow databases in overflow capacity. It is not currently practical to send terabyte data sets over the wire, and the "sneakernet" approach of shipping data on physical media still makes the most sense. Reaching back to base, or replicating data in the overflow capacity, works best for applications with smaller data sets or for those not overly latency sensitive.

- ***Data locality and compliance.*** The current lack of transparency from cloud providers on the exact physical location of their data is such a significant concern that we dedicated Chapter 5 to the subject. As we saw earlier, there are country and regional constraints on how far and where the data can and cannot migrate. Depending on the type and kind of data processed by the cloud application, there might be legal restrictions on the location of a physical server where the data is stored. Missing is a simple API-based mechanism with cloud platforms to query the location of tenant data. The migration of workloads to a public cloud, even if the associated data doesn't move, increases the complexity associated with meeting legal and regulatory requirements for handling sensitive information. How can a service consumer be certain that the virtual machines instantiated in the overflow capacity at the service provider were shut down and the temporary storage securely wiped afterwards?

- ***Management and federation.*** This concept comprises the management, resource allocation, resource optimization, and lifecycle management between a virtualized data center and the overflow capacity in a remote data center. In short, cloud bursting can't be implemented without these logistical capabilities. The extent of interoperability across cloud platforms and the programmability of these platforms determine the extent to which an enterprise can utilize the uniform processes to manage resources. Cloud IaaS offerings are defined, developed, published, provisioned, and managed through the API from the service provider. These APIs must be standardized to enable hybrid cloud users to move workloads quickly and easily across different cloud service providers, without vendor lock-in. The current situation is far from ideal. A number of software tools are available from service providers to import workloads into their infrastructure. Understandably, the tools to migrate workloads *out* of their infrastures are much less available. Conflicts of interest might be avoided if there were third-party tools from independent software vendors. This won't happen until a modicum of API standardization takes place.

Data Center Deployment Models

All the existing cloud deployment models support the cloud bursting usage model. A key objective defined as part of the reference design architecture, then, includes the ability to deploy into and connect to remote data center cloud locations across wide area networks. Additionally, enterprise users expect to gain from the operational flexibility and cost reduction through competitive sourcing. There is the benefit of resource elasticity and response to changeable workload demand. For these workloads, a pay-as-you-go IT using cloud service providers is usually more economical. In this section, we do not deep dive into deployment model configurations. Instead, we focus on the model selected for the reference design architecture.

As indicated in Figure 9-2, there are multiple deployment models possible to support these objectives.

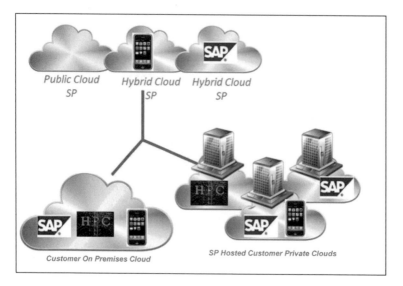

Figure 9-2. *Data center deployment models*

- Seamless and secure integration between geographically disperse customer data centers

- Private clouds on service provider data centers

- Trusted hybrid clouds—hybrid clouds on trusted service provider data centers

- Public clouds

Each model carries its advantages and drawbacks. A strong security foundation was a primary consideration for our reference design. This starts with trusted hardware as determined by hardware roots of trust and is validated using Intel TXT-capable and -enabled hardware. This allows the platform's integrity to be measured and audited on a near-real-time basis. Hence, the choice for our reference design is a trusted hybrid cloud.

Trusted Hybrid Clouds

Given the nature of malicious threats in today's environment and the stringent security requirements in many organizations, IT operations cannot unconditionally trust either their on-premise resources or their cloud service providers' execution environment.

184

Security is a fundamental consideration in server, storage, and network deployments, be it virtualized or bare metal. In a cloud deployment scenario, security needs to be supported and managed by both the service provider and the consumer tenant. This interaction leads to the concept of *trusted hybrid clouds*. Trusted hybrid clouds are built on the concept of hardware-enforced roots of trust. Our reference implementation uses Intel's Trusted Execution Technology (TXT) for this purpose, as well as to implement a real-time attestation capability for the trusted platform.

The proof of concept reference implementation deploys trusted execution environments to establish a root of trust. This root of trust is optimally compact, extremely difficult to defeat or subvert, and allows for flexibility and extensibility to measure platform components during the boot and launch of the environment, including BIOS, operating system loader, and virtual machine managers or VMMs. Chapters 3 and 4 covered the Intel TXT and the attestation process in detail.

As shown in Figure 9-3, the reference design comprehends the deployment model for trusted service provider data centers offering hybrid clouds. Under this model, the customer data center and the cloud service provider both deploy trusted execution environments. Policies and compliance activities using trusted platform attestation are required for enforcement of trust and security in the cloud.

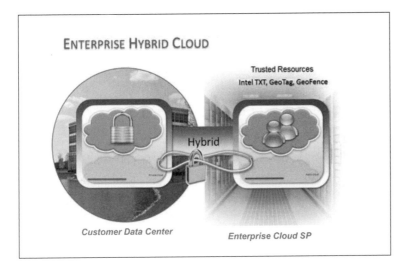

Figure 9-3. *Trusted hybrid clouds (SRC: Virtustream)*

Attestation and policy enforcement are managed by the cloud management layer and include the following.

- *Trusted resource pool,* relying on hardware-based secure technical measurement capability and trusted resource aggregation

- *Platform attestation and safe hypervisor launch,* providing integrity measurement and enforcement for the compute nodes

- *Trust-based secure migration,* offering geolocation measurement and enforcement (geo-fencing) for cloud trusted resource pools and associated compute nodes

- *Instantiation and provisioning of workloads,* operating in a trusted resource pool

- *Dynamic workload migration and API-based enforcement,* moving between trusted resource pools within and across geolocations

- *Visibility and transparency in real-time measurement,* regarding the reporting and auditing of the workloads to support governance, risk, and compliance requirements

- *Best practices for deploying a secure virtualized infrastructure,* following industry recommendations

The reference design demonstrates how an enterprise user workload application can burst into Intel TXT's attested secured resources, as well as prevent application loads from utilizing noncompliant resources under NIST 7904 draft recommended scenarios.

We cover details of the architecture next, with network topology considerations, followed by security considerations for the successful deployment of this reference design.

Cloud Bursting Reference Architecture

Figure 9-4 shows the solution architecture for this trusted hybrid cloud deployment. Site 1 ("Customer Site") represents an IT organization's primary private cloud, running Virtustream xStream cloud management software and managing resource pools of servers running VMWare ESXi. (See the sidebar for details on Virtustream xStream cloud management software.) As can be seen from the figure, there are two resource pools: Intel TXT-based resource pools for security sensitive workloads and non-TXT resource pools for regular workloads. A similar setup (as indicated by site 2, "Cloud Service Provider") is instantiated and maintained at a public cloud environment as well. The workloads from the private cloud (site 1) burst into the resource clusters at site 2. The xStream cloud management software seamlessly federates the identity, controls and configures resources and deployment of workloads, and is fully controlled, monitored, and managed from within the organizations xStream Management portal. To ensure that the management software is running on high-integrity infrastructure, as shown in Figure 9-4, the xStream software components are provisioned on Intel TXT-based trusted pools.

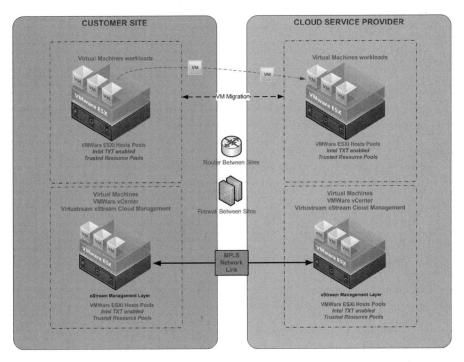

Figure 9-4. *Cloud bursting solution architecture (SRC: Virtustream)*

Here are the key components of the reference architecture, followed by a brief exposition of each:

- Secure environment built around best practices

- Cloud management, or cloud identity and access management

- Separation of cloud resources, traffic, and data

- Vulnerability and patch management

- Compliance, or security policy, enforcement, and reporting

- Security monitoring

Secure Environment Built Around Best Practices

Each computing platform component is built based on standard technical implementation guides (STIGs) from a reputable standards body; in this case, NIST via the NIST SP 800-70 National Checklist Program for IT Products. The cloud data center is built with the STIGs just cited, with multiple security ecosystem components utilizing a *defense in depth* methodology. The framework creates a multi-layered secure computing environment with a high degree of assurance in its security posture.

Cloud Management

Virtustream's xStream software provides management functions with a highly secure and user-friendly self-service cloud management, enabling cloud service provider tenants to move workloads around all the federated cloud service providers' data centers in an efficient and reliable manner. This approach enables cloud bursting and migration of workloads in a secure manner. It manages the resources, identity, access control, reporting, and management within the organization's data center, as well as the hybrid cloud resources in the service provider's data centers. The xStream software provides a very robust set of APIs for interfacing with all the services. API endpoints allow secure HTTP access (HTTPs) to establish secure communication sessions with Virtustream services using SSL.

Cloud Identity and Access Management

The cloud management platform utilizes the least privilege to execute on all operations to ensure that no one user has more than the required privileges to accomplish its respective management tasks in the cloud data center in a controlled manner. Each user carries unique security credentials, eliminating the need for shared passwords or keys and allowing the security best practices of role separation and least privilege.

Access to the cloud environment is denied unless explicitly granted. The default access methodology for all layers of computing are denied unless explicitly given access via an authorization policy managed by the cloud administrator. Custom, secure portals requires dual-factor authentication with role-based access. Identity management is accomplished utilizing LDAP/x.500 directory services with role-based access (RBAC) control and management.

Separation of Cloud Resources, Traffic, and Data

All tenants in the cloud have their related traffic, computing, network, and storage resource separated logically from each other in a reliable and consistent manner, attained by utilizing the xStream management and orchestration platform.

Secure network is segregated into physical zones based on the level of trust associated with the intended purpose, such as management, public DMZ, core, cloud platform, and backup. (There is more detail on the physical zone segregation is in the Network Topology and Considerations section.) Additionally, xStream allows adding another layer of network security to customer virtual machines by creating private subnets and even adding an IPsec VPN tunnel between the client's network and the third-party data center.

Vulnerability and Patch Management

Cloud vulnerability and patch management are handled in an automated method by the cloud service provider for all tenants wanting secure, trusted, and compliant computing. Logging under SIEM, intrusion detection, file integrity monitoring, content filtering, data leakage prevention, firewall audits, web application layer firewalling, and many other security processes need to be considered to ensure the security of the cloud provided.

Compliance

Security policies are defined in the orchestration portal during virtual machine provisioning. Here are some examples:

- *Trusted execution technology enforced policies*: A given virtual machine requires TXT-based boot integrity and attestation and should not be allowed to execute on unverified and non-attested hypervisors and platforms. Figure 9-5 shows how a policy gets set up using the xStream operational portal.

Figure 9-5. Enabling the trust policy

- *Geo-fencing policies*: This type of policy defines where a virtual machine and associated data are allowed to run. A geo-fence is a set of one or more physical locations and geographies for a physical data center, including possible locations within the physical data center down to a physical rack. For example, a VM can only run on physical machines running in a data center in the United States and Canada.

- *Data security policy*: Data center best practices dictate that sensitive, private, and confidential data in the cloud, including but not limited to PII data, must be protected with tokenization and/or encryption technology conformant with FIPS 140-2–level encryption technology. During provisioning, options to encrypt the provisioned disk of a virtual machine or even an entire virtual machine are available to a cloud administrator. Chapter 8 covered the notion of trusted VMs, including tenant-controlled encryption and decryption of virtual machines based on outstanding data security policies.

- *Compliance reporting*: All cloud audit logs and security-related posture data from vulnerabilities scans are correlated to their respective information assurance framework security controls and are maintained as continuous monitoring artifacts in a GRC information system to attest to the controls functioning as designed and in place for auditors to validate. The reference design calls for defining a small set of controls regarding virtual machine geolocation policies. These controls are evaluated on a continuous basis to assess compliance of workloads and data location regarding trust requirements. One example of a control is an authentication event occurring for a privileged user onto a sensitive compute virtual machine.

- *Security monitoring*: To ensure 24/7 continuous monitoring of the cloud environment, real-time security monitoring is built using enterprise class security information and event management (SIEM) tools. xStream SIEM (xSIEM) is used in the reference design to collect and correlate events from all components of the cloud systems. It is important to verify, on a continuing basis, the threat profile of the cloud environment and to provide visibility into the posture of the environment in a continuous real-time manner to the cloud's security operations team and tenant customers. By monitoring the cloud infrastructure with a SIEM, security operations center personnel can react in an informed manner to any suspicious activity performed against any cloud infrastructure or compute workload. The xSIEM tool is equipped to capture any trust policies the cloud management software has executed with regard to placement and migration of workload, whether inside the enterprise data center or burst into the service provider data center. Events are analyzed, categorized, and the appropriate alerts are generated for investigation and possible remediation.

- *Cloud management and orchestration portal*: As shown in Figure 9-6, the xStream management and orchestration portal is the heart of the cloud operations, enabling the tenant and the cloud provider to operate in an efficient manner while allowing the tenant to consume compute, network, and storage in an elastic manner, with the cloud provider managing and providing these resources in a secure and reliable manner.

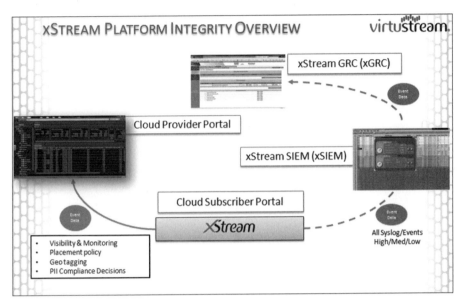

Figure 9-6. *xStream management environment*

Network Topology and Considerations

The network for the reference data center design is built on principles of scalability, redundancy, and security. There are many design considerations in the selection of data center connectivity options. Needless to say, security and isolation are key, but there are more:

- Bandwidth shaping

- Traffic policing

- Performance considerations due to latency

- IP addressing

- Availability and DDOS-related issues

- Time-of-day issues

Figure 9-7 captures the topology for the reference data center network design. The network design architecture includes separate network cores for the enterprise cloud zone and the DMZ zone. This allows a full air gap between those trust zones, and it can facilitate the achievement of certifications for the platform in data centers.

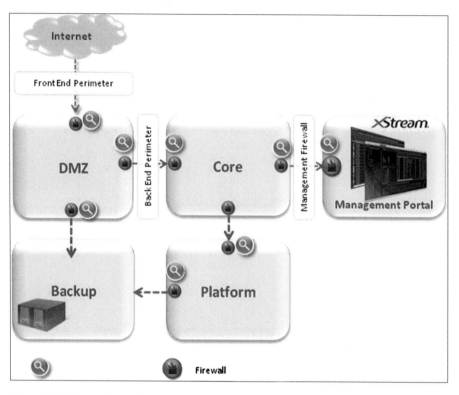

Figure 9-7. *Network topology*

The design caters to the following elements:

- Appropriate level of segregation between virtual machines belonging to different cloud users

- Appropriate level of security for management network

- Standard virtual network design considerations, such as NIC failover design

- Capacity planning for future growth

The design is intended to be a best-practice cloud deployment for using either separate virtual switches or multiple VLANs to segregate traffic and retain inter-site mobility for the network stack. The platform utilizes virtualized converged I/O as a key technology to enable the control of both storage and network-based operations.

At all stages throughout the design, resilience is implied—that is, fault tolerance within the network switch design, multiple connections through multiple firewalls and IPS appliances, and resilient VPN concentrators.

Let's highlight the essential network elements.

- *The demilitarized zone.* All IP VPN traffic lands on a demilitarized zone (DMZ) switch before passing through a port blocking firewall, to strip all non-VPN traffic and to transform VPN traffic to VM VLAN IP traffic accessing the layer 2 switch infrastructures. From here, traffic is addressed to the client-specific vSwitches as per the VM VLAN tags. Before accessing the VM attached switches, all traffic is routed through an IPS device in order to assure quality of traffic from both external access and VM-generated packets.

  The DMZ network incorporates a business continuity management (BCM) function and constitutes the virtualized infrastructure dedicated to meeting the production demands of tenants requiring web facing services. To ensure reliability and availability, one DMZ network is maintained per pair of data centers.

- *Management network.* The tenant management connectivity consists of two routes for internal and external management access. Both routes need to pass through port blocking firewalls before access is granted to the layer 2 switch infrastructure. This is primarily to avoid impact if service provider management workstations are compromised. Remote access is provided through the same port blocking firewall as customer access.

  Storage replication should occur over its own switching and routing infrastructure; firewalls are configured behind each secure connection appliance to avoid compromise of this route to core infrastructure. This traffic will be encrypted and assured throughout transit, and it is preferable that this transit is over a leased line to improve that security.

- *Core network.* Production core network incorporates layer 3 and layer 2 equipment with a high-availability design. The zone is utilized to control, manage, and route all network traffic incoming and outgoing from the customer platform, DMZ, and management network. This zone is the centralized control point for all critical network traffic.

- *Backup network.* This contains all backup devices and related service components with routes from customer platform zones to service all data backup service request and requirements.

- *Platform.* Comprises the production computing infrastructure dedicated to meeting customer production requirements requiring non-web facing services. One required per pair of data centers, data security, resilience, and reliability is a key part of the design of components in this zone.

- *MPLS.* MPLS is an any-to-any WAN technology robust to changes in IP topology and automatic rerouting. MPLS provides a variety of ways of logically isolating multiple virtual connections on a single physical circuit. If possible, a separate VRF (virtual routing and forwarding) MPLS instance can be temporarily created for the temporary traffic, thereby logically isolating the routing domain from the VDI traffic.

  Another method is to use the prioritization techniques available to MPLS to always ensure that VDI traffic trumps any POC traffic on the circuit. These methods may include QoS markings at the IP DSCP (DiffServ Code Point) or at the Ethernet p-bits. Coexistence with any existing quality of service (QoS) markings techniques on the MPLS circuit will be a requirement.

Security Design Considerations

Security is a high priority for customers in a multi-tenant environment. While virtual infrastructures are relatively secure in their basic installation, additional changes are required to adhere to certain security audit requirements. This section provides an overview of some of the security measures considered within the reference design, as they are subject to the wider security protocols required in an offering for managed services.

Hypervisor Hardening

VMware ESXi 5 is a small-footprint version of VMware's hypervisor. This minimal footprint also reduces the attack surface. ESXi implements support for Intel TXT. The capability is managed and controlled by xStream software for trusted compute pools, providing visibility to the integrity of the platform and enforcement of trust policies for deployment and migration of virtual machines. The ESXi installation comes with a number of additional security features:

- LDAP integration

- Management interface firewall

- Lockdown mode

- Logging

These features have to be enabled corrected to ensure hardening. With the high priority attached to security in the multi-tenant paradigm being used in the cloud platform, using ESXi 5.x is recommended. In addition to this, basic security measures such as setting a strong root password should be used and compliance requirements that are necessary for compliance with the security standards selected for the platform are checked.

Firewalls and Network separation

To provide end-to-end separation of client data, it is important to ensure that no element in the infrastructure allows data to comingle or be accessed by another client. This is especially true of the networking design and infrastructure.

In order to achieve this, the reference design prescribes the infrastructure to be entirely separate from the customer VPN landing zone, through to the individual virtual machines and at all points in between. To achieve this, the reference design uses of the following technologies:

- VLAN

- Virtual switches

- Virtual appliances

- Firewalls and routing infrastructure

Every cloud customer is assigned one or more individual VLAN, as needed. Customer network traffic remains isolated from each other within a VLAN. The switch to which a VLAN is attached is also assigned the same VLAN tag.

As shown in Figure 9-8, the only way for machines in VLAN A to talk to machines in VLAN B (and vice versa) is for the router to be configured to allow that conversation to occur. To ensure that the switch configuration is unified across all hosts in a cluster, the reference design uses distributed virtual switches. These ensure that the switch configuration associated VLAN tagged switch port groups are the same across all attached hosts, thereby limiting the chances of a misconfiguration of VLAN tagging on the virtual switch.

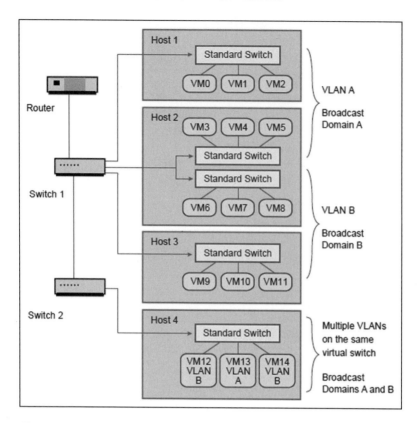

Figure 9-8. *VLAN separation using vSwitches*

In addition to the VLAN tagging, the reference design also makes use of other traditional networking separation and security tools. A key technology is firewalling (see Figure 9-9). Both virtual and physical firewalls are needed to ensure separations throughout the environment, from access to the physical network, including DMZ separation using physical firewall devices, and virtual firewalls to ensure visibility and separation across virtual machines.

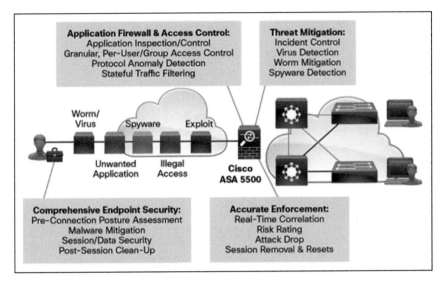

Figure 9-9. *Cisco ASA protection*

Firewalls are required to scale to the highest VPN session counts, throughput, and connection speed and capacity to meet the needs of the most demanding customers. Offering protocol-agnostic client and clientless access for a broad spectrum of desktop and mobile platforms, the firewall device delivers a versatile, always-on remote access integrated with IPS and Web security for secure mobility and enhanced productivity.

The reference design ensures that throughout the network, be it virtual or physical, industry standard separation is enabled, and further guaranteed and improved by the inclusion of specific industry leading technologies that ensure even greater levels of granularity and visibility within the system.

Management Network Firewalling

For additional security, putting the hosts and management servers behind firewalls provides additional security and separation of the management services. Ports will be required to be opened for VMware virtual infrastructure to work.

Virtual Networking

VMware virtual infrastructure implements a virtual networking component that allows for virtual switches and port groups to be created at the software layer and operate as if they were physical infrastructure. There are certain features and ways to configure the networking to improve network segregation and prevent possible network vulnerabilities. These are:

- Use VLAN tagging

- Disable MAC address changes

197

- Disable forged transmits

- Disable promiscuous mode

- Prevent and monitor for spoofing

Note that some of the features need to be enabled for certain customers— for example, for internal IDS scans—but should only be changed explicitly from defaults on an individual basis. As mentioned earlier, all customers will be assigned their own VLAN, and this will remain enabled. As a recommended practice, the reference design calls for use of different vSwitches to physically separate network traffic, disable forged transmits, and segregate management network traffic from virtual machine traffic

Anti-Virus Software

Anti-virus and anti-malware software is always a consideration by any company when security is in question. For the management layer, anti-virus software is recommended on the virtual machine manager server and any other appropriate virtual machines.

The definition of anti-virus policies and the deployment of anti-virus agents by a service provider to the tenant's virtual machines fall outside the scope of this reference design. Tenant segregation and the use of security devices such as firewalls and IPSs—and, if selected, technologies such as virtual firewalls—will ensure that any viruses on a tenant's virtual machines will not spread to other tenants.

It is recommended that approved anti-virus software be installed on management layer virtual machines. Unless specified by the service provider, the tenant is generally responsible for installation of anti-virus software on production virtual machines.

Cloud Management Security

The cloud management layer provides the basis for all management functions surrounding the reference design. It ties into all the other technologies previously listed and provides some additional functionality to assist in the creation of a secure and auditable cloud environment. The security elements required by a cloud management portal are as follows:

- PCI/ISO/FedRAMP/NIST 800-53 associated security controls

- Governance, risk, and compliance (GRC)

- Trusted execution platform

Trusted execution platform is the one element that we have covered in depth in the earlier chapters, so we will not cover that here. Let's cover the other two elements briefly in the next two sections.

Security Controls

The security controls implemented in the reference design are based on NIST 800-53/FedRAMP, GLB, iTAR/EAR, applicable security controls to measure and secure connectivity between data centers.

NIST 800-53

NIST Special Publication 800-53 is part of the Special Publication 800-series that reports on the Information Technology Laboratory's (ITL) research, guidelines, and outreach efforts in information system security, and on ITL's activity with industry, government, and academic organizations. Specifically, NIST Special Publication 800-53 covers the steps in the risk management framework that address security control selection for federal information systems in accordance with the security requirements in Federal Information Processing Standard (FIPS) 200. This includes selecting an initial set of baseline security controls based on a FIPS 199 worst-case impact analysis, tailoring the baseline security controls, and supplementing the security controls based on an organizational assessment of risk. The security rules cover 17 areas, including access control, incident response, business continuity, and disaster recoverability. These controls are the management, operational, and technical safeguards (or countermeasures) prescribed for an information system to protect the confidentiality, integrity, and availability of the system and its information. To implement the needed safeguards or controls, agencies must first determine the security category of their information systems in accordance with the provisions of FIPS 199, "Standards for Security Categorization of Federal Information and Information Systems." The security categorization of the information system (low, moderate, or high) determines the baseline collection of controls that must be implemented and monitored. Agencies have the ability to adjust these controls and tailor them to fit more closely with their organizational goals or environments.

Tables 9-1 through 9-4 show the subset of key NIST 800-53 controls that are implemented in this reference design to conform to a trusted architecture. The NIST 800-53 security controls have a well-defined organization and structure. To make it easy for selection and specification, controls are organized into 18 families. Each family contains security controls related to the general security topic of the family. A two-character identifier uniquely identifies security control families—for example, SI (system and information integration). Security controls may involve aspects of policy, oversight, supervision, manual processes, actions by individuals, or automated mechanisms implemented by information systems/devices. In the context of this reference design, the key controls that are implemented belong to four specific families of controls.

    a.   CM Configuration Management

    b.   SA System and Services Acquisition

    c.   SC System and Communications Protection

    d.   SI System and Information Integration

Table 9-1. *NIST 800-53 Control Family - CM - Configuration Management*

800-53 Control ID	Control Text	Control Comments/Guidance
CM-2 (2)	The organization employs automated mechanisms to maintain an up-to-date, complete, accurate, and readily available baseline configuration.	
CM-8	CM-8d. [Assignment: organization-defined information deemed necessary to achieve effective property accountability] Parameter: See additional requirements and guidance. CM-8 (3) (a) [Assignment: organization-defined frequency] Parameter: [Continuously, using automated mechanisms with a maximum five-minute delay in detection]	

Table 9-2. *NIST 800-53 Control Family - SA - System and Services Acquisition*

800-53 Control ID	Control Text	Control Comments/Guidance
SA-11 (1)	The organization requires that information system developers/integrators employ code analysis tools to examine software for common flaws and document the results of the analysis.	The organization: a. Conducts an organizational assessment of risk prior to the acquisition or outsourcing of dedicated information security services. b. Ensures that the acquisition or outsourcing of dedicated information security services is approved by [Assignment: organization-defined senior organizational official].

(continued)

Table 9-2. (*continued*)

800-53 Control ID	Control Text	Control Comments/Guidance
SA-12	The organization protects against supply chain threats by employing: [organization-defined list of measures to protect against supply chain threats] as part of a comprehensive, defense-in-breadth information security strategy.	Control: The organization requires that information system developers/integrators, in consultation with associated security personnel (including security engineers): a. Create and implement a security test and evaluation plan. b. Implement a verifiable flaw remediation process to correct weaknesses and deficiencies identified during the security testing and evaluation process. c. Document the results of the security testing/evaluation and flaw remediation processes. Supplemental Guidance: Developmental security test results are used to the greatest extent feasible after verification of the results and recognizing that these results are impacted whenever there have been security-relevant modifications to the information system subsequent to developer testing. Test results may be used in support of the security authorization process for the delivered information system. Related control: CA-2, SI-2.

(*continued*)

Table 9-2. (*continued*)

800-53 Control ID	Control Text	Control Comments/Guidance
SA-4 (7)	The organization: (a) Limits the use of commercially provided information technology products to those products that have been successfully evaluated against a validated U.S. Government Protection Profile for a specific technology type, if such a profile exists; and (b) Requires, if no U.S. Government Protection Profile exists for a specific technology type but a commercially provided information technology product relies on cryptographic functionality to enforce its security policy, then the cryptographic module is FIPS-validated.	The organization: a. Limits the use of commercially provided information technology products to those products that have been successfully evaluated against a validated U.S. Government Protection Profile for a specific technology type, if such a profile exists. b. Requires, if no U.S. Government Protection Profile exists for a specific technology type but a commercially provided information technology product relies on cryptographic functionality to enforce its security policy, then the cryptographic module is FIPS-validated.
SA-9 (1)	The organization: (a) Conducts an organizational assessment of risk prior to the acquisition or outsourcing of dedicated information security services. (b) Ensures that the acquisition or outsourcing of dedicated information security services is approved by [organization-defined senior organizational official].	SA-9 (1) (b) [Assignment: organization-defined senior organizational official]. Parameter: [Joint Authorization Board (JAB)] The organization: a. Limits the use of commercially provided information technology products to those products that have been successfully evaluated against a validated U.S. Government Protection Profile for a specific technology type, if such a profile exists. b. Requires, if no U.S. Government Protection Profile exists for a specific technology type but a commercially provided information technology product relies on cryptographic functionality to enforce its security policy, then the cryptographic module is FIPS-validated.

Table 9-3. *NIST 800-53 Control Family - SC - System and Communications Protection*

800-53 Control ID	Control Text	Control Comments/Guidance
SC-12 (2)	The organization produces, controls, and distributes symmetric cryptographic keys using [NIST-approved, NSA-approved] key management technology and processes.	The organization produces, controls, and distributes symmetric cryptographic keys using NIST-approved key management technology and processes.
SC-12 (5)	The organization produces, controls, and distributes asymmetric cryptographic keys using approved PKI Class 3 or Class 4 certificates and hardware security tokens that protect the user'sprivate key.	The organization produces, controls, and distributes asymmetric cryptographic keys using approved PKI Class 3 or Class 4 certificates and hardware security tokens that protect the user's private key.
SC-13 (1)	The organization employs, at a minimum, FIPS-validated cryptography to protect unclassified information.	The organization employs, at a minimum, FIPS-validated cryptography to protect unclassified information.
SC-21	The information system performs data origin authentication and data integrity verification on the name/address resolution responses the system receives from authoritative sources when requested by client systems.	The information system provides additional data origin and integrity artifacts along with the authoritative data the system returns in response to name/address resolution queries.
SC-6	The information system limits the use of resources by priority.	The information system limits the use of resources by priority.
SC-7 (8)	The information system routes [organization-defined internal communications traffic] to [organization-defined external networks] through authenticated proxy servers within the managed interfaces of boundary protection devices.	The information system routes [Assignment: organization-defined internal communications traffic] to [Assignment: organization-defined external networks] through authenticated proxy servers within the managed interfaces of boundary protection devices.

(continued)

Table 9-3. (*continued*)

800-53 Control ID	Control Text	Control Comments/Guidance
SC-7 (12)	The information system implements host-based boundary protection mechanisms for servers, workstations, and mobile devices.	The information system implements host-based boundary protection mechanisms for servers, workstations, and mobile devices. Enhancement Supplemental Guidance: A host-based boundary protection mechanism is, for example, a host-based firewall. Host-based boundary protection mechanisms are employed on mobile devices, such as notebook/laptop computers, and other types of mobile devices where such boundary protection mechanisms are available.
SC-7 (13)	The organization isolates [organization defined key information security tools, mechanisms, and support components] from other internal information system components via physically separate subnets with managed interfaces to other portions of the system.	The organization isolates [Assignment: organization defined key information security tools, mechanisms, and support components] from other internal information system components via physically separate subnets with managed interfaces to other portions of the system.
SC-7 (18)	The information system fails securely in the event of an operational failure of a boundaryprotection device.	The information system fails securely in the event of an operational failure of a boundary protection device.

Table 9-4. *NIST 800-53 Control Family - SI - System and Information Integrity*

800-53 Control ID	Control Text	Control Comments/Guidance
SI-4	SI-4a. [Assignment: organization-defined monitoring objectives] Parameter: [ensure the proper functioning of internal processes and controls in furtherance of regulatory and compliance requirements; examine system records to confirm that the system is functioning in an optimal, resilient, and secure state; identify irregularities or anomalies that are indicators of a system malfunction or compromise] SI-4 (5) [Assignment: organization-defined list of compromise indicators] Parameter: [protected information system files or directories have been modified without notification from the appropriate change/configuration management channels; information system performance indicates resource consumption that is inconsistent with expected operating conditions; auditing functionality has been disabled or modified to reduce audit visibility; audit or log records have been deleted or modified without explanation; information system is raising alerts or faults in a manner that indicates the presence of an abnormal condition; resource or service requests are initiated from clients that are outside of the expected client membership set; information system reports failed logins or password changes for administrative or key service accounts; processes and services are running that are outside of the baseline system profile; utilities, tools, or scripts have been saved or installed on production systems without clear indication of their use or purpose]	

(*continued*)

Table 9-4. (*continued*)

800-53 Control ID	Control Text	Control Comments/Guidance
SI-6	The information system verifies the correct operation of security functions [Selection (oneor more): [Organization-defined system transitional states]; upon command by user with appropriate privilege; periodically every [Organization-defined time-period]] and [Selection (one or more): notifies system administrator; shuts the system down; restarts the system; [organization-defined alternative action(s)]] when anomalies are discovered.	Control: The information system verifies the correct operation of security functions upon system startup and/or restart and periodically every ninety days and notifies system administrator when anomalies are discovered. Supplemental Guidance: The need to verify security functionality applies to all security functions. For those security functions that are not able to execute automated self-tests, the organization either implements compensating security controls or explicitly accepts the risk of not performing the verification as required. Information system transitional states include, for example, startup, restart, shutdown, and abort.

We will briefly mention the controls implemented for each of these families in the next three sections. Column1 provides the 800-53 control ID, column 2 describes the control, and column 3 provides additional commentary or guidance (if any) for each of the controls. Selecting and specifying security controls is based on the maturity of the organization's information systems, how they manage risk, and the system impact level in accordance with FIPS 199 and FIPS 200. The selection of the security controls includes tailoring the initial set of baseline security controls and supplementing the tailored baseline as necessary, based on an organizational assessment of risk, and assessing the security controls as part of a comprehensive continuous monitoring process.

Governance, Risk, and Compliance (GRC)

By continuously assessing the compliance of the systems and the underlying cloud system, a tenant system can be assigned a granular rating traceable over time, allowing visibility into any threats presented by the underlying, normally invisible virtualized cloud infrastructure. The tenant is alerted to any potential threat originating within the infrastructure due to poor server management.

Figure 9-10 shows the xGRC rating system used in the reference design. These ratings allow for easier audit and reporting, as well as a simple method of assessing infrastructure health. The physical and virtual data center's machine data are correlated and fed into GRC Reporting Tools in a continuous monitoring cycle and the related controls are maintained for the specific compliance frameworks—for example, NIST 800-53 or PCI etc. xStream's xGRC provides this functionality in the reference architecture.

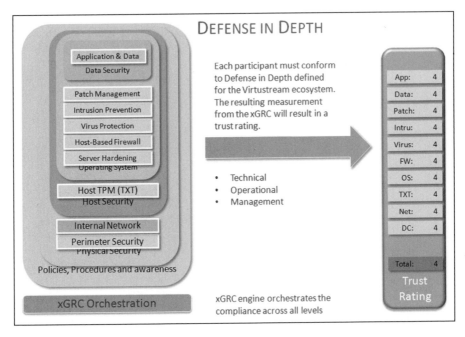

Figure 9-10. xGRC rating system

Practical Considerations for Virtual Machine Migration

In the initial discussion of cloud bursting, we glossed over a number of considerations in the interests of presenting a clear explanation. In particular, with the current state of the art, there are a number of limitations when it comes to migrating virtual machines across hypervisors. This is the problem of *virtual machine interoperability*.[1] The assumed environment for current practical implementations is a private cloud environment connected to the home base through VPN links. The VPN links are necessary to have all virtual machines in the same subnet. Furthermore, all virtual machine movements

---

[1]Open Data Center Alliance Usage: Virtual Machine (VM) Interoperability in a Hybrid Cloud Environment Rev. 1.2; http://www.opendatacenteralliance.org/docs/Virtual_Machine_%28VM%29_Interoperability_in_a_Hybrid_Cloud_Environment_Rev1.2.pdf.

take place across hosts running the same hypervisor environment. There are a number of operational limitations that prevent virtual machine movements across different hypervisor environments or across public clouds with different providers.

Live migration is supported by the most commonly deployed hypervisor environments: Xen, VMware, and Microsoft Hyper-V. This is a case of homogeneous migration, where the source and target hosts run the same hypervisor environment. Homogeneous migration is the first of three possible levels for virtual machine interoperability or compatibility.[2]

To summarize the DMTF definitions:

- Level 1: Workloads under compatibility level 1 only run on a particular virtualization product and/or CPU architecture and/ or virtual hardware selection. Level 1 portability is logically equivalent to a suspend operation in the source environment and a resume in the target environment.

- Level 2: Workloads under compatibility level 2 are designed to run on a specific family of virtual hardware. Migration under level 2 is equivalent to a shutdown in the source environment followed by a reboot in the target environment.

- Level 3: Workloads supporting level 3 compatibility are able to run on multiple families of virtual hardware.

Level 1 maps to homogeneous migration, the type of migration supported today within a single hypervisor environment and the only environment where live migration is feasible. Level 2 supports movement across heterogeneous hypervisor environments; this necessitates an intervening reboot. For this reason, this scheme is known as cold migration. Level 3 allows not only migration across different hypervisors but also across different host hardware architectures, and hence we identify it as heterogeneous architecture migration.

Live migration, when feasible, preserves the most operating states of a virtual machine image of the three schemes, including IP addresses and open file descriptors, and even transactions and streaming data in midstream. On the one hand, live migration may be required by some legacy applications that break after some of the state transitions mentioned above. On the other hand, requirements for live migration are strict: the target host usually needs to be part of a preconfigured cluster; the hosts need to be in the same subnet; and even if physically remote hosts are connected through a VPN tunnel, latency due to the trombone effect may induce failures. Live migration is not possible across heterogeneous hypervisor environments.

Heterogeneous hypervisor migration relaxes some of the environmental requirements compared to live migration. A logical shutdown and restart means that virtual machines in the target environment may end up running with a different set of IP addresses. Open file descriptors may be different, even though they may be reaching the same files; the descriptors may point to a remote file that was previously local. Transactions interrupted during the migration may have to be rolled back and retried. The virtual machine image

---

[2]DMTF, Open Virtualization Format White Paper, OVF version 1.0.0e, paper DSP2017, 2/6/2009, Section 5.

needs to be remapped to run in the new target hypervisor environment. It is not practical to modify the memory image to run in the new environment, and hence the need for a reboot. For applications that can tolerate these environment changes, cold migration offers a broader choice of target service providers.

Heterogeneous architecture migration provides the least support of state preservation. At the same time, it provides the most options in running an application across computer architectures or service providers. It potentially involves reassembling the application in the target environment. Loose coupling becomes obligatory. This applies to advanced methodologies, such as integrated development and operations (DevOps).[3] Heterogeneous architecture migration offers the broadest choices for operating environments, running not only on a variety of hypervisor environment but also across platform architectures. The trade-off is being the least state-preserving of the three levels.

From the discussion above, it becomes clear that cloud bursting options need not include live migration as an obligatory requirement. Loosely coupled application components may be instantiated as levels 2 or 3 cloud bursting components. An example of level 2 bursting could be web server front-end instances connected to the mid-tier through DCOM or CORBA. Examples of level 3 bursting could be web server front-end components connected to the application through REST interfaces, or even instantiating auxiliary services such as content delivery networks or connecting to API managers.

Summary

This chapter on cloud bursting references an architecture design utilized by Virtustream, which marks the beginning of a new era in cloud computing. This is an era when the migration and bursting of workloads to trusted federated cloud partners, whether in a private or public infrastructure, will industrialize a new mode of cloud operations via a highly efficient model to enable the consumption of cloud resources in an elastic manner that doesn't compromise security. The chapter covered the reference design leveraging Intel Corporation's TXT technology to ensure the platform boot integrity and attestation, both in the private cloud infrastructure and the external/overflow capacity. The integration of Virtustream's xStream cloud management platform with Intel TXT via the Mt. Wilson trust attestation authority provides an automated and production-ready cloud platform to accomplish the secure cloud bursting architecture and usage.

This is just the beginning. As discussed in the chapter, there are regulatory compliance issues, quality of service questions, and data locality and governance matters, as well as the immaturity of the monitoring and remediation components. The Virtustream xStream cloud management software used in this reference design and the proof of concept begin to address many of these problems. This and other cloud architectures will continue to evolve as real-world organizational requirements change, and as proofs of concept such as the illustrated proof of concept in this chapter exercise existing technology to its limits, requiring new technologies to be created or improve upon what presently exists.

---

[3]http://www.readwriteweb.com/enterprise/2011/08/devops-what-it-is-why-it-exist.php, http://www.cio.com/article/print/705919.

VIRTUSTREAM OVERVIEW

Virtustream is a leading Enterprise Class Cloud solution provider for global 2000 workloads. xStream™ is Virtustream's Enterprise Class Cloud solution allowing both mission-critical legacy and web-scale applications to run in the cloud—whether private, virtual private or public. xStream uses μVM technology to deliver enterprise-grade security/compliance, application performance SLAs, consumption-based pricing, significant cost efficiency beyond virtualization and the ability to deliver IT in minutes rather than months. xStream is available as software, appliance or a managed service and works with all leading hardware and virtualization software.

Figure 9-11 shows the overview of xStream management software.

XSTREAM CLOUD MANAGEMENT SOFTWARE

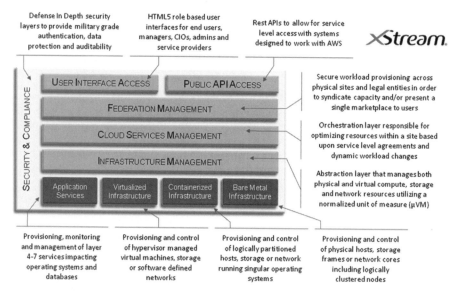

Figure 9-11. *Virtustream xStream Software*

Index